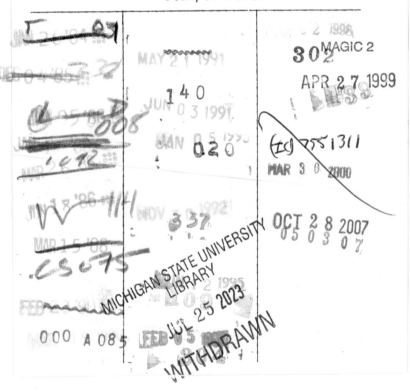

MAPS IN MINDS

REFLECTIONS ON COGNITIVE MAPPING

ROGER M. DOWNS
DAVID STEA

MAPS IN MINDS
REFLECTIONS ON COGNITIVE MAPPING

ROGER M. DOWNS
The Pennsylvania State University

DAVID STEA
The University of California, Los Angeles

Harper & Row, Publishers
New York   Hagerstown   San Francisco   London

To our parents: Charles and Dorothy, Armand and Henriette

Sponsoring Editor: Ronald K. Taylor
Project Editor: Brenda Goldberg
Designer: T. R. Funderburk
Production Supervisor: Stefania J. Taflinska
Compositor: P & M Typesetting, Incorporated
Printer and Binder: The Maple Press Company
Art Studio: Vantage Art, Inc.

Maps in Minds: Reflections on Cognitive Mapping

Copyright © 1977 by Roger M. Downs and David Stea

Library of Congress Cataloging in Publication Data

Downs, Roger M
   Maps in minds.

   (Harper & Row series in geography)
   Bibliography: p.
   Includes indexes.
   1.   Geographical perception.   I.   Stea, David,
joint author.   II.   Title.
G71.5.D68   301.3   76-57221
ISBN 0-06-041733-1

CONTENTS

List of Tables   vii
List of Figures   ix
List of Boxes xii
Preface   xiii
Acknowledgments   xv

Chapter 1 SENSES OF PLACE   1

Introduction   1
Cognitive Mapping and Maps   6
Why Is Cognitive Mapping Important?   12
The Organization of the Book   29

Chapter 2 SPATIAL PROBLEM SOLVING   30

Introduction   30
What Are Spatial Problems?   36
Knowing   40
Whereness   41
Whatness and Whenness   54
What Are the Ways of Solving Spatial Problems?   55
Cognitive Mapping as Spatial Problem Solving   58

Chapter 3 THE MEANING OF COGNITIVE MAPPING   61

Introduction   61
What Do We Mean by "Mapping"?   61
The Objectives of Cognitive Mapping   68
Cognitive Mapping as an Interactive Process   73
The Selectivity of Cognitive Mapping   77
Making Sense Out of the World   83

Chapter 4 THE WORLD IN THE HEAD   99

Introduction   99
The Accuracy and Similarity of Cognitive Maps   99
Whatness and Whenness   107

Whereness 123
Conclusion 144

Chapter 5 A TALE OF TWO PLACES 146
Puluwat: The Art of Navigation 146
Two Views of Boston 156

Chapter 6 THE GENESIS OF COGNITIVE MAPPING 171
Introduction 172
Cognitive Mapping and the Functioning of the Brain 174
The Evolutionary Record 182
The Development of Cognitive Mapping 187
An Attempt at Integration 202

Chapter 7 LEARNING: HOW ENVIRONMENTS GET MAPPED 209
Introduction 209
Learning a New City 214
The Process of Environmental Learning 218
Conclusions 239

Chapter 8 COGNITIVE MAPPING IN EVERYDAY LIFE 240
Introduction 240
The Design of Urban Spaces 241
You Can't Get There from Here 252
Games 258
The Worlds of Fantasy and Imagination 261
Conclusion 261

Bibliography 264
Name Index 273
Place Index 276
Subject Index 280

LIST OF TABLES

2.1 Percentage of Rats Choosing Each of the Long Paths in the Revised Maze   35

3.1 Spatial Expressions in Everyday Language   87

3.2 Symbols and Nicknames for Cities and Countries   92

4.1 Common Responses to the Uncertainty of Natural Hazards   122

LIST OF FIGURES

1.1   "You can't go home again": the pain of returning to a well-remembered place.   3
1.2   Humorous representations, 1: a Texan's view of the United States.   8
1.3   Humorous representations, 2: a Maritimer's view of Canada.   9
1.4   Humorous representations, 3: a Londoner's view of the north of Great Britain.   10
1.5   The importance of centrality.   11
1.6   The Search, and how to avoid it.   13
1.7   Knowledge of place and knowledge of routes are often intimately related.   14
1.8   Residential and touristic undesirability: New York City is a place of fear and wonder to many visitors, fraught with fascination and dread. To the tourist equipped with this map, it appears even more frightening. The shaded areas are considered dangerous both night and day, the black areas during the night.   15
1.9   The dangerous areas of Monroe, a neighborhood of Philadelphia.   16
1.10   Residential desirability, 1: where California students would like (and not like) to live.   17
1.11   Investment possibilities in Baltimore housing as seen by three landlords in 1971.   19
1.12   Selling an image of America, 1: United Air Lines.   21
1.13   Selling an image of America, 2: Greyhound Bus Lines.   22
1.14   Selling western Europe: El Al Air Lines.   23
1.15   Residential desirability, 2: where Alabama students would like (and not like) to live.   25
1.16   Christopher Columbus, whose somewhat distorted map of the world made native Americans "Indians" for over 400 years.   28

2.1   "Round" and "wagging" dances convey the spatial sense of the bee.   31

2.2   "Charting" the direction of food.   32

2.3   Tolman's "original maze" (see text).   33

2.4   Tolman's "revised maze" (see text).   34

2.5   It no longer costs only $9.90 to go from New York to Boston, as in 1972, but the message is abundantly clear: Separation can be measured in monetary terms, as well as in units of distance and time.   48

2.6   An approach to Boston, from the south. At the intersection of Interstate Route 95 and Massachusetts 128, Route 128 runs East-West, but the signs read "North" and "South," respectively. The "South" sign also reads "Boston," which is in fact to the north. Small wonder that drivers become so confused!   52

3.1   Fingers, too, have cognitive maps.   67

3.2   The Empire State Building "dumped" into the Grand Canyon.   74

3.3   Cognized boundaries, 1: various U.S. regions.   89

3.4   "Word images" of places around the globe.   93

3.5   Evoking an image of New York.   94

4.1   A map of Normandy Street drawn by Anthony, a schoolchild in Roxbury, Massachusetts.   105

4.2   Jerome's map: The same area is represented as in Figure 4.1, but the cartographer is different.   106

4.3   The cognitive geography of love: exploring romantic Colonial America.   110

4.4   Juxtaposing conflicting images: the appeal of (and by) South Carolina.   112

4.5   Icelandic orientation: another "pivot of the four quarters."   127

4.6   Yurok orientation: "as long as the rivers shall run."   128

4.7   Richmond (Staten Island, N.Y.) orientation: "up-island" and "down-island."   129

4.8   The annihilation of distance.   139

5.1   The Puluwat Atoll, Caroline Islands, Micronesia.   147

5.2   Star compass (see text).   150

5.3   Etak: a Puluwatan framework for integrating navigational knowledge.   152

5.4   Composite images of Boston derived from verbal interviews (above) and from sketch maps (below).   157

5.5   Cambridge, Massachusetts, north of the Charles River, and its institutions of higher learning (shaded areas).   162

5.6   Boston, with its five-sided Common (shaded area).   165

5.7   Cognized boundaries, 2: various Boston districts.   166

5.8   Mentally "looking" east along Commonwealth Avenue ("inbound"): a sketch from memory.   169

6.1   A Roy Doty cartoon illustrating the hypothesized division of cognitive functions between the left and right hemispheres of the brain.   178

6.2   Some results of a recent experiment of Emil Menzel, subsequent to that reported by Hewes (see text). The maps show the best performances of four chimpanzees who had been carried about an outdoor field and shown 18 randomly placed (hidden) foods. Note that the apes remembered most of the hiding places and that the search pattern approximates an optimum routing, a clear indication of cognitive mapping in action. 184

6.3 Another Menzel experiment, using the same four chimpanzees of Figure 6.2. Two pieces of food were hidden in one third of the outdoor enclosure and three pieces in the opposite third. On 13 of the 16 trials shown, the first area approached by the chimpanzees was the site containing the larger cluster of food. To the "least distance strategy" depicted in Figure 6.2, the apes added another cognitive mapping strategy to maximize the rate of food acquisition. 185

6.4 Filling in the gaps among existing data yielded this inferential developmental sequence of cognitive mapping skills. 189

6.5 Time-lapse motion picture photographs of a preschool child constructing a "toy landscape." The child uses miniature buildings, trees, vehicles, and streets provided by the researchers, and is perfectly free to make whatever he or she wishes on a large sheet of "butcher paper." 193

7.1 All roads do *not* lead to Rome. 210

7.2 In primary school, we are taught that the eye is like a camera; in college, we are taught that it is not. Whatever our resolution of this conflicting information, we retain the idea that the camera offers a *metaphor* for seeing. "What to see" is built into the camera's structure, but it is something that the eye must *learn*. 211

7.3 Two aids to spatial navigation and one to societal navigation. 216

7.4 The actual route to school (A) and probable trip-to-school sketches (B, C, and D) provided by three of the Stock children. "B" is drawn by the youngest, "C" by the second oldest, and "D" by the oldest, who takes a bus to school (see text). 219

7.5 A hypothetical route *map* in which compass directions, street names, and some other cues are considered irrelevant. The corresponding *list* of instructions (a verbal route map) might read as follows: (1) Leave your driveway and turn left; (2) go down two blocks; (3) turn right; (4) go past two traffic signals; (5) turn left at the third; (6) continue for about a mile until you come to a "Standard" gasoline station; (7) turn right; (8) follow the road as it curves uphill; (9) look to your right just past the crest of the hill where you'll see a red house with a white picket fence; and (10) turn into the driveway. 226

7.6 The *actual* form of New York City (from *Flash Maps*). 232

7.7 A "squat" Manhattan, distorted for the purposes of depicting highway entrances and exits. 233

7.8 An even more distorted New York than shown in Figure 7.7, designed to help New Yorkers (and others) find (and even learn) subway routes. 234

8.1 "He's got the whole world in his head." 262

LIST OF BOXES

2.1   Philadelphia: Love It, or Leave It, or Just Don't Go   37
2.2   Near and Far: The Space of Science Fiction   49
4.1   The Mythical "Sense of Direction"   125
4.2   A Ghastly Disorientation   131
4.3   The World of the Straight and Narrow   135
6.1   Piaget I: The Developmental Psychology of Jean Piaget   194
6.2   The Developmental Psychology of Jerome Bruner   201
6.3   Piaget II: The Relationship Between Development and Learning   203
6.4   Piaget and Bruner: Some Comparisons   205
7.1   Aids to Environmental Learning   221

PREFACE

Our ability to understand ourselves as human beings is limited, in many ways, by the ever-present feeling that much of how we behave and how we think is obvious, that these are things that *everybody* "knows." We hamstring ourselves with the disparaging remark that something is trivially obvious. For this reason, we have learned to ignore very many ideas that are both fascinating and important. This deliberate oversight is aided and abetted by the nature of academic research, which encourages the feeling that abstruseness is a virtue. Moreover, academic disciplines are structured in such a way that all-too-many topics slip unnoticed between the interstices of several disciplines. The topic of this book, *cognitive mapping*, has suffered all of these fates. While obvious in one sense, it is *not* trivial. Although we all make continuous use of the ability, we do not necessarily understand how it works, and, unfortunately, the cognitive and mapping ideas have been of only passing concern to psychologists and geographers. Even the name for the concept is unsatisfactory; it makes some intuitive sense but it is scarcely a household word. We are forced to use an unfamiliar phrase because we do not have a popular expression for this ability that allows us to cope with the problems of understanding the spatial environment within which we live.

Despite these obstacles, we can easily make a strong case that cognitive mapping is a necessary requirement for human survival and that it touches far more of our everyday lives than we appreciate at first glance. It has links to architecture and planning, to education, to literature, to language, and to games and toy play. An understanding of these links is not trivial, and so this book attempts to throw some light on the obvious. For example, we do need to understand how we find our way around in a city, how we communicate about places, how children develop an understanding of the world. All of these ideas depend on our ability to comprehend the spatial environment, and thus this book is concerned with exploring the world in the head.

The written record of this exploration has taken far longer to produce than even our most pessimistic estimates had anticipated. And yet, despite the guilty feelings that followed from missing so many deadlines, this book, and its message, continued to fascinate us. Part of our problem was the incredible range of ideas that we were forced to consider. Although we had always believed in the pervasive influence of cognitive mapping, we were surprised by some of the areas where our exploration led us. As authors, we were also hampered by our decision to write a book in which illustrations and examples were an integral part of the text. Wherever possible, we avoided the "academic" literature in favor of such "popular" sources as newspapers, magazines, novels, billboards, and even restaurant placemats. The book uses cartoons, advertisements, anecdotes, jokes, and quotations to make a particular point *and* to reinforce the idea that cognitive mapping touches many parts of our everyday experience. Although we are trained, respectively, as a professional geographer and a professional psychologist, we have not written a book *for* any particular discipline or for any particular course. Instead, we wanted to share an understanding of an idea that is simple, yet vitally important to any human being. We are all confronted with the need to come to grips with the spatial environment in which we live. Just as much as we would argue that we cannot escape this need, we would also argue that we should not ignore the ability that allows us to answer it. Cognitive mapping is too important and too fascinating to be dismissed.

R.M.D.

D.S.

ACKNOWLEDGMENTS

During the long, drawn out gestation period of this book, we have depended on the support and assistance of many people. Although they may not have realized what they were contributing to, we appreciate their efforts. To the best of our collective recollections, the manuscript typing was in the hands of Maria Becerra, Colleen Kristula, Nina McNeal, and Vicki Sanders; the labor of obtaining permissions was borne by Geoff Hamburg, Brooke Harris, Maureen McGee, and Vicki Sanders; the artwork was ably executed by Costis Hadjimihalis, Maurice Herman, Maureen McGee, and Jean O'Laoire; and we received contributions to and comments on the manuscript from Dan Carson, Suzanne Downs, Vikki Fulton, David Hodge, David Ley, Ben Marsh, Cathy McCartan, Jim Meyer, E. Kareem Sadalla, Ed Soja, and Larry Springer. We apologize to those people whom we have inadvertently overlooked. To all of you, thanks; to Mo, Nicolas, and Suzanne, a special thank-you for bearing with us for such a long time.

Acknowledgments for Permission to Reprint Material

These acknowledgments are divided into two major parts, "Quotations" and "Illustrations," and within each part by chapters. Under "Quotations," we gratefully acknowledge permission to reprint the material specified in each case to the individual, organization, or publishing house extending the permission and so indicated; under "Illustrations," we gratefully acknowledge permission to reproduce or recopy the illustration indicated by figure number to the individual, organization, or publishing house extending the permission and so indicated.

QUOTATIONS

CHAPTER 1

To Harper & Row, Publishers, Inc., for *You Can't Go Home Again*, by T. Wolfe, © 1966; to M.I.T. Press, for *The Image of the City*, by K. Lynch, © 1960; to *The New York Times*, for "Free Subway Maps a Best Nonseller," © 1972; to Homerica, for "Relocation Counselling"; to Arlington House, publishers for "Safe Places" advertisement originally appearing in *The New York Times*; to *The Los Angeles Times*, for "Social Map of Beautiful People Places," © 1972.

CHAPTER 2

To the American Psychological Association for "Studies in Spatial Learning, 1. Orientation and the Short Cut," by E. C. Tolman, from *Journal of Experimental Psychology*, © 1946; to *Saturday Review*, for "The National Birthday Mess," by G. Walter, © 1972; to *The Philadelphia Inquirer*, for "Despite Its Foes, Phila. is a City to See and Love," by J. Wooten, © 1973; to *The New York Times*, for "Travel Notes: Airport Tax Faces Challenge," © 1973; to *Newsweek Inc.*, for "What's in a Name," © 1973; to *The New York Times*, for material in the March 8, 1973 issue,

CHAPTER 3

Would You Want to Visit There?" by D. Murray, © 1972; and "In English Area of Montreal, a New Breed," by W. Borders, © 1973; to A. L. Strauss, for *Images of the American City,* © 1961; to *The New York Times,* for "On the Town, But Which One?" by J. Smith, © 1972; to Harvard University Press, for *The Intellectual Versus the City,* by M. White, and L. White, © 1962; to Basic Books, for *The Mind of a Mnemonist,* by A. R. Luria, © 1968.

CHAPTER 4

To T. R. Lee, for "Psychology and Living Space," from *Transactions of the Bartlett Society,* © 1964; to Houghton Mifflin Company, for *O Pioneers!* by W. S. Cather, © 1913; to *The New York Times,* for advertisements © 1972 and 1973; an article appearing on November 15, 1974; and "Superman Rescues Metropolis Again," by A. H. Malcom, © 1972; to Pocono Mountains Vacation Bureau, for permission to reprint an advertisement from *The New York Times,* © 1972; to The Viking Press, Inc., for *Travels with Charley,* by J. Steinbeck, © 1962 by J. Steinbeck; and *The Haunting of Hill House,* by S. Jackson, © 1959 by S. Jackson; to Midatlantic Banks, for permission to reprint an advertisement from *The New York Times,* © 1973; to *The New York Times,* for "Guess What State's Initials are N.J.?" by T. J. Flanagan, © 1973; to *Clifton Magazine,* and R. Symanski, for "No Arby's in Appalachia," by R. Symanski, J. Harman, and M. Swift, © 1973; to *The Social Science Journal,* for "Myth and Reality: Environmental Perception of the Mormon Pioneers," by R. H. Jackson, © 1972; to Harcourt Brace Jovanovich, Inc., for *Main Street,* by S. Lewis, © 1920; to Farrar, Straus & Giroux, Inc., for *The Weekend Man,* by R. Wright, © 1970; to A. L. Strauss, for *Images of the American City,* © 1961; to NTIS, the Academy of Pedagogical Sciences, RSFSR, and F. N. Shemyakin (see Chapter 3 credits); to G. P. Putnam's Sons, for *The Moon Is a Harsh Mistress,* by R. Heinlein, © 1966 by R. A. Heinlein; to *Time: The Weekly News Magazine,* for "Sign Language," © 1972; to *The New York Review of Books,* for *The Mask of State: Watergate Portraits,* by M. McCarthy, © 1973; to *The New York Times,* for "The Specialness of Growing Up in Washington, D.C.," by C. Rivers, © 1972; to M.I.T. Press, for *The Image of the City,* by K. Lynch, © 1960; to William Morrow and Company, Inc., for *A Christmas Story,* by Richard Burton; to John Murray (Publishers), Ltd., for "On Finding the Way," from *The Art of Travel: or, Shifts and Contrivances Available in Wild Countries,* by Sir. F. Galton, © 1872.

CHAPTER 5

To Harvard University Press, for *East Is a Big Bird,* by T. Gladwin, © 1970; to Australian National University Press, and the University Press of Hawaii, for *We, the Navigators,* by D. Lewis, © 1971; to the *Journal of the Polynesian Society,* for "A Return Voyage Between Puluwat and Saipan Using Micronesian Navigational Techniques," by D. Lewis, © 1971; to Sage Publications, Inc., and S. Carr, for "The City As a Trip: Perceptual Selection and Memory in the View from the Road," by S. Carr, and D. Schissler, from *Environment and Behavior,* Vol. 1, No. 1, pp. 9 and 31, © 1969; to Sage Publications, Inc., for "The Sonic Environment of Cities," by M. Southworth, from *Environment and Behavior,* Vol. 1, No. 1, pp. 49–70, © 1969; to Little, Brown and Company, for *Rites of Way,* by A. Lupo, F. Colcord, and E. P. Fowler, © 1971; to Sage Publications, Inc., and G. Fellman, for "A Neighborhood A Highway Would Destroy," by G. Fellman, and B. Brandt, from *Environment and Behavior,* Vol. 2, No. 3, pp.

297–298, © 1970; to the *Journal of the American Institute of Planners*, for "Some Sources of Residential Satisfaction in an Urban Slum," by M. Fried, and P. Gleicher, from *AIP Journal*, Vol. 27, © 1961; to the American Sociological Association, for " 'Sentiment' and 'Symbolism' as Ecological Variables," by W. Firey, *American Sociological Review*, © 1945.

CHAPTER 6

To Aldine Publishing Company, for "The Development of Spatial Cognition: A Review," by R. A. Hart and G. T. Moore, in *Image and Environment*, edited by R. M. Downs, and D. Stea, © 1973; to the Society of Sigma XI, for "One Brain–Two Minds," by M. S. Gazzaniga, from *American Scientist*, Vol. 60, © 1972; to *The Bulletin of the Los Angeles Neurological Societies*, and J. E. Bogen, for "The Other Side of the Brain, IV. The A/P Ratio," by J. E. Bogen, R. De Zure, W. D. TenHouten, and J. F. Marsh, Vol. 37, No. 2, © 1972; to G. W. Hewes, for permission to quote passages from a letter written to J. M. Blaut, July 18, 1971; to Bantam Books, Inc., for "Tonio Kroger," reprinted from *Tonio Kroger and Other Stories*, by T. Mann, English translation by D. Luke, © 1970 by Bantam Books; to *Psychology Today*, for "The Brain," by K. H. Pribram, © 1971 by Ziff-Davis Publishing Company; to the Association of American Geographers, for "Studies of Geographic Learning," from the *Annals of the AAG*, Vol. 61, © 1971; to the Conde Nast Publications, Inc., for "Mimsy Were the Borogroves," by L. Padgett, from *Analog*, © 1943 by Street and Smith Publications, Inc., © 1971 (renewed) by the Conde Nast Publications, Inc.; to *Psychology Today*, for "I.Q. and Point of View," by A. Pinard, and E. Sharp, © 1972 by Ziff-Davis Publishing Company; to *The New York Times*, for "Piaget Sees Science Dooming Psychoanalysis," by J. L. Hess, © 1972; to the American Psychological Association, and H. D. Fishbein, for "Children's Understanding of Spatial Relations: Coordination of Perspectives," by H. D. Fishbein, S. Lewis, and K. Keiffer, from *Developmental Psychology*, Vol. 7, No. 1, © 1972; and "The Course of Cognitive Growth," by J. S. Bruner, from *American Psychologist*, Vol. 19, © 1964; to Clark University Press, for *Processes of Cognitive Growth: Infancy*, by J. S. Bruner, © 1968; to Ziff-Davis Publishing Company, for "Newsline – Child Development: Babies See More Than You Think," by P. Horn, from *Psychology Today*, © 1975.

CHAPTER 7

To *The Pennsylvania Mirror*, for "Wrong Directions," by Paul Dubbs, © 1975; to Harper & Row Publishers, Inc., for *One Hundred Years of Solitude*, by G. Garcia Marquez, © 1970; to John Wiley & Sons, Inc., for a selection by J. A. Michon, in *Cognition in Learning and Memory*, (L. W. Gregg, ed.), © 1972; to *The New York Times*, for "City's Bronx Map Is Drawn Askew," by E. C. Burks, © 1971; to The American Psychological Association, for "Reverse Illusions of Orientation," by M. A. Binet, in *Psychological Review*, © 1894; to Aldine Publishing Company, for a selection by P. Gould in *Image and Environment: Cognitive Mapping and Spatial Behavior*, (R. M. Downs, and D. Stea, eds.), © 1973.

CHAPTER 8

To M.I.T. Press, for a selection by D. Appleyard, from *Planning Urban Growth and Regional Development 8*, (L. Rodwin, ed.), © 1975; to the U.S. Forest Service, for "The Contribution of Environmental Research to Wilderness

Policy Decisions," by R. C. Lucas, in *Journal of Social Issues*, © 1966; to Charles Moore, "The San Francisco Skyline: Hard to Spoil, But They're Working On It," in *Architectural Forum*, © 1965; to the M.I.T. Press, for *Learning from Las Vegas*, by R. Venturi, D. S. Brown, S. Izenour, © 1972; to *The Vancouver Sun*, for "Can I Get There From Here?" by C. Davis, © 1974; to The New York Times Company, for "Jigsaw Puzzles Can Be Merciless," by N. Smaridge, © 1975; to The New York Times Company, for "Labyrinthian Way," by M. Gardner, © 1975.

ILLUSTRATIONS

For Figure 1.1, to United Features Syndicate, Inc.; for Figure 1.2, to Curt Teich and Company, Inc.; for Figure 1.4, to Doncaster and District Development Council, Doncaster, England, G. B.; for Figure 1.5, to North Texas Commission, and Tracy-Locke Advertising and Public Relations, Inc.; for Figure 1.6, to Reynolds Securities, Inc., and Albert Frank-Guenther-Law, Advertising/Public Relations; for Figure 1.7, to the Register and Tribune Syndicate, Inc., Des Moines, Iowa; for Figure 1.8, to David Butwin, and the *Saturday Review*; for Figure 1.9, from the *Black Inner City as Frontier Outpost*, AAG Monograph Series, #7, 1974, to the Association of American Geographers, and D. Ley; for Figure 1.10, from *Spatial Organization: the Geographer's View of the World*, by R. F. Abler, J. Adams, and P. R. Gould, 1971, p. 520, to Prentice-Hall, Inc.; for Figure 1.11, from "Society, the City, and the Space-Economy of Urbanism," by D. Harvey, to the Association on College Geography and the author; for Figure 1.12, to United Air Lines; for Figure 1.13, to the Greyhound Corporation; for Figure 1.14, to El Al Israel Airlines; for Figure 1.15, to Penguin Books, and P. Gould; for Figures 2.1 and 2.2, from *Bees*, by K. Von Frisch, to Cornell University Press; for Figure 2.5, to Amtrak, and Ted Bates, Advertising; for Figure 3.1, to Yellow Pages, Phoenix, Arizona; for Figure 3.3, to Aldine Publishing Company; for Figure 3.5, to the Bank of America; for Figures 4.1 and 4.2, from "Black Youths View Their Environment: Neighborhood Maps," *Environment and Behavior*, 1970, **2** (1), 1970 (June), by F. Ladd, to Sage Publications, Inc., and the author; for Figure 4.3, to Virginia State Travel Service; for Figure 4.4, to South Carolina State Development Board; for Figure 4.6, from *Yurok Geography*, by T. T. Waterman, to the University of California Press; for Figure 4.8, to COMSAT (Communications Satellite) and Ehrlich, Harris, Manes, and Associates, Inc.; for Figures 5.1, 5.2, and 5.3, from *East Is a Big Bird: Navigation and Logic on Puluwat Atoll*, by Thomas Gladwin, © 1970 by the President and Fellows of Harvard College, to Harvard University Press, and the author; for Figure 5.4, to the M.I.T. Press; for Figure 5.5, from the "Semantics of Icelandic Orientation," by E. Haugen, Word, 1957, 13, 447–460, to the International Linguistic Association, Inc.; for Figure 6.1, to *Newsweek*, and Roy Doty; for Figures 6.2 and 6.3, from "Chimpanzee Spatial Memory Organization," by Professor E. W. Menzel, *Science*, 1973 (30 November), **182**, 943–945, © 1973 by the American Association for the Advancement of Science, to AAAS, and the authors; for Figure 7.1 to Publishers—Hall Syndicate, and Hank Ketcham; for Figure 7.2, to Needham, Harper and Steers Advertising, Inc., and Herbert Bayer; for Figure 7.3, an editorial cartoon by Frank Interlandi, to *The Los Angeles Times*; for Figures 7.6 and 7.7, from *New York in Flashmaps*, by Toy Lasker, to Flashmaps, Inc.; for Figure 7.8, to the New York City Transit System.

Chapter 1

SENSES OF PLACE

INTRODUCTION

All through the ghostly stillness of the land, the train made on forever its tremendous noise, fused of a thousand sounds, and they called back to him forgotten memories: old songs, old faces, old memories, and all strange, wordless, and unspoken things men know and live and feel, and never find a language for—the legend of dark time, the sad brevity of their days, the unknowable but haunting miracle of life itself. He heard again, as he had heard throughout his childhood, the pounding wheel, the tolling bell, the whistlewail, and he remembered how these sounds, coming to him from the river's edge in the little town of his boyhood, had always evoked for him their tongueless prophecy of wild and secret joy, their glorious promises of new lands, morning, and a shining city. But now the lonely cry of the great train was speaking to him with an equal strangeness of return. For he was going home again.

*   *   *

He thought of all his years away from home, the years of wandering in many lands and cities. He remembered how many times he had thought of home with such an intensity of passion that he could close his eyes and see the scheme of every street, and every house upon each street, and the faces of the people, as well as recall the countless things that they had said and the densely-woven fabric of all their histories. Tomorrow he would see it all again, and he almost wished he had not come. It would

1

have been easy to plead the excuse of work and other duty. And it was silly, anyhow, to feel as he did about the place.

But why had he always felt so strongly the magnetic pull of home, why had he thought so much about it and remembered it with such blazing accuracy, if it did not matter, and if this little town, and the immortal hills around it, was not the only home he had on earth? He did not know. All that he knew was that the years flow by like water, and that one day men come home again.

The train rushed onward through the moonlit land.

(Wolfe, 1966, pp. 74–75)

Returning after a long absence to a childhood home is a powerful, recurring theme in both literature and popular music. Thomas Wolfe uses the noise of the homeward-bound train to trigger a string of recollections, which are synthesized into a sound and visual portrait of the man's home town. Most of us have undergone a similar experience although we may not have the skill to articulate it so evocatively. Nevertheless, if you close your eyes and recall your own thoughts and emotions on returning home, you will be forced to agree with Wolfe that "you can't go home again." The saying that there's no place like home is such a cliché that we overlook its double significance and meaning. While it is true that our home serves as an anchor point for many of our beliefs and affections, it is also true that there is no longer a place that is identical to, or sometimes even vaguely resembles, our memories of home.

The world that you grew up in, that became part of you, and that is so vividly remembered, has vanished. The portrait that you constructed does not match the world that you see around you. The little "ma and pa" grocery store around the corner has been demolished. The overgrown park that you used to play in has been transformed into a manicured housing development. Streets and alleys that you walked along on your way to school do not exist. The face of the earth has been changed many times since you left home. Your memories are now out-of-date and their very foundations have been shaken.

But we have also changed. We have acquired many new perspectives on the world and now look at things very differently from the ways in which we did as children. The lawn that took so long to mow in the summer and to rake leaves from in the fall now seems to be no larger than the proverbial postage stamp. The railway station, recently abandoned, used to be at the end of a seemingly never-ending walk, but now appears to be only a hop, skip, and a jump away from home.

Returning to a place can be a painful experience, and we can sympathize wholeheartedly with Snoopy's cry of anguish (see Figure 1.1). Memories are treasured, and it comes as a disturbing shock to realize that people and things and places are not what they used to be, that the

Figure 1.1. "You can't go home again": the pain of returning to a well-remembered place.

world as we remember it does not physically exist any longer. Nostalgia can be both happy and sad, satisfying and disturbing. (We are perhaps unaware that the Greek roots of the word are *nostos*, meaning to return home, and *algos*, meaning pain.)

As with the past, so with the present: Wherever we make our home, there are familiar places and familiar ways of experiencing and remembering them. We are proud of our transition from the uncertain newcomer who doesn't know his way around to the confident old-timer who knows the place like the back of his hand. We can find our way easily; some trips can be made blindfolded. Directions are readily given to inquiring strangers. We can conjure up vivid images of the sights and sounds of places that are mentioned in conversation. In short, we feel at home in the place. However, even if this comfortable familiarity does not breed contempt, it is refreshing to see a place through new eyes. A visiting friend can point out views and places that we have never noticed, while the drive along a well-travelled route as passenger instead of driver reveals the blinding effect of much everyday experience. Sometimes we consciously try to break free from these patterned ways of experiencing the world. A new short cut through a well-known part of the city provides a novel understanding of the places that are off the beaten track. The participant in a mystery tour, a popular feature of English working-class social life, enjoys not knowing where he is going. Since only the organizer of the bus tour knows the route, the fun comes from guessing the next place to be visited and from seeing well-known places in a novel and unexpected sequence.

And so also with the future: We pursue many activities and hobbies that lift us, at least temporarily, out of the ruts of our familiar world. We like to learn about exotic and faraway places in the world, a desire catered to by popular magazines such as *Holiday* and the *National Geographic*, by books such as *Kon Tiki* and the innumerable travel guides to everywhere under the sun, and by such films as Lowell Thomas' travelogues and the *National Geographic* series of documentaries. The illustrated travel lecture retains its audience appeal, and people are still lured to the dinners that offer a chance to buy a vacation or retirement place in the sun. We enjoy visiting new places in our role as tourists. Half of the fun of a vacation comes in the planning stage when we wrestle with the choice between the scenery of New England or the beaches of Florida. Often the other half of the fun comes from the *reminders* of the trip: the souvenirs, the fading suntan, and the notorious color slides that are inflicted on unwary friends. These selected memories carefully filter out the unpleasant aspects of the vacation itself: rose-tinted spectacles overlook the airsickness, the customs' hassle, and the missing travellers' checks. Yet our interest is not confined to down-to-earth places in the so-called "real world." Fantasy worlds are equally appealing. J. R. Tolkien's "Middle Earth," Lewis Carroll's "Wonderland," Walt Disney's "Fantasia," and the countries depicted in Jonathan Swift's *Gulliver's Travels* seem no less "real" to us than places that we "know" to exist but that we will probably never visit. The success of Disneyland in California and Disneyworld in Florida is ample testimony to the appeal of fantasy worlds.

Yet this pervasive human desire to reminisce, to explore, to visit, to fantasize, and to learn about places all over the world is much more than the idle curiosity or inquisitiveness that it appears to be at first glance. Rather, it reflects, and is part of, a fundamental human need: *the need to know about the world around us.* We need to know where people and things are, to know how to get there safely or quickly, to be able to estimate how far away or close something is, to know which places to avoid at all costs, and to be able to find the best place to live or at which to open a new business or to visit for a vacation. We need to organize in our minds an understanding of the world in which we live. We must synthesize past and present experiences of our spatial environment with beliefs and expectations about places as yet unvisited or never to be visited. We must accommodate our worlds of fantasy and imagination. These needs to know and to organize are central to a skill and ability that we very rarely consciously recognize. It is part of that "mysterious" hidden second nature, which we sometimes refer to in passing but which we do not stop to analyze. This ability plays a fundamental role in everyday life, affecting work, play, travel, and most other aspects of our normal behavior.

In this book, we want to embark on a voyage of discovery and analysis. Our objective is to explore *inner* space, a little-known region of that dark continent *inside* man's head. Inner space refers to the representation of the geographical environment as it exists within a person's mind. It is the world as people believe it to be. We will try to answer some crucial but rarely asked questions: How do we know the world? What do we mean by the ability to know the world? How do we make sense of the world out there? How do we learn about new places? Does this ability change with age or experience? How do we use this ability in making decisions about and organizing our everyday life? How do we communicate our understanding of the world to other people? How do we try to alter other people's understanding? Can we use our understanding of this ability to design teaching programs for schools or to improve the design of our built environment?

Before we can answer these questions, we must resolve the apparent contradiction between our claim that this ability to think about the spatial environment is fundamental to everyday life, and the statement that these crucial questions have rarely been asked. If it is so important, why do we know so little about it? A part of the answer lies in the nature of the social sciences. The object of our exploration is one of those *terrae incognitae* that falls in between many, and yet squarely within none, of the social sciences as they are currently defined. It is obviously a major concern of both geography and psychology; it is important to sociology and anthropology. Yet, like so many interdisciplinary topics, it has largely escaped the focal attention of all of these disciplines. The questions have not been totally ignored in the past, but it has been only in recent years that any large group of social scientists has invested a significant amount of time in answering them. This book represents, in part, an attempt to give some coherence to their answers; more importantly, it represents our personal understanding of the ability to know the world.

Before we place the entire blame for our ignorance on academics, we must also recognize two other parts of the answer to this contradiction. On the one hand, we are so adept at using this ability to know the world around us that we rarely notice its existence. Knowledge seems to "come naturally" to us, but, as we shall see later, it does *not*. The only time that the ability comes to our attention is when it doesn't work—that is, when we are lost. The impact of such an event is described by Kevin Lynch (1960, p. 4):

> To become completely lost is perhaps a rather rare experience for most people in the modern city. We are supported by the presence of others and by special way-finding devices: maps, street numbers, route signs, bus placards. But let the mishap of disorientation occur, and the sense of anxiety and even terror that accompanies it reveals to us how closely it is linked to our sense of balance and well-being. The very word "lost" in our language means much more than simple geographical uncertainty: it carries a tone of utter disaster.

Fortunately, such disasters are rare and therefore we pay little attention to the ability that helps us to avoid them. On the other hand, our ignorance of this ability is excusable. How can we study or even discuss something for which we do not have a name? In our everyday language, we speak of someone having a good sense of direction, but we have very little explicit idea of what this implies. We talk about our memory (or lack of memory) for names and faces but rarely of our memory for places. Although we need and possess this mysterious ability to think about our spatial environment, we do not have a name for it. It is obviously connected with such familiar psychological concepts as memory and learning, with intelligence and imagination. Yet these concepts are inappropriate for our requirements, and so, instead of the clumsy and vague phrases that we have used so far, we must introduce two terms: these are *cognitive mapping* and *cognitive maps*.

COGNITIVE MAPPING AND MAPS

Cognitive mapping is an abstraction covering those cognitive or mental abilities that enable us to collect, organize, store, recall, and manipulate information about the spatial environment. These abilities change with age (or development) and use (or learning). Above all, cognitive mapping refers to a *process* of doing: it is an *activity* that we engage in rather than an object that we have. It is the way in which we come to grips with and comprehend the world around us. The idea of a process or activity becomes clear if we list a range of everyday situations in which we make use of cognitive mapping: in learning the way from home to school (and back again) as a child; in planning a vacation trip; in deciding upon an efficient route for a multipurpose shopping trip; in searching for a new home; in getting to know a new town; in learning to be a taxi driver in London (or any other city).

A *cognitive map* is a *product*—a person's organized representation of some part of the spatial environment. Examples include a sketch map showing the route to your house; a list of the places downtown that you avoid because they are dangerous; a child's painting of his house and neighborhood; the picture that comes to mind every time you try to cross town on the subway system; and the travel brochure that describes places that are worth visiting. Most importantly, a cognitive map is a cross section representing the world at one instant in time. It reflects the world *as some person believes it to be*; it need not be correct. In fact, distortions are highly likely. It is *your* understanding of the world, and it may only faintly resemble the world as reflected in cartographic maps or color photographs. However, to get a better understanding of the nature of cognitive maps, we must focus on two key concepts from the definition and look at them in more detail. The key concepts are *representation* and *environment*.

In everyday usage, we think of a portrait of a person or a scale model of a building as representations; we speak of somebody making a representation on our behalf. Turning to the dictionary, we find that a representation stands for or symbolizes something; that it depicts or portrays something; that it can be a mental image or likeness or model. Our use of representation shares *all* of these characteristics. We are talking about something that *stands for* the environment, that *portrays* it, that is both a *likeness* and a simplified *model*, something that is, above all, a *mental image* in a person's brain. These images are not necessarily visual in form since, as we will discuss in Chapter 3, blind people also construct mental images of their spatial environment. (The intriguing but complex issue of where and how such representations are formed in the brain will be treated in Chapter 6.) The cognitive map is clearly a representation in every sense of the word—in fact, if we break down the word so that it reads re-presentation, we have another clue. Cognitive mapping allows us to generate mental images and models of the environment, which are *present again,* which we can conjure up and think about almost at will.

However, we still face the question, Representation of what? Environment is now such an overused word that it has lost its precise meaning, and therefore we must specify what particular aspects of a person's environment are of interest to us. In the context of cognitive mapping, we mean the *everyday spatial environment:* everyday in the sense that it is the world that we interact with regularly and that serves as the normal setting for our activities. It includes schools, homes, the local shopping center, friends' houses, the pattern of streets and roads, beaches, picnic areas, restaurants, movie theaters, parking lots, and the doctor's office. These make up the stage or context for much of our everyday or normal behavior. These are important places that we use, need to know about, and therefore need to represent mentally.

In addition, the places that we have listed help us to understand the *spatial* part of our definition of the environment. We use schools, stores, parks, and so on, in everyday life and so we need to know their locations, how far away they are, what's there, how good they are, and how to get to them. Cognitive mapping is our way of acquiring and storing this essential information, of being able to use it to decide where to go and how to get there.

We can also see how our interest in the environment differs from that of other social sciences. Sociologists, and many social psychologists, might focus on a person's everyday social environment: the patterns of people and groups and organizations with which a person regularly comes into contact. Some sociologists are also interested in a much broader and inclusive definition of environment, which encompasses, for example, the type of school system a child attends, the family structure he grows up in, his friendship patterns, and the roles of books, television, and radio as they influence his attitudes and beliefs. Obviously, cognitive mapping is important in determining the overall course of a person's life, but sociologists and psychologists are primarily interested in many *other* aspects of the environment, and tend to ignore its *spatial* aspects.

If our discussion so far has seemed abstract, it must be emphasized that the ability we are trying to grapple with is literally (and metaphorically) down-to-earth. We can get a firmer appreciation by examining

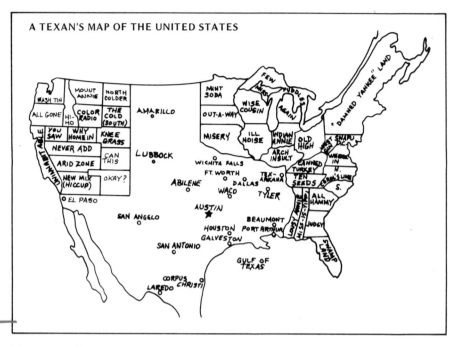

Figure 1.2. Humorous representations, 1: a Texan's view of the United States.

three different cognitive maps (see Figures 1.2, 1.3, and 1.4). Each depicts a cognitive representation of a country and is intended to be amusing: Each gets its humor from a different source. In the case of the Texan's map of the United States (Figure 1.2), there is a play on the spelling and pronunciation of the names of the states (Miss Again and Why Home In), and such regional biases as labelling all of the northeastern states "Damned Yankee Land," and California as "uninhabitable" are evident. The Maritimer's view of Canada (Figure 1.3) places an extreme emphasis on the virtues of home. There is no place in the rest of Canada that can match it; the Maritimes, blessed by a smiling sun, are the home of the world's biggest, best, and finest. "Ye newe map of Britain" (Figure 1.4) pits cosmopolitanism against provincialism, civilization against backwardness. Of course, after laughing, a Texan or a Maritimer or a Londoner would claim that the maps are exaggerations, overstatements, and that they should not be taken too seriously.

But are they overstatements? We often admit that many a true word is spoken in jest, and such is the case with these three cognitive maps. If we look more carefully, and are not sidetracked by the humor, we notice that these maps depend for their success upon their approximation to the truth and contain, if not the whole truth, a good part of it. Each is an attempt to express something about the world—how

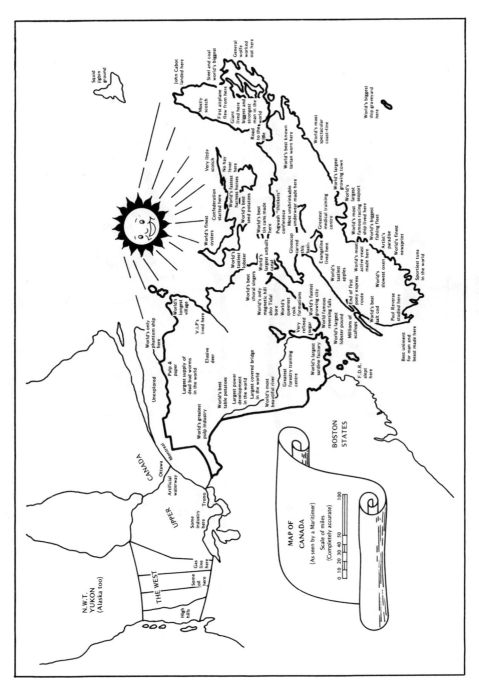

Figure 1.3. Humorous representations, 2: a Maritimer's view of Canada.

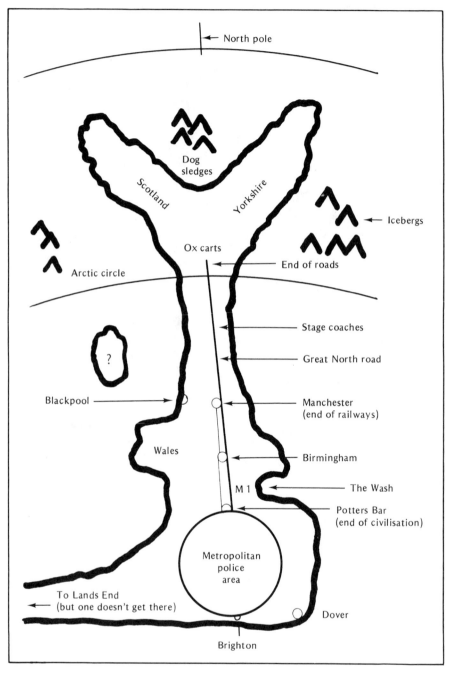

Figure 1.4. Humorous representations, 3: a Londoner's view of the north of Great Britain.

people react to and assess the world around them. These cognitive maps are not much like the cartographic atlas maps of the U.S.A., Canada, or Great Britain with which we are familiar. The shapes of the coastlines are twisted, the areas of the various states or regions are out of proportion, and the relative locations of places have been changed. Despite these alterations, the maps are easily recognized and readily understood. Each one reflects a regional bias to and parochial view of the world; each one compares the rest of the world with home, and finds the rest of the world wanting. The Texan's view echoes the joke that everything is bigger in Texas, expressed more appropriately in this case as, everything is big about Texas except the states that surround it! Texas looms larger than everywhere else in the U.S.A., an effect that is partly achieved by the annexation of a large part of Mexico. This cavalier disregard for national frontiers reflects an attitude which may partially explain why Texans were for many years the most unpopular tourists in Mexico. Such cartographic license is also employed to locate the Southwest Metroplex (Dallas/Fort Worth) "smack dab in the middle" of the U.S.A. (see Figure 1.5). The Londoner's view accen-

Figure 1.5. The importance of centrality.

tuates the positive aspects of the good life in the southeast of England and relegates the negative for everywhere to the north. Everything that matters in Canada is, in the view of at least one mapmaker, located in the Maritime Provinces.

In all three cases, we have a representation of a part of the world as a certain group of people believe it to be, expressing pride of place in the case of Texas and the Maritimes, and an Englishwoman's fear of the unknown area north of London. These examples are amusing, thought-provoking, truthful, and eye-catching, but they are scarcely sufficient evidence to support our claim that cognitive mapping is vitally important and that it is worthwhile writing (and reading) a whole book about cognitive maps.

WHY IS COGNITIVE MAPPING IMPORTANT?

Why is cognitive mapping important and worth studying? There is a range of answers to this question. In the remainder of this chapter we will present four answers and then briefly outline the organization of the book.

COGNITIVE MAPPING AND SPATIAL BEHAVIOR

The principal reason for attempting to understand cognitive mapping is that the world as we believe it to be serves as the basis for much of our everyday spatial behavior. Although the arguments behind this claim are reviewed in detail in Chapter 2, we can appreciate the importance of cognitive mapping if we look at some of the ways in which spatial behavior is dependent on the world as we believe it to be.

First, we rely upon organizing and manipulating our knowledge of the world in order to know where to get things and to find people. We *need* to find supermarkets for food, stores for clothing and furniture, doctors for medical treatment, friends for advice, and parks and beaches for relaxation. We have to know where these essential things are located. If we don't know where they are, we are either forced "to let our fingers do the walking," as the *Yellow Pages* telephone directory advises, or to waste a lot of valuable time and effort before we find what we are searching for (see Figure 1.6).

But it is not sufficient only to know where people and things are. A second role of our cognitive mapping ability is in telling us how to get there. Although we usually speak of astronauts, air crew, and ships' captains navigating, we *also* have to navigate around our own corner of the world. As the child in Figure 1.7 demonstrates, the ability to find the quickest way home is something that we learn the hard way. We all pride ourselves in getting to know our way around a place. This means learning all of the shortcuts, knowing the traffic bottlenecks to avoid in the rush hour, and keeping track of which streets are currently under repair. We are generally flattered to be asked to give directions al-

Figure 1.6. The Search, and how to avoid it.

Figure 1.7. Knowledge of *place* and knowledge of *routes* are often intimately re-
      lated.

though the lost stranger may not always value the advice after he has
tried it out. Our environment is littered with signs, directions, and ar-
rows to help us in wayfinding; tourist information centers and American Automobile Association offices help us to solve spatial problems.
The *Baedeker* guide books, which were so popular with early twentieth
century European travellers, have been replaced by oil company road
maps, tour guides, and even tape-recorded casettes for walking tours
around museums and cities.

   The widely felt need for assistance in wayfinding is reflected in this
embittered assessment:

> . . . it is virtually impossible to understand New York, to find out what is
> going on or how to get there. For some years I believed information was
> deliberately withheld—that New York was a game with all the cards
> stacked against the provincial, the tourist, the foreigner—so that only the
> strongest would survive. Now I know better. New York is simply the es-
> sence of the American Way, a triumph of the spirit of Free Enterprise.
>
> (*New York*, 1972, p. 84)

And when free enterprise steps in to fill the information gap, the public
response is overwhelming:

> Give the people what they want, charge nothing and business will boom.
> The Transit Authority discovered this yesterday when it began to give

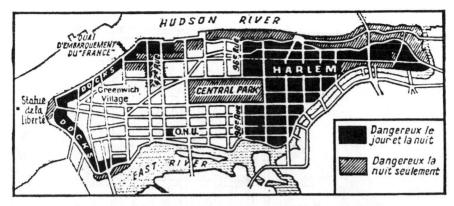

Figure 1.8. Residential and touristic undesirability: New York City is a place of fear and wonder to many visitors, fraught with fascination and dread. To the tourist equipped with this map, it appears even more frightening. The shaded areas are considered dangerous both night and day, the black areas during the night.

away new pocketsize subway maps and found that the demand of straphangers quickly exhausted the supply of many token-vending booths around the city.

*   *   *

A spokesman for the Transit Authority said all booths would be restocked with maps as rapidly as possible. The authority has printed 1.5 million copies of the new maps, but the spokesman said there were no figures available on the number distributed yesterday.

(*The New York Times*, August 8, 1972, p. 37)

There is more to wayfinding than knowing the shortest or easiest route. A tourist intent on sight-seeing would prefer the most picturesque and historic route. However, a tourist might also be advised to take heed of the warning contained in the French newspaper, *L'Aurore*. Urban crime, muggings, and gang harrassment have reached such a level that both visitors *and* city dwellers need to know where it is safe to be and to walk, night *and* day. For this reason, *L'Aurore* published a street map of Manhattan (see Figure 1.8) showing potential French tourists where it was unsafe both day and night, or night only. Yet such maps of safety are not just advisable for tourists to the city. David Ley (1972) interviewed residents of an inner-city neighborhood in Philadelphia about the location of dangerous places: street corners, alleys, bars, and so on. Figure 1.9 is an aggregate mapping of their responses, showing areas of high potential danger as peaks on a stress surface. Patterns of movement within the neighborhood carefully avoid these acknowledged danger points. The shortest route, in terms of physical distance or time, is not necessarily the best if it's not safe.

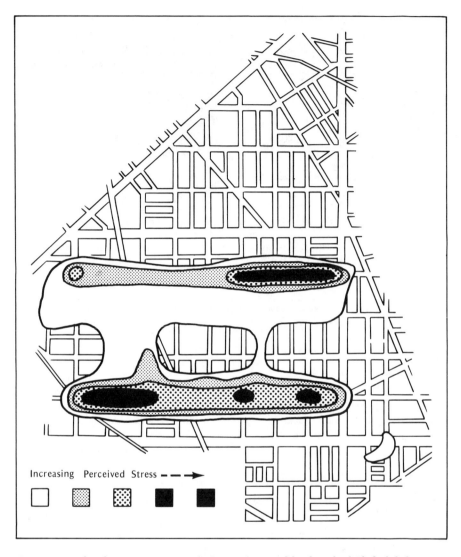

Figure 1.9. The dangerous areas of Monroe, a neighborhood of Philadelphia.

So far, we have seen that cognitive mapping tells us where to get things, and how to get there quickly, easily, and safely. A third role lies in telling us where to locate our basic activities: shopping centers, offices, factories, and, in particular, our homes. Given the increasing rates of social and spatial mobility that all Western societies are witnessing, the choice of a place to live is more than ever a true choice. Constraints of family ties, work place, and housing supply are of decreasing importance. The question, Where would you *like* to live? is far more meaningful, and cognitive mapping helps us to answer it. We choose be-

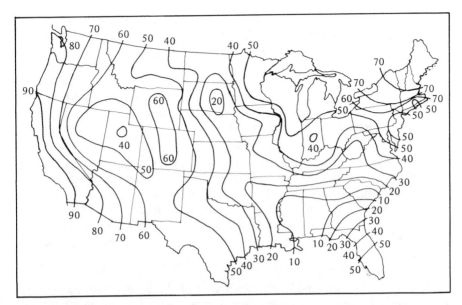

Figure 1.10. Residential desirability, 1: where California students would like (and not like) to live.

tween parts of the country, cities within a region, neighborhoods within a city, and houses within a neighborhood. We sort out in our minds the good and the bad, attractive and unattractive, desirable and undesirable, at all spatial scales.

On a national scale, Peter Gould (1966) has shown how U.S. college students view the states of the U.S.A. as potential places to live. Figure 1.10 is a map of the collective viewpoint of a group of students in California. Scores for each state range from 100 in California itself (the most desirable) to 0 in Alabama (the least desirable). The contour lines indicate the relative level of desirability and form a surface of peaks and valleys. Although we cannot claim that hypothetical questions (where would you like to live if you had complete freedom?) asked of college students give a representative picture, the surface does make intuitive sense. We have the same home bias shown in the Texas and Maritimes maps; there are regional stereotypes that color responses to the South and the Midwest; recreation or resort states like Maine or Florida are high spots of attraction. The residential desirability surface is one reflection of cognitive mapping at work.

However, long-distance moves are an uncertain undertaking, and uncertainty leads to worry and fear. Are we making the right decision? Homerica, a nationally advertised company, can ease the burden:

> We specialize in taking the risk out of relocating. Relocating and buying a home in a strange area is a big step and a misstep could prove extremely

costly. At Homerica we take the time, tension, and chance out of relocating. Counseling families and helping them to select the right neighborhood and home in an unfamiliar area is our business.

For those hardy people who prefer to rely upon their own cognitive mapping skills, a recent book can offer some assistance. *Safe Places*, by David and Holly Franke (1972), is a carefully researched discussion of 46 of the safest communities in the U.S.A.:

> To help you decide which of these communities is the right one for you, the authors knocked on doors in every town ... They sifted fact from fiction, reality from wishful thinking, saving you months—even years—of beating the bushes for a Safe Place of your own. The authoritative information they uncovered—warts and all—is carefully organized to help you make up your mind before you call the moving man and make your escape.

Within a city, we are all acutely aware of the status distinctions between various areas. We dichotomize areas according to whether they are on the right side of the tracks or not. There are fine differentiations on the right side of the tracks between "Nob Hill" or the "Golden Ghetto." The fashionable places to live are well known and envied: It is desirable to have the "right" address. A recent article in *The Los Angeles Times* (March 19, 1972) carries this folk geography one step further, and offers a social map of "beautiful people places" in Los Angeles. The article also reveals the power of suggestion in determining the social ins and outs of the city:

> What labels a place "socially desirable" is not totally explainable: views, gates, protection, high real estate values, clean air, schools, proximity to ocean/hills, chic shops—these can all play a part. On the other hand, areas with none of these to offer attract top Los Angeles leaders. Maybe Beautiful People buy where other Beautiful People buy, or buy where they think they buy.

The social and economic structure of the city is crucial knowledge not only to people seeking homes, but also to businessmen making investment decisions involving stores, offices, and factories. At the heart of all of these decisions is the real estate market. A cognitive map of areas of investment opportunity is essential for survival in this business, and David Harvey (1972) has provided a map of investment potential in inner-city Baltimore, as seen through the eyes of three professional landlords (see Figure 1.11).

The fourth connection between cognitive mapping and spatial behavior recalls our earlier discussion of the human desire to get away from home in order to see the world. Tourism and cognitive maps are inseparable. We must select the places to visit and map out the routes that we will follow. Help in making these choices is never far away. The tourist advertising industry is geared to manipulating and influencing our cognitive representations of places in the hope that the

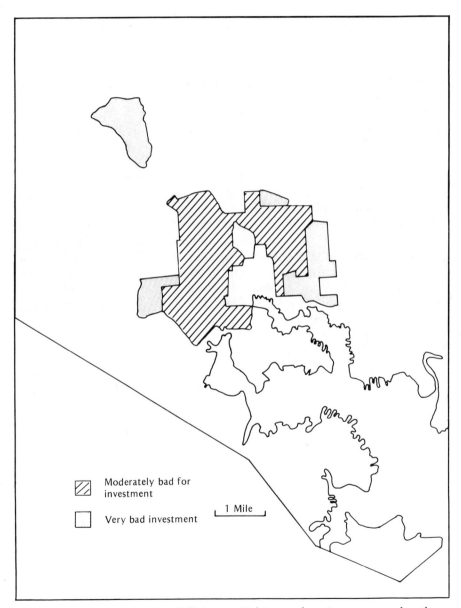

Figure 1.11. Investment possibilities in Baltimore housing as seen by three landlords in 1971.

urge to visit them will prove irresistible. Whether you are the blase world traveller or the confirmed stay-at-home, Florida, the state of excitement, claims to satisfy your every need:

> When you have been everywhere and you've seen everything . . . you discover that, after all, there's no place like Florida. When you haven't been anywhere and you haven't seen much, you'll discover that almost everything you've wanted to see is here in FLORIDA.

We are also tempted by the United Airlines map (Figure 1.12), the Greyhound Buslines map (Figure 1.13), and the El Al Airlines montage (Figure 1.14). They draw upon, reinforce, and accentuate our beliefs about vacation spots by singling out memorable graphic symbols that capture the identity of a place: Big Ben for London, the Capitol for Washington, and the Golden Gate Bridge for San Francisco. As we will see in Chapters 3 and 4, the way in which these advertisements are organized, and the "language" that they use, are both paralleled in our own cognitive maps of the world.

   Even this brief and highly selective discussion should reveal the fundamental interlinking of cognitive mapping and spatial behavior. Although this argument alone should be sufficient evidence to warrant a detailed investigation of cognitive maps and mapping, there are three other reasons that we must touch on. These are the existence of different perspectives on the world, the practical uses of cognitive mapping, and the role of cognitive mapping in structuring experience.

PERSPECTIVES ON THE WORLD

Cognitive maps and mapping vary according to a person's perspective on the world. Although everybody needs to be able to map the world cognitively in order to survive, the precise nature and use of this ability shows significant variations from person to person. Jakob von Uexkull (1957), an extraordinary ethologist writing in the 1930s, attempted to describe the *umwelten*, or phenomenal worlds, of different living creatures. For creatures ranging from the insects to man, he posed the question, What does the creature sense? The worlds experienced by different species are literally worlds apart. The sensory receptors of each species are sensitive to particular types of information from the surrounding environment: to heat instead of light, to color instead of black-white tones, to shape instead of movement. We sometimes overlook the existence of these "other" worlds because of the natural tendency to anthropomorphize, to attribute to every other creature our own human way of perceiving and cognizing the world. We must not make the same mistake with respect to fellow human beings. Their world may not be identical to our own. The universal need for cogni-

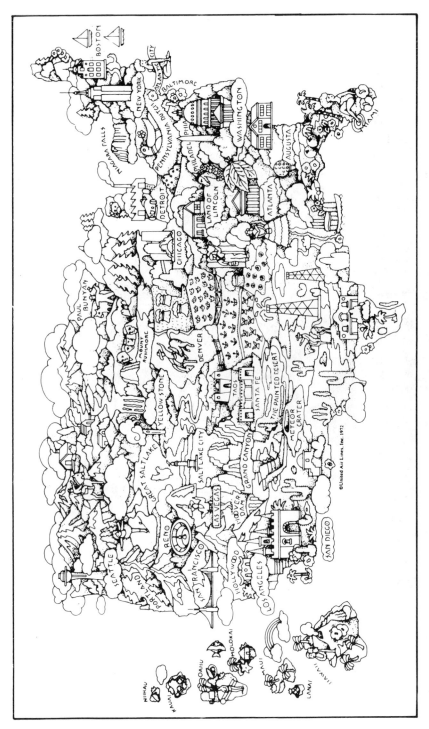

Figure 1.12. "United proudly presents the summer of '72." Selling an image of America, 1: United Air Lines.

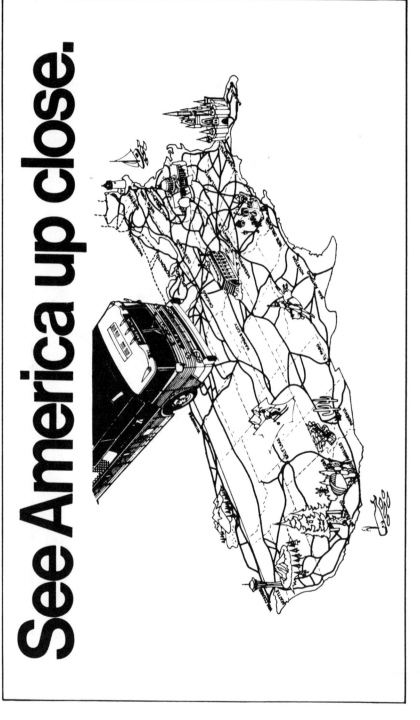

Figure 1.13. Selling an image of America, 2: Greyhound Bus Lines.

Our London-Paris-Amsterdam tour is 90% fun and 10% Jewish.

Figure 1.14. Selling western Europe: El Al Air Lines.

tive mapping should *not* be construed to mean either a universal process or a universal product.

Obviously, human beings share sensory receptors with approximately similar physiological capabilities to receive information. However, the world, as we believe it to be, is a synthesis of different types of information: visual, auditory, olfactory, and kinaesthetic. People mix these information types in varying proportions and place greater emphasis on different sensory modes. Consequently, cognitive maps show tremendous individual differences. Blind and deaf people cognitively map their spatial environments and represent the world to themselves. The mapping ability itself follows the same general principles as that of people with full visual and auditory capacities, although the resultant maps differ. Cognitive maps are not necessarily visual pictures of the world. For some people, sounds and smells play as much of a role in the image of a place as do visual inputs. For others, a picture may not be worth one word, let alone a thousand words. Representations do not have to be in the form of sensory images; word pictures can be just as effective. It is all a matter of style, of a choice of perspective on the world. There is no one universal way of looking at the world that everyone must use. Cognitive mapping is a flexible process that offers us a range of perspectives to suit specific situations.

Perspectives undergo major changes with increasing age; both the ability to map cognitively and the outcome of the process show qualitative developmental changes from birth onwards. The world of the child is not a scaled-down version of the world of adults. As the child passenger and the adult driver discover, there is more than one way to solve a wayfinding problem (see Figure 1.7). To understand the development of cognitive mapping, we must try to see the world through the eyes of a child. And this task is made more difficult because perspectives also change with practice and familiarity. Children and adults alike learn about places, and, as they do so, their representation changes. Eventually the child in the cartoon will learn the direct route from her friend's house to her own home although she hasn't yet made the connection. If the adult driver in the car is a long-term resident of the neighborhood, she will have a very different cognitive map from that of a would-be house purchaser who has just been given the proverbial 10-cent tour by the local realtor. Learning not only affects how much we know, but also how we organize our knowledge. To know somewhere like the back of your hand means more than knowing a lot about a place: It means grasping the complex of relationships between places, people, activities, and routes.

In addition to age and experience, our perspectives on the world are colored by the social group, region, and nation that we identify with. An area that is a run-down slum to a suburban American may be a happy, comfortable, friendly neighborhood to the residents' neighborhood action group. A small area of woodland may be a wildlife sanctuary to conservationists and an investment opportunity to real estate developers. The Texan's map (Figure 1.2) and the Londoner's map (Figure 1.4) are clear expressions of regional bias. In direct contrast to the view from California (Figure 1.10), the Alabama students (Figure 1.15) see residential desirability decreasing all around them although they are tempted by the attractions of California.

All of these variations in perspective emphasize that the world is what we make it, that the world as we believe it to be depends upon our sensory capacities, our age, our experience, and our attitudes and biases. Not only does our spatial behavior depend upon our cognitive mapping ability, but it is also affected by our particular versions and expressions of this ability.

THE PRACTICAL USES OF COGNITIVE MAPPING
Although cognitive mapping forms part of our mysterious "second nature" and is largely out of our immediate awareness, we should recog-

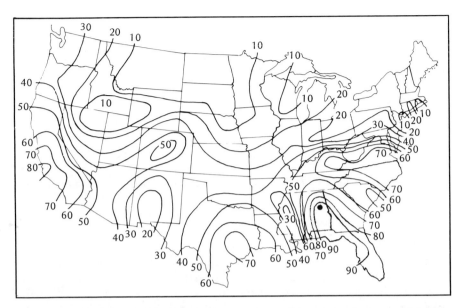

Figure 1.15. Residential desirability, 2: where Alabama students would like (and not like) to live.

nize that it is subject to a series of social pressures which influence and guide and, in some cases, make use of its operation.

Given the fundamental link between cognitive maps and decisions as to what to do where, cognitive maps are a target for advertisers with products and places to sell. Realtors, land speculators, travel agents, resort operators, shopping center developers, and local chambers of commerce are all trying to alter the way that we think about the world around us. But attempts at manipulation are not restricted to such blatant assaults by the advertising industry. Novelists, poets, artists, playwrights, and film directors endeavor to create a setting for their work, a setting that conveys a sense of place. The artistic ability to blend characters and setting draws upon the cognitive mapping skills of both artist and audience. Places "come alive" and we can see the world through the eyes of different characters. Thomas Hardy's Wessex and William Faulkner's Yoknapatawpha County have a reality that transcends our knowledge that they are based upon Dorsetshire and northern Mississippi. For many people throughout the world, America is a land of pony tails, white socks, drive-ins, freeways, skyscrapers, and split-levels—a stereotype constructed from the residual debris of a diet of Hollywood movies and T.V. shows.

Fortunately, there are more responsible sources that promote an understanding of the world. Education, and the discipline of geography in particular, shapes our cognitive maps. However, opinions as to the role (and value) of geography are many and varied. Mark Twain, speaking through Huckleberry Finn and Tom Sawyer, stated a popular belief about geography—that it is concerned with regional differentiation. Huck, during the flying-boat journey over the U.S.A., shouted:

> We're right over Illinois yet ... Illinois is green, Indiana is pink ... it ain't no lie, I've seen it on the map, and it's pink.

Tom endorsed this view of the geographer when he replied:

> ... he's got to paint them so you can tell them apart the minute you look at them, hain't he?
>
> (Quoted in Haggett, 1966, p. 3)

Although we may dispute Mark Twain's claims, geography in our schools and colleges does directly "color" (or change and influence) the form and content of cognitive maps and the operation of cognitive mapping. Teachers believe that they are training children to understand the world around them. But, as we shall see in Chapters 6 and 7, cognitive maps are learned, but are largely untaught. The process of learning to understand one's physical world begins *before* formal schooling. With building blocks and toys, the small child *models* the world as he believes it to be. The journal, *Better Homes and Gardens*, recently suggested a rainy day blanket game for a child trapped without playmates:

> To make the game, take half of an inexpensive blanket and glue on felt cutouts of the areas your youngster knows best—such as shopping center, school, library, airport, Grandma's house. Then the intrepid young traveler can push his toy cars and trucks along the wide highway and start to make-believe.

Children play these games spontaneously, and begin to develop their understanding of the world through their manipulation of models. There is more to toy play than simply idle amusement. An understanding of how this process of cognitive mapping unfolds as children develop is vital if we are to provide toys and teaching programs that are supportive. We must construct exercises that are in tune with the level of cognitive mapping competence that children have attained. At present, such goals are difficult to achieve. We know so little about the development of cognitive mapping in children that we are often guilty of two errors: underestimating the child's ability *and*, on the other hand, confusing it with that of an adult.

But what of the raw material on which this cognitive mapping process operates? In discussing the importance of understanding the mapping process, we have scarcely mentioned the role of the spatial environment itself. In this role lies a distinctly practical justification for the objective of this book. The physical form and arrangement of the environment has a major impact on the success of our efforts at knowing the world. Certain places are easier to comprehend, more readily learned and remembered, and pose fewer wayfinding difficulties. Given this, we can ask what causes these variations. And answers to this question lead directly to the social process of environmental design and planning. Such a goal was at the heart of Kevin Lynch's pioneering book, *The Image of the City*. Lynch argued that enviroments can be made more legible and imageable. At the city-wide scale, we can recognize the importance of landmarks, while at a smaller scale, urban sign and orientation systems can be designed with cognitive mapping in mind. Within multilevel building complexes, we can provide much-needed cues and signs to assist in wayfinding. Such design tactics are a necessary part of the answer to the poignant request that we should humanize our environment. A human environment is one in which we feel a sense of belonging, a sense of being comfortably at home. And a major part of that feeling rests upon the ability to come to terms with the environment, to be able to comprehend it and move around in it successfully.

OUR PERSONAL WORLD

Beyond all of the strictly utilitarian roles of cognitive mapping lies a more personal reason for understanding the process by which we come to know the world. In some very fundamental but inexpressible way, our own self-identity is inextricably bound up with knowledge of the spatial environment. We can organize personal experience along the twin dimensions of space and time. But the dimensions are inseparable—there can be no personal biography of "what" things happened "when" *without* a sense of the place in which they happened. Cognitive maps serve as coathangers for assorted memories. They provide a vehicle for recall—an image of "where" brings back a recollection of "who" and "what." This sense of place is essential to any ordering of our lives.

But it provides more than a filing system for coping with the complexities of the past. The ways in which cognitive mapping touches upon ongoing life are many and varied. We solve abstract problems using spatial representations that we can mentally rotate and manipulate. We use spatial mnemonics to recall a sequence of important ideas. We make use of spatial imagery and metaphors in verbal and written communication. We daydream and fantasize about real and imaginary places. As Stephen Spender wrote, "Different living is not living in different places but creating in the mind a map." This process of creating a mental map is essential to our survival in terms of everyday behavior and to our identity as thinking and communicating human beings.

Figure 1.16. Christopher Columbus, whose somewhat distorted map of the world made native Americans "Indians" for over 400 years.

THE ORGANIZATION OF THE BOOK

The seven succeeding chapters pursue and hopefully capture the essence of cognitive mapping and maps. They expand upon the four answers that we gave to the question, Why is cognitive mapping worth studying? Our argument begins in Chapter 2 with the basic link between the world in the head and spatial behavior. Spatial behavior is a response to the spatial problems that are posed by the two-dimensional nature of the earth's surface. We are forced to move around from location to location, and cognitive mapping provides the means and necessary information for solving spatial problems. Chapter 3 breaks the process of cognitive mapping into its two components. After reviewing the basic operations that comprise mapping, we will show how these operations are carried out in the head. Chapter 4 is concerned with the outcome of the cognitive mapping process. In particular, we analyze the structure and contents of cognitive maps and relate them to the "real world" on which they are based. By studying two specific and dissimilar environments, Micronesia and Boston, Chapter 5 shows how cognitive mapping underlies the everyday life of Micronesians and Bostonians. Chapters 6 and 7 explain the change in a person's cognitive mapping ability over time. Chapter 6 details the developmental sequence that a normal person follows, while Chapter 7 considers learning or the effect of experience on cognitive maps. Chapter 8 introduces the topic of environmental design, and reviews some of the attempts to make practical use of what is known about the process of cognitive mapping.

Before we embark on our voyage of discovery, however, travellers' warnings are necessary. This book is only an exploration—there are no definitive answers to many of the questions that will occur to you. This is not a book *in* any one discipline. Psychology, geography, urban planning, physiology, philosophy, and many other formal branches of knowledge are drawn upon informally. Many of the ideas are speculative. In fact, one good ally to assist in reading this book is probably armchair introspection, an ally normally shunned by scientists. To return to our earlier analogy, we each have our own dark continent, our own personal beliefs about the world. The ideas in this book are designed to help you pierce the gloom. We may, in hindsight, follow the example of Christopher Columbus, who could not possibly have found what he was looking for on his exploration, yet was undeniably successful in the long run.

Chapter 2

SPATIAL PROBLEM SOLVING

INTRODUCTION

The examples and illustrations discussed in Chapter 1 raised as many questions as they answered. The purpose of this chapter is to answer the more obvious of these questions. Why do we need this far-reaching yet mysterious cognitive mapping ability? How do we use it in our everyday life? How does it work? As a first step, let us take a close look at several examples of behavior and try to extract some common threads or principles. However, instead of restricting our study to human beings, we will ascend the phylogenetic scale, beginning with an example of insect behavior.

Von Frisch (1954) published a study of honeybees, which has had a major impact not only on biology but also on wider philosophical attempts to understand living organisms and their behavior. One significant finding, which documents the existence of a symbolic language among worker honeybees, has generated an immense amount of speculation and controversy about the definitions of language and communication. If we ignore this controversy and simply consider the *behavior* of the honeybees, we can begin to answer the question, Why do we need cognitive mapping? Von Frisch observed that once a foraging honeybee discovered a pollen source, the bee returned to the hive and performed a structured pattern of movements on the surface of the honeycomb. He referred to these movements as a "dance." Two specific characteristics of this dance communicated the spatial location of the newly discovered pollen source to fellow worker bees. The topography of the dance—its form—indicates the *distance* of the pollen source away from the hive. A "round dance" means a nearby source and a "tail-wagging dance," a distant source (see Figure 2.1). The number of turns that are made in the wagging dance in a given time period indicate how far away the distant source is: the fewer the cycles, the greater the distance. In addition, by the *direction* taken during the straight part of the wagging dance, the dancing bee conveys the direction in which fellow bees must fly in order to reach the pollen source (see Figure 2.2). On the vertical surface of the comb, the dancing bee orients itself in such a way that the angle between the straight portion of the dance and the direction of the force of gravity is identical to the angle between the flight path from the pollen source and the direction of the sun. The other bees follow the pattern of movements, "interpret" the meaning of the dance, and fly to the pollen source.

Bees are not the only insects with a "spatial sense." Among the many others that display a great variety of spatial abilities is the digger wasp, so-called because it dwells underground. Tinbergen (1951) reports that the digger wasp, on returning from a foraging expedition, finds its burrow by means of immediately surrounding landmarks. More importantly, it is the total pattern of these landmarks, and specifically, the shape of this totality, that provides the location cue. In one experiment, Tinbergen centered a ring of pine cones around the entrance to a wasp's burrow. After the wasp had returned repeatedly to its burrow in the presence of these new landmarks, Tinbergen moved the ring of cones a few feet away from the entrance. Instead of returning to its burrow, the wasp returned to the center of the ring of cones. Tinbergen then constructed a triangle of pine cones around the entrance to the burrow, and replaced the already displaced ring of cones

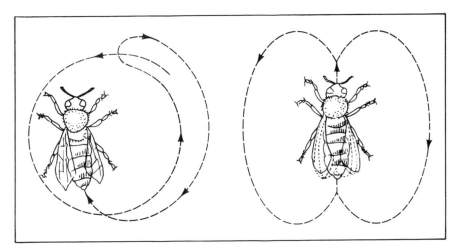

Figure 2.1. "Round" and "wagging" dances convey the spatial sense of the bee.

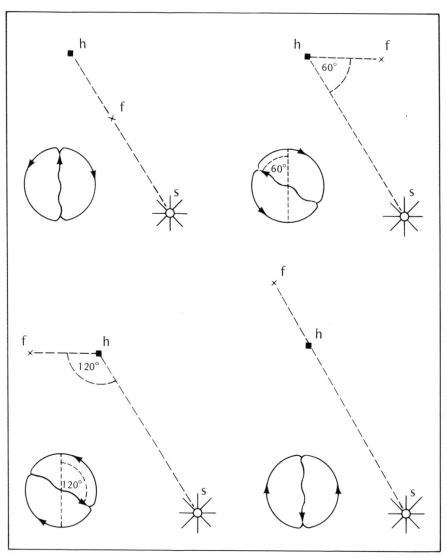

Figure 2.2. "Charting" the direction of food.

with a ring of pebbles, still several feet removed from the insect's burrow. The wasp returned to the center of the ring of pebbles, demon-
strating a response to the shape of an arrangement, rather than to the
specific elements of that arrangement.

Bearing these patterns of insect behavior in mind, let us ascend the
phylogenetic scale to consider one of an ingenious series of experiments reported by a psychologist, Edward Tolman (1948). Although the
subjects were laboratory rats—creatures favored by some psychologists,
but viewed with amused scepticism or disdain by most people—the

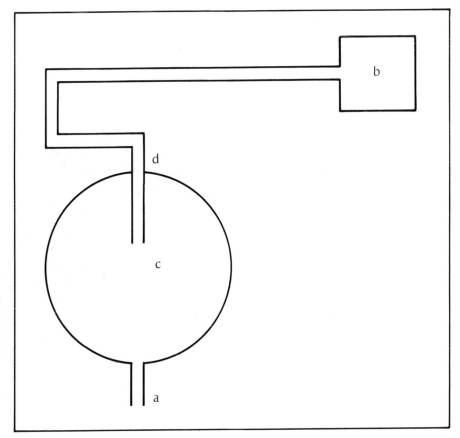

Figure 2.3. Tolman's "original maze" (see text).

rats' behavior shows distinct parallels with that of von Frisch's honey-bees. Moreover, some emerging threads of interpretation are strongly reinforced. The particular experiment about the nature of the learning process involved the maze shown in Figure 2.3. A hungry rat was placed at the starting point (a) and food was placed in the goal box (b). After much searching and hesitation, the rat reached the goal box via the alley (d). The procedure was repeated three times a night for four nights with the same rat until the rat had learned to go directly and without hesitation from (a) to (b). At this time, the rat's world was completely reshaped. He was confronted with the revised maze shown in Figure 2.4. The starting point (A) and the circular table (C) remained the same size and shape; however, the rat had a choice of 12 long alleys and 6 short alleys radiating from (C). None of these new routes was identical in either shape or position to the original alley (D) that the rat had learned to follow from (A) to (B). The goal box (B) was also removed. If a large number of rats trained in the original maze were

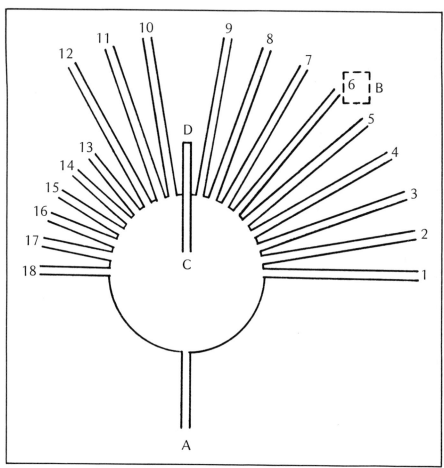

Figure 2.4. Tolman's "revised maze" (see text).

placed singly in the revised maze, the question became: What would they do? After trying the blocked alley (D), each rat returned to the table (C), and explored most of the alleys by going a few inches along each. Eventually, the rat chose to run all of the way along one alley. The cumulated results of these alley choices are shown in Table 2.1. The most popular alley, 6, was chosen by 35 percent of the rats; it ran to within a few inches of the entrance to the original location of the goal box (B).

Without pausing to ask *how* the rats managed to make this choice of path 6 (the answer to the question *why* being obvious), we come to the supposed summit of the phylogenetic scale: the human being. Let us consider someone contemplating the purchase of grocery supplies for the family. Perhaps the Plazaville Shopping Center has a supermarket that is advertising special low prices on desirable food items. Instead of

Table 2.1   PERCENTAGE OF RATS CHOOSING EACH OF
THE LONG PATHS IN THE REVISED MAZE

Path Number	Percentage of Rats Choosing the Path
1	17
2	9
3	2
4	4
5	4
6	35
7	6
8	7.5
9	2
10	7.5
11	4
12	2

(From E. C. Tolman (1948) "Cognitive maps in rats and men." *Psychological Review,* **55,** Figure 17, p. 204. Originally taken from E. C. Tolman, B. F. Ritchie, and D. Kalish (1946) "Studies in spatial learning: I. Orientation and the short-cut." *Journal of Experimental Psychology,* **36,** p. 19.)

(A) in Figure 2.4 being the starting point, we can substitute the term home, and we can replace (B) by the Plazaville Shopping Center. The person must choose a route connecting home to the shopping center, and we would call the resultant behavior a shopping trip.

What general conclusions can we draw from these diverse and, at least in conventional wisdom, unrelated examples of behavior? More particularly, how do they help us to understand the process of cognitive mapping? We need a general framework for interpreting and explaining behavior. To begin with, the bees, wasps, rats, and the person engage in what a geographer would call spatial behavior: Their spatial location is altered through some form of movement. The movement patterns of spatial behavior could be described in terms of such characteristics as origins, destinations, distances, directions, and frequencies of occurrence. We could then attempt to infer some explanation for the observed pattern of spatial behavior. There is an alternative explanatory framework available. Instead of focussing on the essentially superficial characteristics of the spatial behavior of the bees, wasps, rats, and people, we can ask a more fundamental question: *Why this behavior?* In other words, what was the point of the spatial behavior; what did it achieve? To this simple question, there is an immediate but trivial answer. In each case, the spatial behavior allowed the animal to get food, and to return home.

Again, however, we are being influenced by the superficial similarities among these behavior episodes: We must ask what is meant by "getting food." There is a general and, to our argument, basic answer to the question of why this spatial behavior. In each case, the spatial behavior was the result of the animal *solving a spatial problem.* The spatial problem for the honeybee was complex. It involved finding a pollen source, returning to the hive, and then communicating the spatial location of the pollen source so that other bees could take advantage of it. The wasp had the spatial problem of finding its way home. The hungry rat in the revised maze faced the spatial problem of being placed in a partially novel environment and having to choose a path to get to where it believed a food source to be located. The person faced an equally complicated spatial problem, which involved getting to the shopping center, finding the food within the supermarket, finding the car in the parking lot, and returning home. It is our basic argument that, throughout our everyday lives, we are confronted with spatial problems that we must, and do, solve successfully. Given this claim, we must ask the obvious question: *How do people solve spatial problems?* As this chapter will show, the most powerful, flexible, and reliable method of spatial problem solving is cognitive mapping, and so the answer to this question is also one answer to our earlier question, Why cognitive mapping? Other answers will be given in Chapters 3 and 4.

As the examples of spatial behavior suggest, the "we" does not refer solely to human beings: *All* mobile living creatures are confronted with spatial problems. However, in this book, our attention is focused upon *human* spatial problem solving although, as Chapter 6 will also make clear, we can draw parallels between human beings and other living creatures concerning the general characteristics that this spatial problem-solving ability must possess.

The remainder of this chapter considers two ideas. First, we will look more closely at the nature of spatial problems and try to understand the requirements necessary to solve them. Second, we will describe how we can solve spatial problems, and we will evaluate the range of possible problem-solving strategies. While Chapter 1 has introduced and illustrated the intriguing question of the relation between the world, as people believe it to be, and everyday behavior, Chapter 2 presents some of the basic concepts and arguments needed to answer the question.

WHAT ARE SPATIAL PROBLEMS?

Spatial problems require us to make decisions about where to get such things as a pair of new shoes or the cheapest liquor in town, how to get to places such as the drive-in movie theater or the doctor's office, and where to go for a summer vacation or to look for a better apartment. In reaching such decisions we must not only find desirable things and places, but we have to remember that some places must be avoided at all costs: Los Angeles freeways in the rush hours, Philadelphia (nearly always! — see Box 2.1), and houses built on earthquake fault lines or downwind from municipal garbage incinerators. Each decision that solves a spatial problem results in a pattern of spatial behavior.

BOX 2.1

PHILADELPHIA: LOVE IT, OR LEAVE IT, OR JUST DON'T GO

Philadelphia, supposedly the City of Brotherly Love, must qualify as the least-loved city in the U.S.A., and the place that consistently receives the worst press. Samples are easy to find:

> New York sports columnist Jimmy Cannon called Philadelphia "a wino of a town. . . . There is no room for class in the whole metropolis." Dorothy Parker called it "a cemetery with lights."
>
> (Walter, 1972, p. 81)

But there are *some* exceptions, as this reporter for the *Philadelphia Inquirer* explains:

> What can you say about a 300-year-old city that plays bocci, cricket and stickball on the same Sunday?
>
> That its streets are as filthy as its air, that its subways are rotting, that its cabs aren't running, that it really does shut down on weekends, that some parts of it aren't all that safe, that it gets bad press and sometimes deserves it—and that I like it.
>
> That wasn't supposed to happen. As a matter of fact, the odds were against it, because, in case you didn't know, friends, there's a vast anti-Philadelphia lobby out there, waiting in the dark and armed to the molars with Fieldian sneers, Phillies jokes, and veiled warnings against the mayor, the water and the women—and it's awfully difficult not to listen. Still, after what is loosely defined as nearly three months of work, I have suddenly discovered that I really like this place.
>
> (Wooten, 1973, p. 1–B)

Of course, the cynics would respond that time will tell and that familiarity will breed contempt. It is true that you can't trust the locals:

> A few years ago . . . a now-extinct movement called Action Philadelphia, Inc., decided, in its words, to "put firecrackers under the city to get it moving again." Its first move was to erect alongside one of the major highways leading into the city a huge billboard that proclaimed: PHILADELPHIA ISN'T AS BAD AS PHILADELPHIANS SAY IT IS!
>
> Some wag with a can of spray paint immediately undid all this by appending the slogan: NO. IT'S WORSE!
>
> (Walter, 1972, p. 81)

Nor can you trust native sons who have left Philadelphia. The comedian W. C. Fields was reputed to have said many things about his old home town, and not one of them was flattering. Included in the litany of disparaging remarks are the following: "I was born in Philadelphia, God rest its soul"; "I'd rather be dead in California than living in Philadelphia"; and "Philadelphia is the only town that closes on Sundays." Other expatriates are equally uncharitable:

> Even prominent Philadelphians take pokes while they are abroad. The soon-to-be-retired Ambassador to the Court of Saint James's, Walter H. Annenberg described Philadelphia to British reporters as "a bush-league London."
>
> (Walter, 1972, p. 81)

Even those people fortunate enough to be leaving Philadelphia are disgruntled and cynical. After the city government imposed a $2-per-person airport use tax, the following report appeared:

> Many travellers were "very bitter," a spokesman for Trans World Airlines said, and one traveler was heard to say, "It's worth $2 to get out of Philadelphia."
>
> (*The New York Times,* July 16, 1973, Section 10, p. 4)

Perhaps we should commiserate with those apocryphal and unlucky competition winners since we know that the first prize is one week in Philadelphia, and the second prize is two weeks. And if you think that these comments are unfair, perhaps even libellous, you could always consult a Philadelphia lawyer. . . .

These decisions are made necessary by the properties of the surface of the earth on which we live. We can see *why* these are necessary decisions if we state two simple propositions and draw one inevitable conclusion. First, everybody and everything has got to be somewhere, and being somewhere means being at a particular place or *location* on the earth's surface. Second, it is physically impossible for two people or things to occupy exactly the same location at the same time, and therefore separation or *distance* between people, places, and things is inevitable. Given these two unavoidable and universal facts of life, the conclusion comes in the form of an everyday expression: You can't be in two places at once. This expression is far more than just another amusing truism. It captures the essence of the spatial problems that we confront daily, which dominate and permeate every aspect of our existence to such an extent that, paradoxically, they go unrecognized. Since we cannot be in two places at once, we have to move either ourselves or other people and things from place to place, depending upon who plays the role of Mahommet and who is the mountain. Such movements begin at the scale of walking from room to room in a house, progress to the journey to and from work or school, include trips to the laundromat or drugstore and weekend visits to the country, and extend as far as long-distance migrations from city to city or vacations in Hawaii.

One way to grasp the pervasiveness of spatial problems is to think about an average day in your own life. How often are you trying to get "there," where people or things you want to reach are located, or how often are you trying to get other people or things "here," where you are located? Activities such as arranging and attending meetings, collecting people in the car pool for work or school, or delivering parcels and messages are all attempts to solve complex spatial problems. The coordination of certain people and things, at certain places and times, is such a frequent event and so easily taken for granted that we never think how remarkable a feat it is. Nor do we appreciate how much time, thought, and effort we devote to the solution of spatial problems.

Spatial problems are an inevitable, ever-present part of our daily life, and yet we do not take the trouble to analyze them. If we look carefully at what is involved in organizing and carrying out such varied spatial activities as a visit to the supermarket or a sightseeing tour around a city, some common needs are apparent. To solve any spatial problem, we need two basic types of information about the world around us: whereness, or knowledge of the spatial location of something or someone, and whatness, or knowledge of which things or people are at a particular location. Without both types of information, it is difficult, if not impossible, to make a decision and to solve a spatial problem. Whereness and whatness information are complementary. In searching for whereness information, we know what we are looking for, but need to know both where it is and how to get there. Whatness information tells what is at a particular location and why anybody would want to go there. Included in whatness information is a subclass of information, whenness. We need to know not only where a place is and what is at that place, but also when certain things will happen there or how likely it is that things might happen there.

Simple definitions are often misleading; at first glance the meanings of whereness, whatness, and whenness are self-evident. This feeling is a partial reflection of the amazing skill and facility with which we successfully solve spatial problems in everyday life. Yet if we are to understand just how and why we are successful and, in particular, the nature and operation of the cognitive processes that we employ in spatial problem solving, we must take these simple definitions apart. We will ask what do we mean by "know"? What underlies the concept of whereness? How can we distinguish among such terms as location, direction, and orientation? What constitutes whatness? While the question of how information is processed cognitively will be dealt with in Chapters 3 and 4, we must get a better understanding of the basic information requirements for spatial problem solving.

KNOWING

In our discussion so far, we have begged the key question, What does it mean to "know"? In its deepest sense, this is a thorny philosophical issue, which we would prefer to bypass. Knowing and understanding are, however, related to cognition, as understood by psychologists. As with many terms, there are both everyday and technical meanings that we must disentangle. In education, for example, definitions of knowing range from the product of simple rote memorization to the deepest comprehension of a body of profound subject matter. Disagreement concerning the nature of knowing is reflected in the common response to a student reciting a passage of poetry — "He doesn't understand a thing he's read" — or an equally common reaction to an academic "grind" or "drone" — "He only knows what he's taught."

To indicate our own usage of the word "know," let us consider a frequent comment on someone's response to a common spatial problem, wayfinding: "He knows where he's going," or "He knows his way around." This type of statement means different things to different groups of people.

A first group would view the statement as one describing the consequence of some genetic endowment, and would paraphrase it to read that "he has a *natural* sense of direction." The obvious parallel is with the mysterious and, as yet only partially explained, homing instinct in birds and animals. The implication is that this person has always known where he is going, and would know under any conditions. He is *made* that way. The juxtaposition of the two statements, "He knows where he's going *because* he has a natural sense of direction" has no additional explanatory value.

Others, adopting a view more closely akin to structuralism in psychology and philosophy, hold that an internal cognitive structure, even a "template," exists, which facilitates such knowing, although perhaps it does not work equally well at all times and in all environments. This is the orthodox or *state* description of cognitive mapping. A person simply "has" a cognitive map that facilitates knowing. In this view, a child *necessarily* knows less than an adult about where he's going, since greater knowing is invariably a product of further physiological and psychological development. The course of development is, by whatever means, innately prescribed; it is an inevitable *property* of the individual.

A third group considers knowing as predominantly the result of experience, of sensory-motor interaction with the environment, of learning. In essence, this group treats knowing the environment as a *process* that is part of the general problem of knowledge, which it views as acquired through learning. Environmental learning, however, is seen as beginning at a very early age — setting the stage, so to speak. Later in life, through a variety of interactions with a variety of spatial environments, the adult is better able to predict what a new environment is going to be like after just a brief experience with it. He generalizes on the basis of past experience, but he also has specific past interactions with his current environment to rely upon as well. Thus, according to this view, he knows his way because he knows many ways *and* has learned something about *this* way as well. And it is this third view of knowing, fundamentally, to which we subscribe.

WHERENESS

Now that you know what we mean by "know," we can ask what it means to know about the whereness, whatness, and whenness of the world around us. Whereness is one of those apparently self-evident concepts that are far more complex than we realize. We have defined it as where something or someone is located. If we know someone's location, then we can work out (or derive from this knowledge) how far away he is (distance) and which way he is (direction). The key to understanding whereness, therefore, is location, yet location itself is a difficult idea to pin down. To begin with, we must distinguish between *identity* and *location*.

IDENTITY

Many places have an identity in the sense that they possess names that serve as labels: for example, Chicago's Loop; London street names such as Petticoat Lane or the Strand; the Plazaville Shopping Center; or Columbus Circle in New York. Chronologically assigned house numbers in Brazilian *favelas* (the higher the number, the newer the house) establish identities. They serve to distinguish the place from other places, but they say nothing per se about where the identified place is located in space. Identity alone does not even necessarily convey uniqueness since there may be many places with the same identifying label. Many U.S. cities have a Broadway. We need to know whether a town called Miami is in Florida or Ohio, or whether Newport is in Monmouthshire or on the Isle of Wight, in Rhode Island or Kentucky, and so on.

This is not to suggest that identities are unimportant and that people do not attach tremendous symbolic significance to them. Several recent incidents attest to the very opposite. Identities are part of the world and part of the way in which we view the world. *Newsweek* (March 19, 1973, p. 45) contained this story:

What's in a name?

Four years ago, the Sino-Soviet border dispute erupted in a series of brief armed clashes over the ownership of an obscure island in the Ussuri

River. The quarrel has simmered ever since — its most recent outbreak is a linguistic tiff over the names of some equally obscure towns in eastern Siberia. Recently, Moscow ordered the substitution of Russian names for nine towns that have had Chinese-sounding names since the days when the area was under Chinese control. Though the region passed to the czars back in 1860, the Chinese have long insisted that its seizure came under an "unequal treaty" forced upon a helpless China. In a bitter attack ... on "social imperialist policy," China denounced the Russians' nomenclatural fiddle as "aggression." The renaming of the towns, the Chinese charged, was a "big lie" and an effort to tamper with history.

The New York Times (March 8, 1973, p. 5) reports the official Chinese press agency as claiming the following:

> The renaming of places can in no way alter history. ... Even if all the maps existing in the Soviet Union today are burned up and all the names of places changed into Russian ones, all the maps and atlases published in other countries cannot be burned and all the names cannot be changed.

Obviously the Chinese do not believe in the saying that sticks and stones will break your bones but names will never hurt you! The suggestion that the Russians might change their cartographic maps is not so far-fetched as it might seem. In the second edition of the Soviet World Atlas, published in 1967, identities were preserved but locations were changed. Towns, railroad lines, lakes, and rivers were moved from their true locations in order to confuse an enemy attempting to target missiles.

The preservation of spatial identity is an emotionally charged issue, as the City Commission of Atlantic City (New Jersey) was forced to realize. The seemingly innocuous proposal to change the names of Baltic and Mediterranean Avenues met a nationwide storm of protest because these two names are immortalized on the boards of the property game, Monopoly. Mr. Edward Parker, a member of the company that manufactures the game, argued:

> Baltic and Mediterranean are not just local street names. They must be included in the category containing such thoroughfares as Broadway, Trafalgar Square and the Champs-Elysées. Who would ever suggest changing their names? Baltic and Mediterranean Avenue belong to America.
>
> (*Newsweek*, January 22, 1973, p. 66)

> While I certainly agree with the logic of having a street name remain the same for its entire length, I feel that this is a special case whose repercussions could probably shake the very foundations of American tradition ...
>
> (*The New York Times*, January 9, 1973, p. 43)

Whether or not we agree with such a cataclysmic viewpoint, names do matter. We do become emotionally attached to these identifying labels. But, they express neither uniqueness nor location, with the exception of places such as Centre County, Pennsylvania, or Four Corners, Arizona, which, until its emergence as a scene of environmental conflict, was better known as the only point in the United States where four states meet. Labels are important and necessary, but not sufficient. In some cases, they may not even have any meaning, as the following comment by a nineteenth century Australian Surveyor-General suggests:

> Once a name was adopted, however, it was to be retained regardless of its original meaning: "Map names altho' derived originally from Aborigines are for the use of Englishmen, and once adopted it matters little what they mean, our use of them when they fit our mouths, is, to distinguish geographical features."
>
> (Heathcote, 1965, p. 34)

LOCATION

The specification of location requires something more than an identifying name; what is needed is a *location description*. This can take one of two forms: (1) *state* and (2) *process*. A state description of location tells where something is located in terms of a well-known and commonly understood system of coordinates. A process description is a set of instructions telling how to get to a particular location. A simple micro-spatial example of the distinction between state and process descriptions is provided by an analogy drawn from a chess game. The location of any chess piece can be described either in terms of the designation of the chessboard square on which it is located (state) *or* by the sequence of moves through which it got there (process). Thus, we can say that a pawn is occupying Q5 (a state description that depends upon an understanding of the coordinate system of a chessboard) or that it got to where it is by the moves "pawn to K4, pawn takes queen's pawn" (a process description). A chess book will often include both: a limited set of state descriptions ("snapshot" illustrations of the board at critical turning points during the chess game) and a complete set of process descriptions ("shorthand" statements of all of the sequential moves that have been made).

In geographical macrospace, the same state-process distinction holds. One form of state description is a set of cartographic map coordinates (e.g., latitude and longitude in degrees, minutes, and seconds). A second form is a street intersection (e.g., 5th Avenue and 42nd Street), or block designation (on the 2600 block of St. Paul's Street). The first form of state description refers to a universally agreed-upon set of coordinates that are imposed on the earth's surface and that have a well-known point of origin. The second refers to a street pattern locally familiar to the residents, in these examples, of New York City or Baltimore (Maryland). In certain situations, maps based on coordinate systems are used without any identifying place names:

> One pilot said that he often thought of himself as a long distance truck driver. A crewman said that bombing South Vietnam from a B-52 was "like delivering the mail." The maps used by the crews show almost no place names. One general said that kept the maps uncluttered. It also keeps them impersonal. The targets are given code numbers and are marked by intersecting map coordinates. "For all you know," one pilot said, "you could be bombing New York City."
>
> (*The New York Times*, October 13, 1972, p. 12)

People living in Salt Lake City, Utah, or Bogotá, Colombia, can utilize even simpler state descriptions of location. In Salt Lake City, the house number indicates the number of yards that it is removed from the Mormon Temple, so the street address (e.g., 3501 North West Temple Street) uniquely locates the house. In Bogotá, the house number is itself sufficient for precise locational purposes, since the combination of digits uniquely denotes the nearest street intersection, and the distance of the house, in meters, from that intersection.

As an example of a process description, consider the problem of an out-of-town visitor to New York who wants to get to the Main Branch of the New York Public Library. Since this name establishes only identity, our visitor does not necessarily know that the library is located at the intersection of 5th Avenue and 42nd Street. He is among those rare people who arrive in New York by train, coming into Pennsylvania Station, and he has no idea of his initial location, except that it is somewhere within Manhattan. The first passerby from whom he requests directions is in a hurry and simply says, "Take a taxi," a form of process description, but hardly one useful to a person with less than a dollar in his pocket. The second passerby gives him the following set of instructions: "Go out that door," pointing eastward, "and walk three blocks. Then turn to your left, walk seven blocks, and you'll see the library right ahead of you, and to your left." The visitor, ambling toward the indicated exit, need know nothing at all about the "coordinates" of the station or the library on the Manhattan street grid in order to follow this set of instructions. A real-life example of the use of process descriptions reinforces the aptness of the chessboard analogy. An assistant at the New York City Information Center said:

> ". . . one block up and two over," . . . "It's like a chess game here." . . . "So many blocks this way, so many another way."

Perhaps Alice, in one of her adventures through the looking-glass, was in the real world after all:

For some minutes Alice stood without speaking, looking out in all directions over the country—and a most curious country it was. There were a number of tiny little brooks running straight across it from side to side, and the ground between was divided up into squares by a number of little green hedges, that reached from brook to brook.

"I declare it's marked out just like a large chess-board!" Alice said at last. "There ought to be some men moving about somewhere—and so there are!" she added in a tone of delight, and her heart began to beat quick with excitement as she went on. "It's a huge game of chess that's being played—all over the world—if this *is* the world at all, you know."

(Dodgson, 1939, p. 150)

These, then, are two fundamental forms of location description. We use both in cognitive mapping, depending upon how the environment is organized, how well we know it (process descriptions at first and state later), and how old we are (process first and state later). As an illustration of the effect of age on the knowledge of location, recall the child in the cartoon in Figure 1.7 and her difficulty in getting home again. Although the problem of how location is handled cognitively will be treated in Chapters 3 and 4, there are some aspects of locational problems worthy of further mention here.

Both state and process descriptions depend upon frameworks of understanding, which people *impose* upon the world. The frameworks are not some absolute property of the world, which we discover. The coordinate systems, whether compass based or city-block based, are designed by people for their own use. This means that we must understand the logic of the system and become familiar with its north and south codes, its large numbers, and its halves (i.e., 135 1/2 East College Avenue). However, not everybody agrees that the numbering system is even necessary:

And since she tries to keep in touch with her mother, even though neither of them is very good at writing, there are those numbers to keep in mind. Whoever got *that* idea anyway—of putting numbers on houses? Where do the numbers on her street start? Where does the street start, for that matter? In Dorchester County, South Carolina, so far as she knows, "there's not a number there on any home." She never had a post office box number, nor does her mother even today: "I write her name; I write the town; I write South Carolina—and it gets there faster than letters from her get to me."

(Coles, 1971, p. 7)

To use the Bogotá and Salt Lake City numbering systems described earlier, we must understand the principles underlying them. Location descriptions, therefore, depend upon a system of understanding that we must all agree upon and know in order to use. Such understanding is not always present. Many of us might echo Alice's question as she fell down the rabbit-hole:

> ". . . but then I wonder what Latitude or Longitude I've got to?" (Alice had not the slightest idea what Latitude was, or Longitude either, but she thought they were nice grand words to say.)
>
> (Dodgson, 1939, p. 17)

State and process descriptions of location are neither always equally useful nor always interchangeable. In general, where the layout of available paths is sufficiently regular so that both types of description can be employed, state descriptions offer greater flexibility in two important senses. First, a knowledge of origin and destination and of the overall layout of an area usually permits the choice among a number of alternative paths, while a process description refers to one specific path connecting origin and destination. Second, it is more parsimonious and simple to learn the "rule system" that governs the pattern of the urban fabric (which is necessary for state descriptions) than to try to reach many different places in the city by memorizing a large number of specific paths or process descriptions. Flexibility and simplicity are important in spatial problem solving. But where there is no regularity to the available paths and their identity labels, a situation exemplified by the street pattern of English towns and some older New England cities, both modes of location description may not be equally feasible. It is impossible to use a state description unless a determinable pattern allows us to specify a state in terms of coordinates. Thus the intersection of 5th Avenue and 42nd Street in mid-Manhattan (the "regular" or "gridiron" part) is a state description, whereas the intersection of Allen and Division, or Chatham Square in the lower, "irregular" part of Manhattan is merely an identity and *alone* does *not* specify location. A process description is *always* possible (except for some places in New England where it's said that "you can't get there from here") and, in patternless or amorphous places, is sometimes the *only* possibility.

There are other situations in which process descriptions may be advantageous. This is especially true where *how one got there* is an important piece of data, about which a state description says nothing. To analyze the outcome and strategy of a chess game, one must know the sequence of moves that led to that outcome. To use fixed route public transportation, one must know more than merely the identity of the destination. The specific routes, route numbers, transfer points, and so on are all important pieces of process information. Indeed, the exact location (state description) of the destination is often irrelevant and effectively useless. Addresses for rural mail delivery are process descriptions for the information of the postman travelling his fixed route. They use merely "RD 1," a route on which the addressee lives rather than a specific address given in terms of a coordinate system. Urban addresses, on the other hand, are state or quasistate descriptions. The post office organizes these in such a way as to establish efficient postal delivery routes, which are usually process descriptions again.

One way to bypass the choice between state and process descriptions of location is via redundancy: use both. Member-clubs of the American Automobile Association, for example, issue *both* standard road maps *and* a collection of strip maps called a "Triptik." Either map could provide both state and process descriptions. However, because the standard road map is better for state descriptions and the Triptik better for process descriptions, the AAA provides something of both for every driver. (As indicated in Chapter 7, there are different personal preferences for ways of specifying location.) Certain city guides (e.g., the *Guia Roji* for Mexico City) contain both city maps and a thick book providing a guide to the public transportation lines connecting most points with most other points in the city.

DISTANCE

Once we know locations, we can work out *distances*, since distance is simply a measure of the amount of spatial separation between two locations. Such simplicity is again misleading. The problem of how we express this separation (i.e., what units of measurement we use) is complex. On the one hand, we have "absolute" measures of distance, including familiar units such as miles and yards, kilometers and meters. These measures are based on arbitrary but commonly agreed upon fixed units. On the other hand, we have "relative" measures of separation, which depend upon our ability to overcome the effects of separation. Overcoming separation exacts a toll, which we can view as a *cost*: Hence we have time measures ("it'll take you about an hour to get there") and monetary measures ("it's a 25¢ bus ride from here": see also Figure 2.5). These relative or cost measures of distance are in large part a function of the tools available to us for overcoming distance (see Box 2.2). Some direct aids to travel, such as jet aircraft, reduce large distances to absurdly short periods of time. New York is simply not very far from San Francisco if one has the air fare. Other indirect aids, such as television, annihilate distance by making two occurrences (one where the filming is taking place and the other in the T.V. tube) effectively simultaneous. García Márquez (1970, p. 3) has provided an amusing description of the effects of another, somewhat more "primitive" tool, on distance:

> In March the gypsies returned. This time they brought a telescope and a magnifying glass the size of a drum, which they exhibited as the latest discovery of the Jews of Amsterdam. They placed a gypsy woman at one end of the village and set up the telescope at the entrance to the tent. For

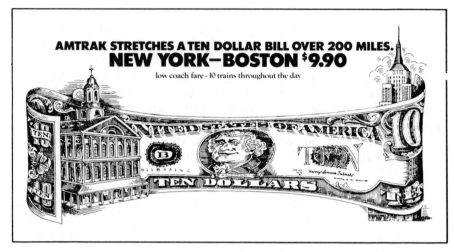

Figure 2.5. It no longer costs only $9.90 to go from New York to Boston, as in 1972, but the message is abundantly clear: Separation can be measured in monetary terms, as well as in units of distance and time.

the price of five reales, people could look into the telescope and see the gypsy woman an arm's length away. "Science has eliminated distance," Melquiades complained. "In a short time, man will be able to see what is happening in any place in the world without leaving his own house."

Our interest, in this book, is with two aspects of cognitive distance. First, we want to know what types of units of measurement people use in everyday life to cope with the problem of thinking about and expressing distance. Second, we want to understand the factors that affect people's estimates of distance. This requires answers to the question of how accurate are distance estimates compared to "real world" distance measures. We must ask about the effects of familiarity, of the characteristics of the locations being considered, and of social and cultural influences. As an illustration of the complexity and subtlety of cognitive distance estimates, consider these experiences:

Some walks overtaxed my own strength. There was no way, other than going myself, by which I could learn how many miles I was being asked to walk. One "not far" excursion put me to bed for a couple of days after a twenty-five mile round trip without food or water, whereafter I set out on a "far" journey equipped with lunch and water, only to find it less than four miles in all. At first, I thought that their use of these words was incontrovertible evidence that they had no idea of distance. Then I figured out that "far" referred not only to space, but to time and social distance as well. The words "Yabo's homestead is far" might mean that his homestead was a long distance off or that he was but remotely related to the speaker. As far as Udama was concerned, it was "far" because her husband Kako disliked Yabo. Everyone agreed that it was further from Yabo's to Kako's than from Yabo's to Poorgbilin's, but everyone also agreed that it was no further from Poorgbilin's to Yabo's than from Poorgbilin's to Kako's. All this seemed to mean that Yabo and Poorgbilin got on together much better than Yabo and Kako, but that Poorgbilin got on equally well with both—a fact which seemed to rank, in local opinion, as something of a feat.

In any case there was only one thing of which I could be sure in advance: if people wanted me to come, they would tell me "It's not far"; if they didn't want me to come, they would tell me "It's far," and if that failed to discourage me, they would add that there was water on the path; an even less reliable statement, for I sometimes found a river, sometimes general muddiness, and sometimes no water at all.

Consequently, when Atakpa invited me to go with her to collect her cousin Amara—"not far at all"—I suspiciously demanded details. Atakpa assured me that if we left in the early morning we would easily return in time for my lunch; also, since Amara was ill but could still walk back to Yabo's without any difficulty, I should have no trouble whatsoever. I believed Atakpa was telling the truth, in an impressionistic way, and I agreed to go, but I gave orders that Monday and my lunch were to accompany me. Just before high noon and after three and a half hours on the path, I congratulated myself on my forethought.

(Bowen, 1964, pp. 52–53)

An additional way of looking at distance is as a measure of the desire to maintain or to overcome separation. Thus, distance has a value attached to it, which can be positive or negative. A suburban housewife may want to be near her mother and far from the ghetto; her strategy for house choice will seek minimization of separation or distance from one place and maximization of separation from another. Distance, then, is not always a "barrier to be overcome." It is often a barrier to be maintained, a positive benefit as well as a cost. We will return to the questions of the *cognitive* aspects of distance estimation in Chapter 4.

DIRECTION

The last component of whereness knowledge is *direction*. The terms direction, directions, and orientation are discussed together here because they so frequently appear together and they are readily confused.

A considerable difference exists, for example, between direction and giving directions. Directions given to an individual are, in general, simply process descriptions of location—a statement of how to get somewhere. A direction, by contrast, can only be specified with reference to a coordinate system. Thus, the direction of a vector in mathematics or

BOX 2.2
NEAR AND FAR:
THE SPACE OF SCIENCE FICTION

We have heard, read, and via motion picture and television, seen much concerning space in science fact and science fiction. But the space dealt with is usually *outer* space, the space of planets in our own solar system, outside our solar system, or even outside the galaxy. The nature of space on earth, in the sense of this book, is touched upon but rarely. Fortunately, a few writers have discussed space on earth in the context of dystopias, which are misbegotten attempts at constructing "perfect societies." One eloquent exploration, E. M. Forster's *The Machine Stops,* written early in this century, is a milestone of literary fantasy.

This remarkable tale is set at an undetermined time in the future, when nearly all people have retreated underground. They live in individual cells, which they rarely leave, and have all their needs cared for by a vast, little-understood, and often deified Machine. A woman is asked by her son to pay him a visit. She does so with great reluctance, since she is repelled by the need to leave her isolated cell, to come into contact with others, to travel, and to experience anything directly. When she arrives, her son blasphemously asserts that progress in their time has been reduced to the progress of the Machine. He tells her of his recent illegal visit to the surface of the earth. In doing so, he deals with the relations among sense of space, human movement, and concepts of distance:

> You know that we have lost the sense of space. We say "space is annihilated" but we have annihilated not space, but the sense thereof. We have lost a part of ourselves. I determined to recover it, and I began by walking up and down the platform of the railway outside my room. Up and down, until I was tired, and so did recapture the meaning of "near" and "far." "Near" is a place to which I can get quickly *on my feet,* not a place to which the train or the air-ship will take me quickly. "Far" is a place to which I cannot get quickly on my feet; the vomitory is "far," although I could be there in thirty-eight seconds by summoning the train. Man is the measure. That was my first lesson. Man's feet are the measure for distance, his hands are the measure for ownership, his body is the measure for all that is loveable and desirable and strong. Then I went further: it was then that I called to you for the first time and you would not come.
>
> (Forster, 1972, p. 128)

physics is the angle that it makes with the horizontal or x-axis in an xy plane. Direction on the two-dimensional surface of the earth is speci-fied in degrees of path deviation from a northward-pointing compass needle.

The former concept of direction is fine for physical scientists and mathematicians, and the latter for mariners and geographers. However, for the majority of us, who control only autos, bicycles, and shoes among available means of transportation, the idea of direction is not very useful. Except for very short-distance moves, we are forced to change direction frequently in our travels, for none of us can go as the (proverbial) crow flies. In Manhattan, where streets run either north-south or east-west, it is not much of a help to be told that a potential destination "is northwest of here," since available paths do not allow movement in that direction. In the city of Puebla, Mexico, such a state-ment of direction would be even more misleading because the major streets, although labelled North, South, East, and West, are rotated at an angle of 45° from true or magnetic north. In Boston, London, or Paris, where streets run every which way, compass directions are of even less utility, and may even hamper the wayfinding process. As an example, consider Figure 2.6, which depicts the intersection of Interstate High-way 95 with Route 128 near Boston, in eastern Massachusetts. The in-tersection is signed in a most interesting but confusing way, one sign saying "Route 128 South" and "Boston," and the other "Route 128 North." In reality, Route 128 runs east-west at the intersection, and Boston is almost due north, rather than south. Such a cavalier disregard for compass directions is only a modern extension of an older New England tradition, as the following newspaper report suggests:

East is east and west is south

East is east and West is west, but evidently nobody told the colonial set-tlers of Massachusetts. The automobile legal association reported this week that South Chatham is west of Chatham. West Dennis is south of Dennis, West Yarmouth is south of Yarmouth. South Wareham is west of Wareham and West Wareham is to the north. North West Duxbury is east of West Duxbury and East Bridgewater is north of Bridgewater. West of Falmouth is nothing but ocean so West Falmouth is—what else?—north of Falmouth.

(The San Francisco Chronicle, August 24, 1967)

Thus, precise vectors are not helpful and, in an imprecise and gen-erally irregular world, exact direction lends an unwarranted aura of precision to rather inexact concepts of wayfinding. New York City is due east of Newark, New Jersey, only if Columbus Circle in Manhattan is the goal (the point from which all distances to New York are mea-sured). It is northeast of Newark if by New York City one means a loca-

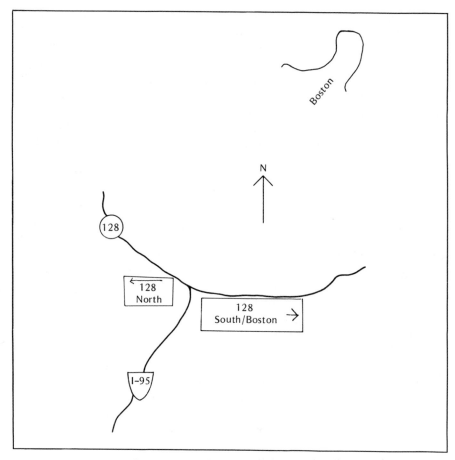

Figure 2.6. An approach to Boston, from the south. At the intersection of Interstate Route 95 and Massachusetts 128, Route 128 runs east-west,
but the signs read "North" and "South," respectively. The "South"
sign also reads "Boston," which is in fact to the north. Small wonder that drivers become so confused!

tion in the Bronx, and due south if one means a place on Staten Island.
Over short distances, the fact that locations such as New York are diffuse reduces the utility of compass directions to such an extent that
they are a hindrance rather than a help. Sometimes, directions are not
even necessary, as Alice discovered in Wonderland:

> "Cheshire-Puss," she began, rather timidly ... "Would you tell me,
> please, which way I ought to go from here?"
> "That depends a good deal on where you want to get to," said the Cat.
> "I don't much care where—" said Alice.
> "Then it doesn't matter which way you go," said the Cat.

"—so long as I get *somewhere*," Alice added as an explanation.

"Oh, you're sure to do that," said the Cat, "if you only walk long enough."

(Dodgson, 1939, pp. 64–65)

But more "folksy" indications of direction *are* of use to people, as is illustrated by the following tale.

David Weaver tells of a summer when he was working on a boat off the Maine coast. One day, a thick fog had gathered; he was on deck when he heard the sound of an engine not too far off. After a time, a lobster boat emerged from the wall of fog.

"Which way to Witch Harbor?" asked the fisherman, only, being from Maine, he pronounced it "hahbuh," and both which and witch sounded quite the same.

Weaver excused himself and went immediately to the chart room, from which he emerged a few minutes later with a set of nautical instructions involving bearings, and so on. As he started to relate these directions to the fisherman, the latter interrupted him: "Don't give me any of that mish-mash. Just point." We are often reduced to such primitive direction systems as pointing or those based on the human body (such as left-right, front-back). These directions refer to coordinate systems, which are commonly agreed upon and understood, but which do not have a fixed point of origin. The point of origin moves with a person, a fact that causes immense confusion and uncertainty. Some people have difficulty with distinguishing between left and right and even those of us who know the distinction must know *whose* left, mine or the person giving the directions?

So far, we have differentiated direction from directions; we must still resolve the unfortunate confusion between direction and orientation. We view the concepts of orientation and location as being essentially similar. Orientation means knowing, or understanding, location and the spatial relations between locations. In its common usage, orientation is rooted in state descriptions; hence, in a coordinate system. However, we are oriented when we know where we are now (our present location), and we can tie together this location with a series of other locations. The ties with other places can be expressed either using process or state descriptions. Most importantly, orientation is basically a cognitive act, since these other places can lie well beyond the perceptual range of any of our senses. We can imagine what is beyond the hill and can link these unseen places with our current location. Orientation refers to the tie between our knowledge of the spatial environment and the environment itself, between cognitive map and real world. We are lost when we are unable to make the necessary link between what we see around us and our cognitive map.

WHATNESS AND WHENNESS

In contrast to the surprising complexity of the essential nature of whereness, *whatness* information is simple to describe. Whatness information tells us something about the characteristics of the objects or people at a particular location and allows us to identify and to recognize "what" is there. Not only can we identify and recognize a place when we arrive there but we can also decide in advance whether we should go there or avoid the place. Whatness information both describes and evaluates the objects or people, and can be thought of as a series of attributes. *Attribute* is an apt term because of its alternative meaning of "something given to"; the characteristics that we are concerned with are constructions made and imposed on the world by people.

For example, in the case of a suburban neighborhood, a description and evaluation expressed in such attributes as middle class, safe, attractive, and well cared for would enable us to build up a mental representation of the neighborhood. Alternatively, if the attributes included segregated, manicured, anonymous, and sterile, we would construct a very different representation of the neighborhood. In both instances, the representation would be a description or characterization of the area, *and* an evaluation of what it would be like as a place in which to live. It would tell us what it is, what it is *not*, what sort of things and people we would expect to find there, and what sort of things we would expect to happen. In this way we can draw a relationship between places in our environment and their potential role in our behavior.

However, information that only describes and evaluates what is at a location is not sufficient in many situations. We must also know when certain things or events can or will happen at a place; hence, the need for *whenness* information. Some things occur in a regular, predictable pattern: the opening and closing of stores and offices, the departure times of transport systems, and, we hope, the collection of mail and garbage. Other events, such as the beginning of the Fall season in New England or the onset of the monsoon in India, are regular though less predictable in a precise time sense. At the other extreme, we have events that are irregular and unpredictable both in terms of *when* they will occur and *where* they will occur: These include muggings (see Figures 1.8 and 1.9), rainbows, floods, droughts, blizzards, hail storms, and tornadoes. If the suburban neighborhood mentioned earlier is in coastal California, we might need to know how close (distance) the place (location) is to a geological fault line or a steep, unvegetated slope so that we can estimate the likelihood of experiencing earthquake or mudslide damage.

Obviously there are innumerable ways of characterizing the whatness and whereness of a location. No single, limited set of attributes can provide adequate knowledge for solving all spatial problems. The nature of the problem itself determines which attributes are relevant or irrelevant, important or unimportant. The problem also determines what is considered to be an *object.*

An object is identified and defined by an integrated set of attributes (whatness and whenness) and bits of locational information (whereness). However, an object at one *spatial* scale can become an attribute at another. Consider the following sequence based upon what is important to a person engaged in solving the problem of where to migrate. At a regional or national scale, cities are the objects of interest and the attributes might include the city's unemployment rate, proximity to recreational areas, and cultural amenities. At an intraurban scale, the neighborhoods in the chosen city are the objects of interest, and such attributes as racial or ethnic makeup, quality of schools, and accessibility to shopping facilities are important. Finally, at the intraneighborhood scale, individual houses become important, and we would consider the number of bedrooms, lot size, and the presence of amenities such as a basement or a brick fireplace. The scale of analysis of the spatial problem at hand defines what is an object and what is attributive and locational information. Given this argument, we can see that the ability to solve spatial problems rests upon the constructive manipulation of whatness, whereness, and whenness information. We must draw upon the stored bits and pieces of experience in order to synthesize a cognitive representation that is useful in guiding our spatial behavior. Exactly how this representation-behavior link is forged is the concern of the remainder of the chapter.

WHAT ARE THE WAYS OF SOLVING SPATIAL PROBLEMS?

Since we cannot avoid spatial problems in our everyday lives, we must solve them. Since our survival and happiness depend upon finding successful solutions, we must develop ways of problem solving that are highly reliable and accurate. On the other hand, since we face countless spatial problems on a daily basis and yet never have enough time to do everything that we want to, our problem solving must not only be reliable and accurate, but also as fast and as flexible as possible. If on our way home we come to a blocked street, we must make a quick decision as to which alternative route to take. Moreover, we possess neither the massive data processing capacity of an advanced series computer nor a gazetteer-like memory; consequently, problem solving must be as simple and undemanding as possible.

This awesome list of requirements and constraints is partially offset by the repetitive nature of frequently encountered spatial problems. Our problem-solving ability can take advantage of the repetition of both specific problems (e.g., journeys to work or to shop) and classes of problems (e.g., giving directions). Nevertheless, the ability must be reliable, fast, and simple. Our next step, therefore, is to describe the possible forms of spatial problem solving that people can employ, and to compare and contrast them with respect to the basic requirements that we have established.

To do this, consider a small child who is hungry and decides that she wants a cookie. The spatial problem involves either getting the cookie to where she is, or getting to where the cookie is located. Although we cannot describe and trace the exact thought sequences and feelings that are going through her head, we can list the possible *strategies* for solving this spatial problem that are available to our hungry little girl. Despite the contrived nature of this extremely simple problem, it is representative of the basic nature of all spatial problems, and it allows us to see that there are six possible strategies.

First, there is the obvious but highly unsatisfactory alternative of simply not trying to get a cookie—this is the least desirable alternative because she stays hungry. It is also an option that is not always available to us in everyday life. Many problems *must* be solved.

Second, she can change the dimensions of the spatial problem and substitute some other type of food for the cookie—perhaps there is some fruit or candy available in a bowl on a nearby table. Although such a substitution solves the immediate problem of hunger and is reliable, fast, and simple, it is of no help for a future occasion when there is no substitute food available or when she wants a cookie more than anything else in the world.

A third alternative also attempts to avoid movement and depends upon persuading an intermediary to bring the cookie to her. She asks her mother to get her a cookie. This solution substitutes verbal for spatial behavior. Two consequences may follow such a request. Her mother may give her a cookie, and again the problem is solved quickly and simply. As a result, verbal behavior is reinforced and the next time the problem arises the most likely course of action is to ask Mother. But suppose that her mother is not at home next time? This strategy, although fast and simple, will not necessarily succeed in the future: it is not reliable. The other consequence of the request to Mother is the reply: Yes, you may have a cookie; go and get it yourself. The reply is kind but not too helpful. It does not solve the child's spatial problem since she has to know *how* to go and get the cookie.

The next three strategies all involve spatial behavior; if the cookie will not come to the child, then the child must go to where the cookie is located. The fourth strategy depends upon what we might call a "windfall" or locational luck. If the child is standing in the kitchen at the moment of hunger and she can see the cookie jar on a nearby shelf, the spatial problem is again solved simply, quickly, and reliably. This would be a workable strategy for any other future occasion on which she could see the cookie jar. We can better understand how this strategy works and at the same time develop a vital distinction, which is necessary for our argument, if we turn to a problem situation in which the child is locationally unlucky. Perhaps she is playing in a place—the garden or her bedroom—from which the cookie jar is not visible. What does this mean and, more importantly, how is her problem-solving ability affected?

If she is in her bedroom, obviously the cookie jar in the kitchen is not visible. She is cut off by walls and doors, which act as *physical barriers*. These barriers prevent her from receiving information about both the whereness and the whatness of the cookie jar. Similarly she is cut off from other types of sensory information, which could serve as clues to the whereness and whatness. She cannot hear the cookies, she cannot smell them because the sealed, glass jar itself acts as a barrier, and she cannot feel where the cookies are because she cannot touch them. In this last instance we can see the effect of another type of barrier: separation or distance. Our senses are effective only over certain distances, irrespective of the intervention of physical object barriers (i.e., walls, buildings, trees, etc.). Each sensory receptor has a spatial limit beyond which it cannot distinguish cues or information, with vision being the most spatially extensive and touch the least extensive. If our child is cut off by distance and/or object barriers from *direct* sensory contact with the cookie jar, she must adopt alternative strategies of problem solving.

In the fourth strategy she could see the cookie jar and was easily able to solve the problem by linking motor actions (walking, stretching out an arm, removing the lid of the jar, etc.) with direct sensory feedback. This feedback involves vision, proprioceptive cues (i.e., signals from the operation of various muscles in the body), and touch. This problem-solving strategy is one based upon *perception*, and relies on the use of direct sensory information cues from the goal object in question (i.e., the cookie jar).

The "bedroom or garden problem" cannot be solved in this way, and therefore, our child has a choice between two further strategies of spatial behavior. The fifth in our sequence would be a random walk. She can move around the house in a structureless though not aimless way, going in and out of rooms with no *predetermined pattern* directing her spatial behavior. Her aim is to get within sensory range of the cookie jar. The solution is likely to be time consuming and the probability of success low. She may give up out of frustration or dinner may fortunately intervene, thus solving the hunger problem. If she is lucky, she may bump into the cookie jar, but can she depend on this the next time that she faces a similar problem? Will she have to take "pot luck" again? This random walk solution may be momentarily successful in terms of simplicity, but it does not answer the long-term requirements of speed, flexibility, and reliability.

Fortunately, the old saying that to be out of sight is to be out of mind is not necessarily true. We are not doomed to live in a world that is bounded by the limits of immediate perception. If we are locationally unlucky and cannot sense our spatial objective, we can turn to a sixth problem-solving strategy, which uses our cognitive mapping ability. Two fundamental characteristics distinguish spatial behavior based on a random walk process from spatial behavior based on a cognitive mapping process. Cognitive mapping allows us to substitute *cognition* for perception and a *plan* for the patternless wandering of the random walk.

Cognition overcomes the lack of direct sensory information about the whatness, whereness, and whenness of places in our environment by taking advantage of past experience. We recall stored information from memory and manipulate it to solve the spatial problem. The key to the manipulation is the plan. The plan is simply a guide for spatial behavior, a prescription for a sequence of actions that will result in solving the spatial problem. It is the outcome of a series of interrelated cognitive operations.

How does the hungry child use cognitive mapping to solve the cookie problem? In outline, the process of the development of the plan consists of three component steps. It can begin with the knowledge that the cookies are in a jar, which is kept on a kitchen shelf. This is an answer to *where* the cookies are located. Next, the child readily solves the problem of identifying *where* she is—in her bedroom. Finally, she asks herself the key question for solving the spatial problem: How do I get from the bedroom to the kitchen?

In developing the plan, therefore, the child uses her cognitive mapping ability to work through a series of steps including recalling (from memory or past experience) the spatial location of the cookies, identifying from direct perceptual cues where she is at present, recalling the spatial links (corridors, turns, doors, etc.) between her bedroom and the kitchen, and manipulating all of this information to give a series of behavioral instructions (go out of the door, turn left, walk down to the end of the corridor, etc.). In this case the instructions, or plan, amount to a process description of location, which will allow her to get from one place to another.

COGNITIVE MAPPING AS SPATIAL PROBLEM SOLVING

We chose the rather contrived example of the child and the cookie because it offered a very simple introduction to the links between cognitive mapping and spatial behavior. In particular, the example spotlighted the essential roles of cognition and plans in reaching a solution to a spatial problem. However, the simplicity of the wayfinding problem can be misleading and may cause us to overlook more complex uses of cognitive mapping. Wayfinding depends in essence upon a knowledge of the spatial relations between places. The emphasis is upon manipulating whereness information to form plans. Once we have mastered the spatial pattern of interrelationships, the twin problems of orientation and wayfinding become so simple to solve that we dismiss them as trivial. We are not consciously aware of the problem-solving process, and this lack of awareness encourages the mistaken belief that the answers "come naturally to us." We are assured of fast, simple, and reliable solutions to wayfinding problems. Flexibility is achieved because we usually know several alternative ways of getting from place to place. That such flexibility is attained only gradually as the result of development and learning is clear from the difference between the child and the adult in Figure 1.7. But what of more complex spatial problems that involve more than just wayfinding?

Consider the situation of a middle-class family who have recently arrived in an unfamiliar city. The first, and most basic, of the many spatial problems that they face is that of finding a new home. (For a discussion of how the family gradually learns to cope with other spatial problems, see Chapter 7.) Choosing a place to live is simultaneously a question of deciding upon *what* and *where*. Unlike the cookie problem, the spatial location of the desired objective is unknown; consequently, the problem-solving process is of a higher order of complexity. It involves far more than the manipulation of whereness information to form a plan for wayfinding. In a sense, there are a series of interlinked subproblems that must be solved with the assistance of the family's cognitive mapping ability.

To begin with, the family maps out an area of the city within which they will search for possible homes. On the basis of past experience with typical American cities, they exclude the entire inner city from consideration. They share a common cognitive representation of the whatness of the inner city that labels it as a place to avoid. Their expectations as to the whatness of the inner city have probably been confirmed by a very brief drive around the city immediately after they arrived. With only a brief glimpse of a place, we can make a reasonable guess as to what it is like because we *know* that certain whatness attributes tend to be associated with certain types of places. Cognitive mapping has, therefore, solved one spatial problem: It has reduced the area within which the family will search.

In searching for a home in the suburbs, the family will keep several whereness characteristics in mind. On the one hand, they want a place that will minimize the distance to schools, parks, and shopping facilities. On the other hand, the place must maximize the distance to expressways and garbage incinerators. They also construct a mental image of their "dream house," a picture that consists of a synthesis of desirable whatness characteristics. As one subplan for action, they gather information on specific houses from friends, newspapers, and realtors. This produces a list of places to visit, a list that involves solving a way-finding problem in order to inspect each possible house. Eventually, they find a house that satisfies enough of their whatness and whereness requirements for them to decide to buy it. The process of cognitive mapping, therefore, solved the spatial problem, although the process itself was far more complex than simply that of wayfinding. It generated a set of alternative locations and helped in the choice between the alternative houses.

Instead of the purchase of a house, we could have considered a variety of similar spatial problems: the choice of a vacation spot, the location of a new branch office, or the siting of a fire station. In each case, the decision is the outcome of a process of cognitive mapping. Plans are developed on the basis of cognition. We use the experience of the past, in the present, to solve the future. We learn which types of whatness, whereness, and whenness information are most useful. We learn that some problems can be solved by plans, which we can call heuristics. Heuristics are rules of thumb, which generally work; for example, we tend to look for elevators in the corners of buildings or we know how to change direction in a grid-form city by making a certain number of left or right turns.

Our ability to cope with many of the demands of everyday life is intimately linked with cognitive mapping. Although there is a range of spatial problem-solving strategies, we can differentiate among these strategies on the grounds of speed, simplicity, reliability, and flexibility. Cognitive mapping is one of the most effective and generally useful strategies. In some situations, it is the only strategy that has any chance of success. However, we have not discussed just how it works in detail. Nor have we emphasized its other roles in our lives. We know that it is tied in with graphic and verbal communication, with the roles of advertising and education, and with our own personal place in the world. We will turn to these questions in the next chapter.

Chapter 3

THE MEANING
OF COGNITIVE
MAPPING

INTRODUCTION

We defined cognitive mapping as the mental process through which people come to grips with and comprehend the world around them, and a cognitive map as a person's organized representation of part of the spatial environment. A representation is something that stands for the environment, that portrays it, and that is both a likeness and a simplified model. Although these definitions were sufficient for our introductory exploration of the problem-solving role of cognitive mapping, we must now ask more penetrating questions. These revolve around the central issue: How do we translate the world "out there" into cognitive maps in the head, and make use of these maps in everyday life? The answer emerges from a careful study of the meaning of the term, cognitive mapping. First, we will look at the general technique of *mapping* and investigate the component parts (or operations) that comprise the mapping process. Second, we will consider the *cognitive* version of the process, focussing on the psychological characteristics of the mental activity.

WHAT DO WE MEAN BY "MAPPING"?

To many people, mapping conjures up visions of surveyors, armed with theodolites and measuring chains, patiently and meticulously recording data that leads to cartographic maps of the Amazon basin or to site plans of a nearby housing development. However, this vision is but one specific application of a general, and widely used, process called mapping. Mapping involves the use of a set of operations, which translate information taken from the spatial environment into an organized representation so that, at a later date, this representation will be useful to us.

Representations can be stored either externally or internally. External representations include such physical things as a street map that helps us to find a friend's new house, a travel brochure for planning a vacation, or a data matrix containing traffic flows, which can be manipulated by a regional planner to suggest the location of new highways. Each of these external representations has a concrete, material form of existence: paper and ink, or punch cards for a computer. In contrast, internal representations are stored in our memory, and exist somewhere in our brain. The precise location and form of physiological storage are uncertain and highly controversial. Nevertheless, internal representations *do* exist: We draw upon these representations to give someone directions, to picture our hometown, and to describe the places we visited on our last vacation. One *common* feature of both external and internal representations is that the represented spatial information helps us to solve spatial problems, or, in a technical sense, is functional in terms of spatial behavior. Therefore, to ask what we mean by mapping or representing is to ask *how spatial information about whatness, whereness, and whenness gets acquired, organized, and stored in such a way that it will be functional when required.*

The *way* in which spatial information is organized and stored is the *mode* of representation, where we use mode in its literal sense of fashion or style. Just as Parisian clothing designers or Detroit automobile makers have developed innumerable annual changes in fashions or styles, so, too, are there many alternative modes of representing the spatial environment. For example, consider this list of representations of spatial information about a city such as New York or London: a street directory, a schematic map of the Underground or Subway system, a tape-recorded walking tour, a guide book of places to visit and routes to follow, some souvenir picture postcards, an illuminated street map, the person at the tourist information booth. All of these different modes represent information about the whatness, whereness, and whenness of New York or London. All of these modes contain organized and stored information about the spatial environment. All of these modes are useful in solving particular types of spatial problems. They are *functionally similar* but, at the same time, *formally different*. The results of organizing and storing spatial information differ dramatically among the street directory, the tape-recorded tour, the souvenir photos, and Ms. *X*, the woman at the information booth.

Thus we can see both the functional similarity among the examples and the formal differences. But, if we look again, we can see yet another underlying similarity, this time in the *process* of representing or mapping. Although 1976 dresses and cars differ in form from those of 1975, the general process of dressmaking or car manufacturing remains the same. In mapping, the process similarity lies in the way that we use the representation to communicate something about the spatial environment. The first stage of the mapping process involves *mapmaking* or encoding; the second stage involves *map reading* or decoding. Thus the *process* of mapping comprises two parts, mapmaking and -reading, while the *product* of mapmaking is the organized representation, which may be stored internal or external to the representing individual.

The obvious question is: How do people make and read maps? Returning to the processes of dressmaking and car manufacturing, we find that they are controlled and determined by sets of instructions or rules stating: (1) *what to do,* (2) *in what order to do it,* and (3) *how it all goes together.* Dressmaking depends upon cut-out patterns together with written sewing instructions, while car manufacturing relies on blueprints and assembly line job specifications. What happens in mapping? If we consider the modes of representing information about New York or London, we find sets of rules or instructions for both mapmaking and map reading. In the case of the illuminated street map, someone had to *decide* what part of the city to include, what places to emphasize, and what streets should be named. All of these decisions utilize rules for mapmaking. On the other hand, a telephone directory is useful only if you know someone's name and address, can understand what the numbers mean (and can remember them!), and can tell whether a call is local or long distance. These are some of the requirements for using a telephone directory, or an example of map reading. We can analyze all of the modes of representation in terms of the rules for making maps and reading them. Obviously, in most cases, the rules or instructions are not as explicitly spelled out as they are in dressmaking. You just have to "know how to do it." Nevertheless, the process of doing it (mapping) is controlled by a set of rules.

However, the rules for making a tape-recorded walking tour are different from the rules for taking a color photograph of the Empire State Building or Big Ben. Knowing how to follow a guidebook tour is different from knowing how to ask questions at an information booth. These differences should not surprise us because, as we said, representations are functionally similar but formally different. The *specific* sets of rules for making and reading different representations vary; however, we can ask, Are these rules similar in some ways that are important to our argument?

If we think of rules as guidelines to making decisions for mapmaking and -reading, there are four major decisions that we face:

1. What are we interested in representing?
2. What viewpoint or perspective are we taking?

3. At what scale is the representation?
4. How do we construct the representation?

We can summarize these decisions as questions of (1) *purpose,* (2) *perspective,* (3) *scale,* and (4) *symbolization.* A decision on each of these questions leads to a set of rules for mapmaking. We must also know the same set of rules to read that particular representation. We can understand these decisions if we look more closely at two representations: the street map and the tape-recorded walking tour.

In producing the street map, we have to decide upon its *purpose.* Who is it for: Will it be for pedestrians or drivers, for strangers to the city or current residents, for sightseeing or everyday living? The answer to this question is crucial since it determines both *who* the representation is useful to, and *what types* of spatial problem it can assist in solving. Perhaps the purpose or value of any map is revealed in this discussion of the map and chart department of *Time* magazine:

> Researchers Isabel Lenkiewicz and Adrianne Jucius compile all the information for the maps and charts. Lenkiewicz majored in cartography and geography in college but stresses that "there are no schools where you can really study journalistic cartography. It's much more important to be interested in a wide variety of subjects than to know how to draw a map." Jucius and Lenkiewicz also deal with telephone callers requesting special geographical information. One caller posed a question that no one minded answering: "Are you the guys who make complicated things simple?"
>
> (Davidson, 1973, p. 2)

Purpose also guides the answers to the remaining three questions. In the case of the street map, the decision about *perspective* follows popular convention. Cartographic maps are usually based on a vertical or bird's-eye perspective. On the other hand, we might question the value of convention, as this report of a courtroom exchange suggests:

> May looks wilted when we return from recess. In the corridor, Archie explained how, due to the geography of San Quentin, May must have been partly, if not entirely out of sight of the parking lot where he claims to have seen the yellow van. Moore produces photos. The road to the parking lot. An aerial view of San Quentin. May is ironic about the second picture: He was an inmate, not a bird.
>
> (Millett, 1972, p. 114)

Directly linked with the purpose and perspective decisions is that concerning the *scale* of the street map. Scale is simply a measure of the size of the representation relative to the size of the environment being represented, and depends upon what part of the spatial environment is of interest. Some children's toys are "larger than life" (gigantic stuffed animals, for example), but in the environmental context that we are discussing, representations are always smaller than the environments represented. However, variations in scale are an important consideration. The choice presents a trade-off between the detail that one can include as against the areal extent that can be represented. In a street map at one scale, we could represent individual houses within a four-block area, while by selecting a smaller scale, we might represent a much larger area, but we would not be able to distinguish individual houses. The pitfalls of choosing the wrong scale can be seen in this seventeenth century discussion of cartography:

> . . . In that Empire, the Art of Cartography achieved such Perfection that the Map of one single Province occupied the whole of a City, and the Map of the Empire, the whole of a Province. In time, those Disproportionate Maps failed to satisfy and the Schools of Cartography sketched a Map of the Empire which was of the size of the Empire and coincided at every point with it. Less addicted to the Study of Cartography, the Following Generations comprehended that this dilated Map was Useless and, not without Impiety, delivered it to the Inclemencies of the Sun and of the Winters. In the Western Deserts there remain piecemeal Ruins of the Map, inhabited by Animals and Beggars. In the entire rest of the Country there is no vestige left of the Geographical Disciplines.

Who is the map for and what do they need to know? Clearly, purpose and scale are intertwined.

Finally, we must choose our *symbols*. If we want to indicate a railway station or park or street, how do we do it? Once again, convention helps us to decide. Railway stations are usually red circles or rectangles, parks are green shapes approximating the park's outline, and a street is indicated by a pair of black parallel lines. This stage of mapmaking involves the choice of symbols that will *externally* stand for (represent) the original object in the spatial environment. We frequently use two different types of symbols together so that they reinforce each other: for example, a red rectangle and a printed name, Grand Central or Paddington Station. There are occasions when people welcome a change from the conventional, as Lewis Carroll suggests in this comment on the Bellman who was captaining the ship in "The Hunting of the Snark":

> He had bought a large map representing the sea,
> Without the least vestige of land:
> And the crew were much pleased when they found it to be
> A map they could all understand.

"What's the good of Mercator's North Poles and Equators,
Tropics, Zones, and Meridian Lines?"
So the Bellman would cry: and the crew would reply
"They are merely conventional signs!"

"Other maps are such shapes, with their islands and capes!
But we've got our brave Captain to thank"
(So the crew would protest) "that he's bought us the best —
A perfect and absolute blank!"

(Dodgson, 1939, p. 683)

We can see the same four decisions or choice of rules in the case of the tape-recorded walking tour. The purpose is to guide visitors around the city, pointing out one expert's impressions of the significant and interesting views and landmarks. The perspective is "eye level," that of the average man on the street. The representation concentrates on things visible at eye level. In terms of scale, the tape casettes are much smaller than the city, and, more importantly, are serially organized in a way in which the city is not. The symbols employed are verbal. However, the words themselves may refer to a variety of sensory impressions: sights, interesting smells, the sound of the docks, and the feel of walking along a bumpy or cobbled street.

Thus the set of rules involved in both stages of representing an environment (mapmaking and -reading) is the result of four decisions about purpose, perspective, scale, and symbolization. *All* representations share these common features, although the results of specific decisions together give the representation its particular form. To emphasize this point, we will call the specific set of rules for making and reading a particular representation or map its *signature*. There is a clear and deliberate parallel with a style of handwriting or the painting of an artist such as Rembrandt or the playwriting style of Shakespeare. Experts in the field of art can usually identify a painting as being the work of a certain artist because of its style or distinctive characteristics such as brushwork and color combinations. Similarly, Shakespeare's plays share a distinctive style or signature. Representations of the spatial environment also have a signature. The typical signature of a cartographic map is the use of a vertical perspective, with a scale of, say, 1:50,000, and with blue lines for rivers, red dots for towns, and so on. The signature is the set of rules that control the process of mapmaking and -reading.

In our discussion, we may seem to have strayed far from our interest in how people cognitively represent the world around them. However, this discussion of representing or mapping answers the earlier question of how spatial information gets organized and stored in a functional way. The examples of representations we discussed were nearly all external, physical objects of some sort: maps, tape casettes, photographs, and books. But what about the person in the information booth? Her job is to offer help and information to people with spatial problems. She must constantly use her cognitive mapping ability, recalling from memory the coded and stored information on whatness, whereness, and whenness. Sometimes she turns to city directories, street maps, or the *Yellow Pages* for assistance (see Figure 3.1). Part of her cognitive mapping ability is knowing *where* to look for information. The recalled information is manipulated to help solve the spatial problems of the gen-

BY THE TIME YOU GET TO PHOENIX, WILL THEY BE WAITING?

You've mapped out your expansion program. Decided on Phoenix. Lined up distributors. Placed some advertising. And waited for Phoenix to put you on the map.

If you've expanded your market and not your Yellow Pages program, you may have a long wait. When people are looking to buy, the Yellow Pages is usually the first place they look, and sometimes the only place. The harder it is for them to find your product, the easier it is for them to find your competitor's.

The Yellow Pages is one advertising medium that can pinpoint your market precisely: whether it's Phoenix or Fargo. Whether it's regional or national. Once you get to the Yellow Pages, you're certain of getting to virtually all of your prospects. So that by the time you get to Phoenix, they'll be waiting.

3 OUT OF 4 PROSPECTS LET THEIR FINGERS DO THE WALKING.

Figure 3.1. Fingers, too, have cognitive maps.

eral public. The results of the manipulations come in several forms: a sketch map, a set of verbal directions of how to get somewhere, a guide book, a description of places to visit. She uses a wide range of signatures for information storage (mapmaking) and information manipulation (map reading and plan making). Her ability to think about the world around her and to solve spatial problems is no different from our own in its basic operation: She is simply better at it because of constant practice!

Cognitive mapping is a very effective and flexible ability, which employs a range of signatures to cope with spatial information. In the next part of this chapter we will show how the mapping process and these signatures are handled cognitively. However, it is always difficult to pin down and dissect a process. Our language is more capable of expressing static things than discussing elusive change. This difficulty is compounded when the process, cognitive mapping, is an internal, mental activity that cannot be observed directly. We are forced to draw inferences from and to speculate about the *outcome* of the process. We can get fleeting but imperfect glimpses at the ongoing operation of the process by watching somebody draw a sketch map or by asking people to think aloud while solving a wayfinding problem. Consequently, the evidence that we can use to answer the question, What is cognitive mapping? consists of a curious amalgam of anecdotes, quotes from both fiction and advertisements, scattered empirical studies, introspection, and a belief that "it must work something like this!" In presenting the answer, we will adopt two perspectives. The first focuses on the objectives or purposes of cognitive mapping, and the second emphasizes the controlling characteristics of the process.

THE OBJECTIVES OF COGNITIVE MAPPING

Cognitive mapping is a directed activity. It does not proceed helter-skelter since *purposes, rightly or wrongly conceived, are always an integral part of the mapping process.* Terms such as purpose, goal, or objective are indistinguishable in that they all refer to the desired outcome of the cognitive mapping process. This desired outcome can take one of two major forms. First, the process generates plans for solving specific spatial problems, which, when translated into guides for action, result in some pattern of spatial behavior. However, spatial behavior is not the only outcome of cognitive mapping. A second and equally important purpose involves generating frames of reference for understanding and interpreting our spatial environment. We can think about the world around us; we can construct worlds of fantasy and imagination; we can toy with different ways of expressing spatial ideas as words or pictures. Such activities *may* eventually lead to spatial behavior, but this is not a necessary outcome. The crucial point is that, in both cases, *cognitive mapping can only be understood as a purposive and hence goal-directed activity.*

We are unaware of the power and effectiveness of our cognitive mapping ability. It rarely fails us, even in widely divergent environmental conditions and contexts. We can find our way around both in daytime and at night, although the specific cues used may change. We can cope with twisting street patterns in the older part of the city and with the multilane freeway system on the outskirts, with the crowded interior of a shopping mall and with the backpacking trails in a national park. Although we are not equally competent and successful in every instance, we resort to the same ability—cognitive mapping. The ability is widely used and this is reflected in its pervasive influences on our everyday language, our educational system, the press, the advertising business, and the environmental design disciplines.

The most striking evidence of the flexibility and power of cognitive mapping is its capacity for adjusting to the loss of various senses. People who are congenitally blind use a cognitive mapping ability surprisingly like that of sighted people, although the types of information used and the representations formed are very different. There is a natural tendency, because of our emphasis on the visual sense, to regard the world of the blind as impoverished and lacking in detailed discriminations. Two representations of the same route from a bus stop to home, one by a blind person and the other by a sighted person, shatter this fallacy. The blind person relates:

> After descending from the bus you have to walk straight ahead a little on Kalyayevskaya Street, with the houses being on the right; you have to be on your toes at the corner of Sadovaya and Kalyayevskaya streets; you have to cross Sadovaya Street first, and then Kalyayevskaya Street; now I walk on the left side of the street; passing a house I come to a small square where I have to cross a streetcar line; there is no need to be in fear on this square as there are few automobiles here; near the next house there are always a good many people as this is a trolley bus stop; next there is a house with a projection; some distance from this house there is another house with a projection and a gate through which I must pass; the gate may be identified by the deep depression in the sidewalk; on the right side of the courtyard there is a house which must be by-passed; behind the house there is a vacant space; here you must walk along the fence for in rainy weather there are puddles; after a few steps to the right there are the steps which lead to my house.

Compare this with the route description given by a sighted person:

> Descending from the autobus, I cross the Sadovaya circle, and walk on the left side of Kalyayevskaya Street. Passing the 13th division of the mi-

litia, I enter a courtyard, and there I see a small two-story house on the right side.

(Khopreninova, 1956, quoted in
Shemyakin, 1962, pp. 229–230)

The sighted person could not remember many details on the route that were of major wayfinding importance to the blind person (e.g., the depression in front of the gate). Both representations are an outcome of the same cognitive mapping process, successfully used for solving the identical spatial problem. They are functionally similar and formally different.

Cognitive mapping can also cope with environmental change, whether the changes are permanent or temporary. We tend to overlook the rate of environmental change, but a recent Rand McNally advertisement for an atlas reminds us of its magnitude and cumulative impact:

Whatever happened to Alice?

Alice, Colorado went the way of 200 other small communities in the past ten years — gone from the face of Rand McNally maps. A turnpike gobbled up Bill's Place, Pennsylvania while DeSoto Beach, Florida is now part of the missile base at Cape Kennedy. . . .

At Rand McNally we're used to changes. In fact, there were over 40,000 made in our city and state maps last year. Businessmen and travelers demand up-to-date, accurate information on their maps, and we supply it.

Our cognitive mapping ability is engaged in a parallel up-dating activity. It is also *flexible* enough to adjust quickly to temporary changes in the world:

One of the traits that make Long Islanders such an independent and hardy breed is their ability to sense an impending traffic jam on the Long Island Expressway and resourcefully navigate alternate routes.

(The New York Times, July 22, 1973, Section 4, p. 4)

Yet despite the power, effectiveness, and flexibility of cognitive mapping, we rarely notice its operation. Such an observation leads directly to the thorny issue of awareness or consciousness. Can this ability really be present if we are unaware of its operation? The answer is yes. If we bear in mind that one role of cognitive mapping is that of enabling us to solve spatial problems, we can view such solutions as ranging along a continuum from habitual actions at one end to conscious actions at the other.

The *habitual problem solution* is best exemplified by the familiar belief that you know somewhere like the back of your hand and can make certain journeys blindfolded. You can walk (or even drive) home think-ing about some personal difficulty without ever being aware of how you solved the spatial problem of getting from work to home, and with-out any memory of that particular journey. However, the lack of a con-scious memory does not mean that your cognitive mapping ability was dormant. You were looking ahead, both literally and metaphorically, to anticipate where to cross the road, where to turn, where to stop and buy an evening newspaper. A sequential plan was being executed and your spatial progress monitored. Had you been snapped out of your thoughts by some person or event, you would have known immediately where you were in relation to home or work. You were well oriented. Such an habitual problem solution is simply the result of learning, of the cumulated experience of many similar journeys in the past. But this learning and these past experiences have been organized by the same cognitive ability that is controlling your spatial behavior on the way home. Since you are unaware of its operation, you tend to dismiss it.

Three illustrations reinforce this argument. The first points to the in-credible strength of habitual problem solutions — to the *force of habit:*

> In Pratolini's autobiographical novel, he gives a striking example of people who in their daily walks continued to follow streets that no longer existed but were only imaginary tracks through a razed and empty section of Florence.
>
> (Lynch, 1960, p. 126)

The second illustration reminds us of both the effort that goes into solving even the most simple spatial problem *and* the pervasive nature of spatial problems themselves:

> People manage to make their adjustments. There are spurts and lags, nat-urally. Some habits and customs are mastered more quickly than others. Some undreamed-of luxuries try the mind and soul more than others do. In Cleveland a man . . . laughs about a few of his recent tribulations and compares them to what his ancestors had to go through . . .: "I can't keep up with the light switches in this city. I think it's harder for me to figure out these lights than it was for my kin way back to cut a path through the hills and settle there. Everywhere you go here there's a switch. On and off, that's what you have to think about when you go into a room. Now who's supposed to know every minute of his life where the switch is? I've been up in this place over a year and I forget, . . .
>
> (Coles, 1971, p. 8)

The third illustration of the force of habit is perhaps the most obvious: sleepwalking. We can move around our house in the dark when we are either completely asleep or drowsy. We know how many steps to take before we have to turn right; we can avoid bumping into unseen furniture. We seem to operate by the "feel" of things. Our spatial behavior is under the control of a plan, but if we were asked later to describe it, we would have difficulty putting it into words. We might be able to draw a sketch representing the route. Nevertheless, the plan does exist and it is one reflection of cognitive mapping at work. (The question of the form of cognitive representations will be discussed later in this chapter.)

In contrast to habitual solutions where we are unaware of our cognitive mapping ability, *conscious problem solving* is an active process that dominates our thinking. We deliberately seek information from our memory (internal representations) and all available external sources; we generate and evaluate alternative solutions to a problem. Orienteering, which has been likened to a car rally on foot, provides a classic example of the conscious solution of spatial problems. John Disley (1967, p. 68) writes:

> The rapid sifting of evidence and the weighing-up of the pros and cons of alternative plans is what the sport of orienteering is all about. Each way of going from one control to another will have certain advantages as well as compensations. The experienced orienteer develops a sensitive calculating mechanism which computes distance against height to be climbed; path running against forest scrambling; and ease of route-finding against complex navigation. Finally, when the variables have been "costed-out" on a time basis, the whole equation needs to be considered in the light of his own fitness.

Everyday life provides numerous parallel situations, which require a similar calculating mechanism: the Long Island Expressway, Christmas Eve in a large shopping center, and travel in State College before and after a Penn State football game. We can even use our cognitive mapping ability to rehearse spatial problem solving in advance:

> Folsom's wife, Vicki, once applied imagery to help her master left-hand driving before touring England and Scotland. Inflight and just before falling asleep, she saw herself in a car designed for left-hand drive. She drove the roads, imagining she was coming out of a one-way street, entering into complicated turns or traffic patterns. "And," she added with a grin, "*the system really works!*"
>
> (Wells, 1971, p. 25)

However, in both habitual and conscious problem solving, it is important to remember that we are learning in two senses. First, we are adding to and confirming our *knowledge* of the whatness, whereness, and whenness of the spatial environment. Second, we are developing and confirming our *strategies* (or heuristics) for solving spatial problems. These strategies can be transferred (or generalized) from one problem situation to another, and hence our problem-solving abilities become more flexible and extensive. Examples of general strategies might include a thorough understanding of the city block system, which would lead to rules for route choice, directional change, and counting block distances, or a search strategy for finding a new apartment, which involves gathering information from friends, newspapers, and realtors. Although the underlying nature of these learning processes will be discussed in Chapter 7, they reflect and emphasize the purposive nature of the entire cognitive mapping process.

In achieving these purposes, cognitive mapping displays three principal characteristics: It is an *interactive*, *selective*, and *organizing* process. Although we will treat each characteristic separately, the ongoing process is controlled by all three simultaneously, subject to the requirements of the spatial problem at hand.

COGNITIVE MAPPING AS AN INTERACTIVE PROCESS

In claiming that cognitive mapping is an interactive process, we are stressing that it rarely proceeds solely by way of armchair contemplation. Rather, the problem solutions themselves and the developing nature of the ability itself emerges from continual interaction with those spatial environments being mapped. At the heart of this claim is the idea of an information feedback process in which *learning by doing* is crucial. The nature of the interaction itself affects both the type of spatial information obtained and the sources through which it is obtained. This point will become clear if we consider a series of examples.

Held and Rekosh (1963) developed a series of ingenious experiments, which showed that *correct, or veridical, perception is dependent upon direct interaction between the perceiving organism and the environment being perceived.* Motor activity (e.g., spatial behavior) is essential for linking the external environment to the internal representation. Thus, for example, visual inputs alone may be insufficient to comprehend (grasp) the environment:

> On first look, of course, the Grand Canyon is impossible to see. What your eyes report, instead of the Grand Canyon, is a painting, a mural. It simply lacks reality. You confront a vast gorge 18 miles across and 30-odd miles in length, studded with towering buttes and splashed with blue, rose, deep purple, and brown. Everyone knows all about that because everyone has seen the photographs dozens of times. The trouble with looking at it in actuality is that you have nothing to relate it to, nothing to measure it by. What the National Park Service ought to do to help people appreciate the Grand Canyon, I concluded, would be to dump the Empire

State Building into it. That would really help us tourists comprehend the extraordinary dimensions of what we are looking at.

(Honan, 1973, p. 24)

One of the roles of cognitive mapping is to develop frames of reference into which we can place environmental information. Honan points to the problem of scale, in this case the need for something whose size is known to serve as a base of comparison. Yet, as Henry Wright, the son of the designer of Radburn, suggests, the problem of scale and the lack of direct, immediate interaction can be compounded:

Such descriptions of Radburn account for the seminal importance of the Radburn idea. In the great majority of instances, those who were influenced by Radburn planning probably never visited Radburn itself, and might have been a bit disappointed if they had, if only by its small size. They fell in love with the Idea—the ideal.

(Wright, 1972, p. 196)

Both Honan's mention of photographs and Wright's concern over the lack of direct, face-to-face contact are fused in a commentary on a recent exhibition of photographs:

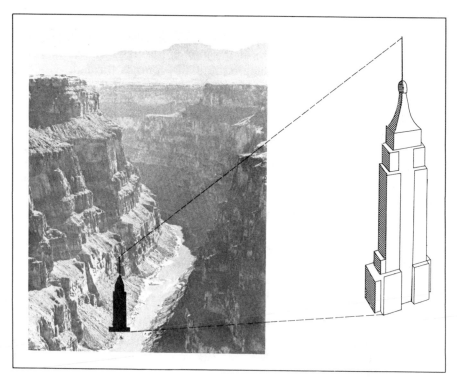

Figure 3.2. The Empire State Building "dumped" into the Grand Canyon.

. . . photography as art has had a lot to do with the way we perceive the world and react to it, and to some extent the accepted image of our environment is one that the art of photography has given us . . .

They (photographers) have taught us a way to look at the world, and in turn, we see the world their way.

And that is the rub. The curious thing about images of the environment is that they inevitably structure reality. Our perception is trained by them. . . .

In architecture and urbanism the photograph has become as valid as the thing itself.

(Ada Louise Huxtable, The New York
Times, Nov. 25, 1973, Section 2, p. 26)

As a consequence, our reaction to photographs is somewhat ambiguous. We tend to distrust them: the camera itself may not lie but . . . Hence, the island of Bermuda produced an advertisement that claimed:

There is a place that looks exactly like these postcards. Oddly enough it's where we took the pictures.

These pictures were not retouched. So, if they are some of the reasons that you come to Bermuda, you will not be disappointed.

Actually, we can promise you countless scenes like these, because, in reality, Bermuda is a 21-square-mile picture post-card.

(Time, July 17, 1972, p. 3)

And even direct, face-to-face experience can lead to strange views of the world, as Huck Finn demonstrates in his description of a balloon ascent:

By and by the earth was a ball—just a round ball, . . . The Widder Douglas always told me the earth was round like a ball, but I never took any stock in a lot of them superstitions o' hers, and of course I paid no attention to that one, because I could see myself that the world was the shape of a plate and flat. I used to go up on the hill, and take a look around and prove it for myself, because I reckon the best way to get a sure thing on a fact is to go and examine for yourself, and not take anybody's say-so. But I had to give in now that the widder was right. That is, she was right as to the rest of the world, but she warn't right about the part our village is in; that part is the shape of a plate, and flat, I take my oath!

(Twain, 1929, pp. 15–16)

For blind people, sound is a major source of spatial information that is vital to the process of orientation and wayfinding. It is most effective when it results from *personal interactions* with the environment. Recognition of location can come from the characteristic sounds of a squeaky door. Distance can be gauged from the knowledge that the sound of footsteps increases in pitch as the person approaches an obstacle (Gatty, 1958). Whatness can be inferred from the differences in sound produced by brick walls in contrast to hedges (Southworth, 1969). A blind person is not groping in the dark in any environment that he is familiar with: His own spatial behavior provides a sensitive reflection of the whatness, whereness, and whenness of the world.

Direct interaction with the environment is a vital feature in both developing and successfully solving problems using our cognitive mapping ability. The practical force of this claim became apparent in New York City. After a world-wide study of urban taxi systems, the chairman of the Taxi and Limousine Commission concluded:

> ... London's taxi drivers were true professionals. "They travel around the city on motorcycles, memorizing the streets for 15 months before they can take the exam for a license," he said with awe.
>
> (The New York Times, Nov. 24, 1972, p. 35)

The value of this interactive learning experience is clear from a story in the same newspaper a few months later:

> **The Empire What Building?**
>
> Years ago, if a New York cabbie drove his passenger around Central Park three times on the way to the airport, the assumption was that he was trying to raise the fare. Today it could mean the driver simply can't find his way out of Central Park. Complaints from passengers indicate that a growing number of the city's cabbies are novices who have had trouble finding locations such as La Guardia Airport and the Brooklyn Bridge. The reason, according to the City Taxi Commission, is a shortage of cab drivers. The result is a small corps of on-the-job trainees far less familiar with the city's streets than many of their exasperated passengers. One man reported that he told a cabbie to take him to Columbus Circle. "Where's that?" the driver asked.
>
> (The New York Times, July 8, 1973, Section 4, p. 5)

The necessity for personal interaction is not just a consequence of the complexities of modern urban existence. Leo Marx describes how Mark Twain experienced a parallel situation:

> The theme of "Old Times" is "learning the river." Here the narrator, Mark Twain, tells of his initiation into a unique American vocation: Mississippi piloting. He insists that this job has to be learned by an apprentice on the spot; no books, no school, no theory can equip him. What he has to learn is a new language—nothing less than the language of nature. It is not simply the general technique of piloting, but a particular piece of geography which he must possess. He must "know the river" by day and

by night, summer and winter, heading upstream and heading down-stream. He must memorize the landscape. And this knowledge forever distinguishes him from the uninitiated. To the trained pilot the river is a book that delivers its most guarded secrets; but to ignorant passengers it is only a pretty picture.

(Marx, 1964, pp. 320–321)

Even the specific type of direct interaction can have an effect on both the form and the contents of our cognitive representations of the world. There is a major difference between *active* and *passive* ways of explor-ing a place. The world experienced by someone on foot or on a bicycle is very different from that of a passenger in a bus or car. It is not sim-ply the mode of travel that is important: It is the person's ability to control the spatial sequence and speed of his experience. We develop a very restricted view of a place if we are unable to satisfy the urge to look around the corner. For most people, parts of their world are ac-tively known and parts are known only passively. The passive world is that of the straight and the narrow while the active world is one that we feel at home in.

Before leaving this discussion of the interactive nature of cognitive mapping, we should touch on some studies that will be discussed in detail in Chapters 6 and 7. James Blaut and David Stea have studied the possibility that toy play may perform a vital role in the devel-opment of the cognitive mapping ability in young children. Although four- and five-year-olds cannot be spatially mobile in an extended envi-ronment, they can interact with the environment by actively *modelling* it with toys. These toys permit the child to learn to understand, to com-prehend, and to cognitively map the properties of this environment "in the large." Later in life, of course, many of these same mapping activi-ties (manipulation, modelling, etc.) occur as purely *cognitive* activities.

THE SELECTIVITY OF COGNITIVE MAPPING

To claim that cognitive mapping is selective in its operation is at first sight to belabor the obvious. To operate in any other way would be im-possible. We must be selective in order to cope with the sheer volume of possible information about the spatial environment. Selectivity takes two forms. First, we must be selective in terms of what spatial informa-tion we choose to encode and store: This mapmaking requirement in-volves decisions about what types of information we store, how we symbolize it, how we arrange and order it, and how we attach relative value or importance to it. Second, we need a selective map reading pro-cess in terms of what information we retrieve and what strategies for manipulation we elect to follow. At the heart of these requirements is the concept of criteria. What are the criteria for selectivity?

There are two major criteria: (1) functional importance, and (2) distinctiveness or imageability. *Functional importance* reflects the fact that we know or remember what is generally useful to us in our everyday patterns of spatial behavior. We do *not* remember everything about the route from home to the shopping center; even if perfect knowledge were possible, it is unnecessary. Instead we remember information about crucial decision points along the route: the stop signs, the traffic lights, appropriate turns and lane changes that, together with a set of car-driving rules, allow us to drive from home to the shopping center. Long-distance truck drivers focus on weighing stations, potential speed traps, and places to eat. Our cognitive maps, therefore, reflect functional importance.

Given this dependence on functional importance, cognitive maps mirror closely the spatial patterns of regular activity. Peter Orleans (1973) has shown how knowledge of the spatial extent and structure of the urban area of Los Angeles reflects the spatial behavior and mobility of various socioeconomic groups. There is a *direct* link between functional importance, cognitive maps, and territory as the following quotation from Eldridge Cleaver illustrates:

> Stacy's loyalty went to Crescent Heights. To him, his neighborhood was the center of the world. Isolated somewhat from the rest of Los Angeles, in the way that each part of that scattered metropolis is isolated from every other, Crescent Heights was a refuge. If Stacy had been captured by beings from another planet, who cast him into a prison filled with inhabitants from all the planets, and if he were asked by the others where he lived, he would have said: "I'm Stacy Mims from Crescent Heights." ... Stacy loved Crescent Heights. He did not feel comfortable or secure anywhere else. When he ventured out of the neighborhood, on infrequent trips downtown or to the East Side or to Watts, he was always relieved when the trip was over and he was back among the familiar sights and sounds of Crescent Heights. Even school was still far enough away that he felt alien and uncomfortable until he was away from school and back on his own stomping grounds.
>
> (Cleaver, 1969, pp. 122 and 124)

The spatial and social isolation of a territorially based group of people is reflected in the way that they view the "outside world." Robert Forman (1971, p. 6) captures this isolation in the comments of European immigrants about U.S. cities at the turn of the last century:

> So great was the sense of insulation from larger society that some immigrants hardly seemed to think of themselves as having left the Old Country. Thus women in Boston who ventured a few blocks outside the Italian colony would say, "I have been down to America today," (Firey, 1947, p.

211) and a Croatian in Chicago could mention that men might live in his neighborhood for years and only go out into the "real America" once or twice (Abbott, 1936, p. 115). Culturally then, the immigrant could continue to live in Italy or Croatia or Poland as transplanted to the New World and become "Americanized" more nearly at his own pace and on his own terms.

We can get a final sense of functional importance if we consider people's graphic representations of their knowledge of an environment. When children draw pictures of their home areas, locations and buildings are drawn to a scale reflecting their relative importance to the child. Thus, their own homes are by far the largest objects, with either their school or their friends' houses next in size. Even in adults, familiar or positively valued areas and landmarks are likely to be drawn proportionally larger than other places. This reminds one of the Crusader-era maps of the world described by Wright (1925), in which Jerusalem always occupies the central position and is often depicted with every house shown in detail.

Distinctiveness or *imageability* reflects the contrasts in and arrangements of the spatial environment itself. Donald Appleyard (1969a), in a study of Cuidad Guyana (Venezuela), asked the obvious but deceptive question, Why are buildings known? The answer lies in three characteristics: form, visibility, and use. Use is obviously a reflection of functional role and is an example of our first criterion of selectivity, importance. Form and visibility can be encapsulated in the phrase, standing out like a sore thumb! In a similar type of study, Carr and Schissler (1969) found that knowledge of areas on either side of the driver's journey to work is a function of relative exposure time and visual dominance. However, in an area of low imageability, the question of selectivity becomes more interesting. De Jonge (1962) focussed on an area of monotonous, undifferentiated apartment blocks in a Dutch city, and found that people deliberately sought out distinctive features such as brightly colored curtains and window box displays as an aid to solving wayfinding problems.

Although functional importance and distinctiveness or imageability are the major criteria, there are occasional but significant modifications to the selection process. Value systems can lead to an unspoken agreement to ignore certain aspects of the environment:

Perhaps the most amazing feature of Nintoku's tomb is the fact that modern Japanese refrain from noticing it. It sprawls like New York's Central Park across the valuable real estate of Osaka's suburbs but no guidebook mentions it, and none but Court ceremonialists ever cross its three concentric moats to climb its wooded slopes . . . Hungry antiquarians from the West have noted from afar that the sides of the mound are strewn with bones. . . . But whenever they suggest an official scientific investigation to their Japanese colleagues, they are met evasively with a sudden change of subject.

(Bergamini, 1971, p. 193, footnote 5)

The tomb is a 100-foot high mountain with an area of 80 acres, scarcely something that could be overlooked by accident!

Deliberate oversight is not restricted to the classical Japanese mind. The modern American planner is equally capable of deliberate selectivity based on social value systems. However, as Robert Goodman (1971) suggests, the influence is more sinister and perhaps pernicious. Goodman quotes from an *American Institute of Architects* publication—a sponsored book on urban design in which "gray areas" are discussed. These areas are not quite slums; they are the unglamorous but necessary service areas of the inner city:

> Perhaps the real defect of the gray zone is that we see too much of it. We pass by large extents of it on our new elevated auto expressways as we soar above the streets toward the center city. We pass through much of it as we proceed along our center city's major arteries. We see it as we approach the center in the morning on the way to work and in the evening on our way home. Its too frequent sight taxes our patience. *The answer may lie in the application of theatrics to the urban scene.* If the gray area is too frequently visible, too depressing because it is too much in our presence, perhaps we can arrange our major routes to avoid it, to bypass it, to give us views of the parts of the city we hold in higher esteem. In the Renaissance, architects were able to recast the service elements of buildings into what appeared to be blank walls which could form entrance courts or the walls bordering a long passage. Could we not do this on the larger scale of the city? Could we not conceal, or at least play down, that which distorts the image of our central city's better self?
>
> (Goodman's italics: Goodman, 1971, pp. 111–113,
quoting Spreiregen, 1965, pp. 215–216)

It is difficult to conceive of a more unpleasant application of the "out of sight, out of mind" philosophy. Unfortunately, this philosophy has been put into practice, as this comment about Mayor Drapeau of Montreal suggests:

> Although Drapeau has concentrated on projects that bring prestige and pleasure to Montreal, he has shown much less active interest in some accute social problems that afflict his city.
>
> Nothing is more eloquent in this respect than the hundreds of brightly colored fences and walls vivid with drawings that were put up in several

districts of the city to help distract the visitor's view from the slums that are often hidden underneath.

(Ryan, 1974, p. 16)

One other form of selectivity is *augmentation*, selective cognitive addition to the environment of elements that "ought to be there." Appleyard (1970, p. 112) has described this process:

> Inference did not always lead to accuracy. After three months in the city, a newly arrived European engineer drew in three railroad lines instead of the actual two. His previous experience told him to expect a railroad linkage between the steel mill and the Orinoco mining port, a connection that did not yet exist. Abstraction and inference enable an inhabitant to cope with larger areas and more complex environments more rapidly and with greater mastery, but he may miss the detail in his skimming of the information given.

How does the process of augmentation and inference work? It involves the intelligent linking of two factors: some cognitive representation of the spatial environment and a set of rules. The rules are generalizations derived from past experience, usually taking the form, "This is what you would expect (or not expect) to find at a particular type of place." Thus, ma and pa grocery stores are generally located on the corners of blocks in the older part of the city; you can usually find a gas station that is open 24 hours a day near a freeway interchange; you won't find ranch-style houses in the inner city, and so on. Whatness, whereness, and whenness information is intertwined to form typical representations of parts of our environment. J. B. Jackson's (1957) article, "The Stranger's Path," outlines the probable sequence of scenes and businesses encountered by a stranger as he enters any small American city.

The joint outcome of rules and some spatial information from the representation is the *generation of expectations*. Jerome Bruner refers to this process as "going beyond the information given." He presents a graphic example of inference at work in a study involving the teaching of the geography of the North Central U.S.A. to a class of fifth graders. The students were given a blank outline map of the area, which marked only rivers, lakes, and natural resources. They were asked to *figure out* (infer) where the main cities, railroads, and highways would be located. Following this, they held a general discussion to see how their choices could be justified:

> The discussion was a hot one. After an hour . . . permission was given to consult the rolled up wall map. I will never forget one young student, as

he pointed his finger at the foot of Lake Michigan, shouting, "Yipee, *Chicago* is at the end of the pointing-down lake." And another replying, "Well, OK: but Chicago's no good for the rivers and it should be here where there's a big city (St. Louis)." These children were thinking, and learning was an instrument for checking and improving the process. To at least a half dozen children in the class it is not a matter of indifference that no big city is to be found at the junction of Lake Huron, Lake Michigan, and Lake Ontario. They were slightly shaken up transportation theorists when the facts were in.

(Bruner, 1959, pp. 187–188)

On occasion, inference can give way to imagination, and fact to fancy:

In the small separate room, where the walls were gradually being covered by strange maps and fabulous drawings, he taught them to read and write and do sums, and he spoke to them about the wonders of the world, not only where his learning had extended, but forcing the limits of his imagination to extremes. It was in this way that the boys ended up learning that in the southern extremes of Africa there were men so intelligent and peaceful that their only pastime was to sit and think, and that it was possible to cross the Aegean sea on foot by jumping from island to island all the way to the port of Salonika.

(Márquez, 1970, p. 16)

Cognitive mapping is not simply a passive process, the operation of which is dictated by the physical pattern of imageability of the spatial environment. Nor is it a process that simply selects information from what is available in the spatial environment. It is an *active* and *constructive* process, often going beyond the information given. Cognitive mapping is one reflection of our intelligence. It is obvious, therefore, that the apparent simplicity of the selective characteristic of the process is deceptive and misleading.

However, a discussion of the *criteria* of selectivity alone is insufficient. We must also consider what influences these criteria: Where do they come from? The answer lies in two different theoretical positions with respect to cognitive processes in general. Copy theory ascribes a dominant influence to factors existing in the environment itself. Experience with the environment is ultimately reflected in direct "copies" of that environment stored in the brain. The copies are stimulus dependent, and it is this theory that leads to the criterion of distinctiveness or imageability.

In contrast, the constructivist theory ascribes a dominant influence to factors existing within the individual. Human cognitive functioning is a constructive process in which specific environmental information is deliberately sought out. Key, critical features of the environment become incorporated into a person's environmental knowledge. This argument underlies the criterion of functional importance and is reflected in anthropological studies of human wayfinding in natural environments. Groups such as the Tuaregs, Eskimos, Aborigines, and South Sea Island navigators operate successfully in widely divergent environmental contexts and yet share similar approaches to spatial problem solving (see Chapters 4 and 5). The constructive nature of human cognition is exemplified by recent events in Northern Ireland. Catholic areas of Belfast had been barricaded off and entry was denied to both British troops and Protestants. Although the barricades were forcibly removed and access reestablished, a Belfast Catholic was quoted as saying that the areas would "still be no go in the mind."

MAKING SENSE OUT OF THE WORLD

The third major characteristic of cognitive mapping is its organizing nature and, to appreciate this, we must return to the objectives of the entire process. In essence, *we are trying to use the past, in the present, to solve the future.* Therefore, in addition to the need for selectivity, we must pull together, organize, and synthesize innumerable bits of information on whatness, whereness, and whenness. This information is mostly the result of many unstructured experiences that are disjoint in both a temporal and spatial sense. There is little systematic exploration of our everyday world. Without some capacity for reorganization, our experiences of the spatial environment would be literally incomprehensible. We must overcome this incomprehensibility, reducing and simplifying our experience into some meaningful, and hence, useful form of ordered knowledge. This is achieved by an organizing process, which influences both the storage of information in memory and its recall in appropriate situations.

Organization is best expressed by the idea of making sense out of things, by the effort after or the search for meaning. Sense (organization) is *not* given by the environment out there. The world is not a jigsaw puzzle that awaits assembly in the mind. Only in part does the organization depend upon the inherent properties of the spatial environment itself. This occurs to the extent that the world is, in Kevin Lynch's term, *legible,* or *self*-organizing, such that one is provided with a readily available framework within which to organize experience. Obviously an environment with a pattern of high continuity, with a number of distinctive and yet clearly interconnected parts would be legible. A grid layout for a city would fit such a description; but such a legible structure would represent only one possible *skeleton* of an organization for a person. The skeleton must be fleshed out with *personal* meaning: John lives there; here is a convenient 24-hour drug store; that corner is dangerous because of the pedestrian traffic; don't walk there because of a teenage gang; and so on. In this way, our cognitive representations recognize that the spatial environment is *full of personal meaning* and, in themselves, become *meaningful*.

Legibility can help in the task of organizing, but it is not the answer to the problem. In many situations, we must perform the organizing with only minimal assistance from the environment. Our cognitive mapping must not only be selective, but also be able to synthesize and organize experiences. We must look at the contents and structuring of cognitive representations of the environment. How does our cognitive mapping ability encode and decode information? What signatures do people use in representing their spatial environments? These questions can be answered by focussing on two ideas: the *units, or contents of representations*, and the *arrangement, or organization, of representations*.

THE CONTENTS OF REPRESENTATIONS

The units or contents can be viewed as categories or concepts:

> To categorize is to render discriminably different things equivalent, to group the objects and events and people around us into classes, and to respond to them in terms of their class membership rather than their uniqueness.
>
> (Bruner, Goodnow, and Austin, 1956, p. 1)

Bruner, Goodnow, and Austin distinguish between *identity* categories, which refer to *forms of the same thing*, and *equivalence* categories, which treat discriminably different things as *the same kind of thing* or as *amounting to the same kind of thing*. Thus, we can experience Chicago on many different occasions, in all weathers and seasons, at different times of the day or night, following different routes, both driving and walking. However, all of these disjoint experiences are recognized as reflecting, reinforcing, and adding to the identity category that we label as Chicago. In contrast, we use several different shopping centers, which vary in size, layout, attractiveness, convenience, and utility, and yet these disparate experiences can be viewed as reflecting a single equivalence category, labelled shopping center. That the formation and existence of categories is the result of a constructive, organizing ability is clear when we realize that the experiences of Chicago can also be taken to reflect an equivalence category, city, and the experiences of one specific shopping center reflect an identity category, University Plaza.

Identity and equivalence categories are the raw material from which we construct cognitive representations. They lie at the heart of solving spatial problems: Orientation depends upon matching an identity category with the world that we see around us. Fantasy worlds are synthesized out of novel juxtapositions of identity and equivalence categories. Communication, whether written, verbal, or graphic, employs a vocabulary of shared categories. Part of learning a new city or neighborhood involves modifying existing categories and generating new ones, especially new identity categories. However, we must remember that not even identity categories are perfect reflections of the spatial environment. They are *not* duplicative. They are not visual snapshots nor even cartographic maps. Instead, they are highly *generalized and simplified reconstructions* of our environmental experience. They are the result of the processes of interaction, selection, and organization, which have occurred intermittently and simultaneously. They are an essential, first step in making sense out of the world.

THE FORM OF REPRESENTATIONS

If our knowledge of the spatial environment is achieved through the development and use of categories, then what *form* do categories take? What do they "look" like? Again, this is a difficult question. Categories cannot be observed directly. We can only infer their existence from what people say or do, from verbal or spatial behavior. Consequently, we can only speculate on the physiological form they take in the brain. We can, however, by introspection claim that they exist in two modes in conscious recall and in our communication with others. We can elect to express our spatial knowledge in either of *two media*, as imagery or as words. The "or" in the previous statement is a crucial reflection of one of the strengths of cognitive mapping: flexibility. Words and images can be substituted freely for one another and are complementary. Your knowledge of Chicago can be equally well a series of visual images of buildings and street scenes *or* a series of verbal descriptions of the same buildings and street scenes. Translations from one medium of expression (or signature) to another are virtually instantaneous. The verbal mode has obvious advantages for interpersonal communication. However, sensory imagery is literally more personal and sometimes more powerful. Not only can we visualize places, but we can recall their feel and their distinctive sounds and smells in highly affective, sometimes emotive terms. Not only do we have a mind's eye but a mind's ear, a mind's nose, . . .

Our ability to represent spatial information as either words or images poses serious problems for research into the process of cognitive mapping. In effect, we must ask a person to use his cognitive mapping skills so that he can express to us the characteristics of the very same cognitive mapping process! This apparently paradoxical statement makes more sense if we consider the basic approach to collecting data. We ask a person to recall and manipulate his categories of spatial knowledge, to organize the knowledge around a specific theme (e.g., the city of Chicago or his neighborhood), and then to translate this organization into a specified form using a particular signature (e.g., a sketch map or a one-paragraph description). It is an indication of the power and flexibility of cognitive mapping that we can easily follow these instructions. But this flexibility and ability to translate makes it difficult to say this is *how* a person *knows* Chicago (or his neighborhood). If you ask for a sketch map, then the graphic medium of expression constrains the external form of the representation. This mode of external representation has its own signature, and we cannot necessarily conclude that it reflects the *cognitive signature* employed for the *cognitive internal representation* of Chicago. Similarly, the verbal medium has its characteristic signature, and the verbal description necessarily reflects the constraints of the signature. In some contexts, a picture may be worth a thousand words: Conversely, we can better express our evaluative feelings about a place in words. And should a person be forced to make a mental translation from one medium to another, the resulting external representation will probably reflect his translating skills and not necessarily how he knows Chicago or how he cognitively represents what he knows.

The problem of translation can be clarified if we think of our spatial knowledge as a *vocabulary* and our cognitive signatures as a *grammar*. The set of identity and equivalence categories that represent our understanding of whatness, whereness, and whenness comprise a vocabulary, a set of units for expressing spatial knowledge. There is also a set of rules or a grammar that controls the manipulation and use of this vocabulary. Thus, for example, heuristics are learned rules or strategies for solving certain types of spatial problems: wayfinding in a grid-form city or searching for a new apartment. Any representation (internal or external) is the result of an application of a cognitive signature (or grammar) to spatial knowledge (or vocabulary). We can illustrate these ideas of vocabulary and grammar in two instances. First, Table 3.1 is a collection of phrases and expressions from everyday language, which reflects the use of spatial imagery. Second, a specific application of spatial imagery shows how vocabulary and grammar are synthesized in expressing ideas:

> He keeps on zigzagging. He keeps on struggling with the mixed feelings he has . . . he is quite concerned with *position*, with where he stands and others do; and so he uses rather often what I suppose could be called topographical or geographic imagery. He is "all over the place" in what he has said; and he can recognize that fact. He is "all over the map." He is "in the middle." He is "in the center," and "between the extremes." Indeed, he is always going up and down, crossing himself back and forth, as he talks: "I'm taking you and me for a ride, I guess. My kids tell me sometimes that I'm crossing the road when I talk with them, going back on what I just said."

> (Coles and Erikson, 1971, p. 46)

Table 3.1 SPATIAL EXPRESSIONS IN EVERYDAY LANGUAGE

Direction

I don't know which way to turn
I don't know where I am going
I don't know which way is up
I don't know where I'm at
I don't know which way to go next
Get Lost!
Getting nowhere fast

Routes

Drive someone around the bend
Lead someone down the garden path
Keeping on the straight and narrow
Off the beaten track
On the track of *or* on the right track
In the footsteps of
Going around in circles

Location

Where it's at	Right in the center of things
Where the action is	Getting to the bottom of things
Where it's all happening	Being on top of things
Far out *or* way out	Being above it all
All over the place	That's beneath me
On top of the world	Being out of it
This is really nowhere	Being into something

Home

There's no place like home
Home is where your heart is

Places

(City X) is the armpit of the nation
First prize is a week in (City X), second prize is two weeks in (City X)
Sending a person to Coventry
Sending coals to Newcastle
Putting someone in his or her place *or* knowing your own place

Seeing

I can't see where I am going
In the mind's eye
I can't picture what you mean
I can't see my way clear to
Seeing is believing
I see what you mean
Out of sight, out of mind
Seeing the light at the end of the tunnel
Can't see the wood for the trees

Mapping

Mapping things out in my mind *or* head
I haven't got it mapped out yet
Putting (place X) on the map
You don't have to draw me a map
(Place X) is off the map

The difficulty of conducting research into how a person knows a spatial environment is compounded by the fact that cognitive mapping is a *reconstructive* organizing process. Cognitive representations do not exist as static forms mysteriously tucked away in our brain. We should not view our memory as a sort of cognitive atlas that we can turn to, nor as a series of picture postcards and colorslides that we can look at, nor even as a written tour guide that we can read. Cognitive representations should be viewed as structures that can be easily *generated* and reconstructed on demand. The result of the reconstruction is a *cognitive structure*, or a cognitive map, of some aspect of the spatial environment. We can generate many such structures, which reflect part of our understanding of Chicago or our neighborhood. These *may* be in the form of visual images; however, we can translate these using a variety of words and phrases, the choice of which depends upon the instructions given and the mood of the person involved. There is no *one* all-embracing representation of our spatial environment. Your answer today to the request, describe your home town, can be very different from your answer yesterday. You may focus attention on very different categories of information, expressed and organized in different ways. Yet both answers reflect your spatial understanding and knowledge.

THE ROLES OF COGNITIVE STRUCTURES

In the remainder of this chapter, we will look at some major types of cognitive structure and show how these structures assist in spatial thinking and problem solving. The first example of a cognitive structure is one frequently used in the news and communications media: It involves a division of the world into the East, the West, and the Third World. Such a classification reflects socioeconomic attributes, culture, and geopolitical affiliation. We have three loosely defined equivalence categories that play a vital role in both describing and interpreting events. It allows us to say that something is the sort of thing you would expect to happen there. One of the key roles of cognitive mapping is in generating *a frame of reference for interpreting events* in our spatial environment. Frames of reference exist at all spatial scales. At a national level we refer to the Northeast or East Coast, the South, the Midwest, and California as geopolitical units (see Figure 3.3). In this respect, we can see another role of cognitive mapping: It generates *predictive frameworks* in which we can suggest what will or might happen. The U.S. geopolitical units allow predictions about partisan voting patterns, social attitudes, and life styles. Cognitive mapping is vital in developing a "lookahead" capacity. For example, when we select a new home and neighborhood, we want to be able to evaluate how we will fit in, and how the neighborhood might change. With relatively few clues, we make extensive predictions as to what to expect in places that we have never been to before.

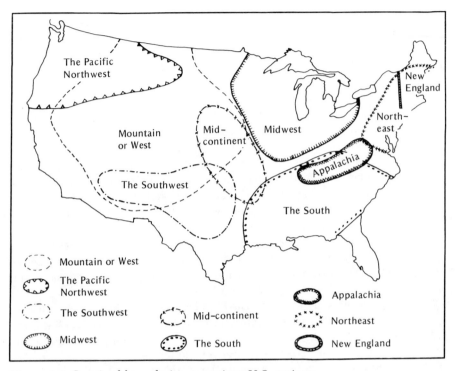

Figure 3.3. Cognized boundaries, 1: various U.S. regions.

We can understand this lookahead capacity if we see how cognitive mapping generates *analogue models* for organizing our spatial knowledge. Perhaps one of the simplest analogue models is reflected in the following newspaper column filler:

Shape of China Sea like peanut

The South China Sea is shaped vaguely like a huge peanut with two large bumps along its western edge. They are the Gulf of Thailand, bordered by the Malay Peninsula, Thailand, Cambodia and South Vietnam, and the Gulf of Tonkin, bordered by China and both North and South Vietnam.

(*The Centre Daily Times*, July 7, 1972, p. 12)

A more familiar and useful analogue model is the conventional spatial representation of a typical North American city as a doughnut, which reflects a fundamental separation into inner city and suburbs. This is literally and metaphorically a difference between black and white, encouraging two powerful stereotypes. The influence of such a mapping is perhaps responsible for the now-infamous comment that "once you've seen one slum, you've seen them all." With each equivalence category is associated a host of whatness attributes: race, income, environmental quality, crime rate, school system, life styles, and so on. But, more than just a descriptive frame of reference, the doughnut model generates predictions and expectations, and *guides behavior*. It prescribes *what* to do *where*, and how to act in certain situations:

> In order to get to [St. Patrick's Cathedral], it is necessary to pass through the southwestern fringes of Harlem, a section of New York that most white out-of-towners would just as soon avoid. Heaven only knows what preconceptions tourists bring with them about Harlem. It would be nice to report that [Company X] uses its good offices to point out that while Harlem may not exactly be paradise, it is still, after all, the most important black community in the United States, and that whatever its problems, there is a vibrancy and a tempo there that can be found in no other section of the United States. But such is not the case.
>
> "According to newspaper reports," the tour guide said ominously . . . , "this is one of the worst areas for dope in the city, so I'm going to have to warn you not to take any photographs. *Please* keep your cameras out of sight."
>
> The cameras quickly vanished under sweaters, into purses, under seats. Some of the passengers didn't even look out of the windows but stared straight ahead in silent apprehension, stagecoach passengers in the middle of hostile Apache country. But nothing happened. No grenades were thrown or bullets fired and the bus was not overturned.
>
> (*The New York Times*, September 24, 1972, Section 4, p. 24)

The parallel with the gray areas, which "distort the image of our central city's better self," is all too obvious.

The two-component doughnut model can be finely subdivided into a series of such equivalence classes as downtown (or the Central Business District), the ghetto or the slums, skid row, the wrong side of the tracks, Nob Hill, and various ethnic neighborhoods such as Little Italy or Chinatown. In this form the model exerts a powerful shaping influence on what we write (and read), how we think (and interpret), and how we decide (and behave). This shaping influence of cognitive mapping is so extensive and pervasive that it is not until we investigate further spatial stereotypes that we can uncover its manifestations.

Stereotypes are generally accepted categories that are part of the common currency of communication and understanding in a culture. They are useful tools in our search for an economical means of organizing spatial knowledge. They allow us to cope and simplify, but at a cost. We become, in Stephen Carr's phrase, victims of conventionality. We capture the idea of "nowheresville" in Podunk, or "Hicksville." Such ascribed status naturally leads to the reverse desire to "put somewhere on the map." In the past, places wanted to avoid being a one horse town; now:

Brighter image sought for Hartford

The Hartford Chamber of Commerce has proposed that the city spruce up in an attempt to become more than just an automotive "pit stop" between New York and Boston. "We need to say 'Hey, we aren't just a gas station between two cities' " ... Among the proposals are brightly painted curbs, designer-created police uniforms and fire hydrants decorated to look like toy soldiers, as well as revitalization of the city's night life.

(*The New York Times*, April 22, 1973, p. 54)

Chambers of Commerce are noted for their booster tactics, but perhaps none can surpass the recent claim by the Atlanta Chamber in its reference to "Atlanta, the world's *next* great city" (italics added).

There are innumerable identity stereotypes for places:

There is a widely held theory on both coasts of America that between the Hudson River and the Rockies there is a huge glacial scour called the Middle West, as flat as your hand and inhabited by men who spend most of their time at Rotary meetings, women who spend most of their time baking and children who play all day with Penrod and Sam.

(*The New York Times*, July 23, 1972, Section 10, p. 1)

North of the border (another identity stereotype!) we have Westmount in Montreal:

Even if Westmount is just "a myth, a state of mind," as one man familiar with it maintains, it is nevertheless known all across Canada and its name is still used, both favorably and unfavorably, as a shorthand to describe the world of the Anglo-Saxons who used to make all the decisions. In less prosperous English-speaking neighborhoods of Montreal, Westmount is a landmark of achievement, a goal to be attained. And in poorer French neighborhoods, it is still sometimes a symbol of what is bad about the people often called "les maudits Anglais"–"the damned English."

(*The New York Times*, February 10, 1973, p. 8)

The "English" English are no less charitable with their derogatory equivalence stereotype that the "wogs" begin at Calais (France). It is at this point that we can see the double meaning of the phrase, victims of conventionality.

PLACE AND SYMBOL

Our attempts at cognitive organization are often encapsulated in *symbols* that offer a quick, shorthand method of characterizing a place. To be successful, a symbol must be immediately recognized by people as standing for a particular place. The meaning and value of a symbol goes beyond the immediate recognition of the identity of a place. It acts as a trigger to help us recall the characteristics of that place, the specific set of whatness, whereness, and whenness information that gives it a unique identity. Given the symbol, we can fill in the necessary detail.

Most major cities possess a distinctive symbol. Table 3.2 lists international cities together with their verbal symbols. We can also translate symbols into memorable and graphic pictograms (see Figure 3.4). The most commonly employed graphic symbol for New York City is shown in Figure 3.5: This is an approximation to the New York skyline seen from the Battery. Yet Anselm Strauss (1961, p. 9) makes an interesting observation about this symbol:

> So well understood is this symbol that a movie can establish its locale by doing no more than flashing a picture of these skyscrapers on the screen for a moment and then directing the camera into the opening episodes of the film. This coded, shorthand expression is at once understood by the

Table 3.2   SYMBOLS AND NICKNAMES FOR CITIES AND COUNTRIES

Nicknames for Cities

Detroit: the motor city
Cleveland: the mistake by the lake
Chicago: the windy city
New York: the big apple, Fun City, Sin City
Boston: Beantown
Pittsburgh: the steel city
Milwaukee: the beer capital of the world
Philadelphia: the city of Brotherly Love
St. Louis: the gateway to the West

Graphic Symbols for Cities

Seattle: the Space Needle
St. Louis: the Gateway Arch
Washington (D.C.): the Capitol, the Monument
San Francisco: the Golden Gate Bridge
New York: the Empire State Building, the Statue of Liberty
Philadelphia: the Liberty Bell
Copenhagen: the Little Mermaid Statue
Paris: the Arc de Triomphe, the Eifel Tower
Athens: the Parthenon, the Acropolis
London: Big Ben, the Tower of London
Venice: canals, gondolas
Sydney: the Harbor Bridge

Graphic Symbols for Countries

Italy: the Coliseum, the Leaning Tower of Pisa
The Netherlands: tulips, barges, canals, clogs, windmills
India: the Taj Mahal
Egypt: the Sphinx
Switzerland: the Alps, skiing, chalets

audience. This familiar expression of the city's "essential" nature is as much accepted by native New Yorkers as it is by outsiders. Yet it is exceptionally difficult—and even unusual—for a New Yorker ever to see this part of the city. This sight is ordinarily available only for those who come into New York harbor from the sea. It is occasionally visible from an airplane, but if native New Yorkers wish to see this part of the city, they must take a ferry into the bay . . . in order to inspect the skyline.

Symbols change their meaning over time. Vincent Canby, the film critic for *The New York Times*, argues that New York has now become

Figure 3.4. "Word images" of places around the globe.

the metaphor for what looks like the last days of American civilization. This new metaphor is reflected in a change of symbol:

> The opening of Passer's "Law and Disorder" exemplifies the difference between the New York film of today and the New York film of the thirties or forties. Passer starts his film with a long, leisurely, horizontal pan shot along the New York skyline, then cuts to a series of uproariously outrageous crimes taking place within that city. The oldtime movie about New York might open with a stockshot of Manhattan seen from the air, followed by a slow pan down the side of a tall building (sometimes

Fortune doesn't list us.
But we're the largest totally international bank in New York.

BANK OF AMERICA, NEW YORK

Figure 3.5. Evoking an image of New York.

the Empire State Building), ending with a quick dissolve to a California studio and a familiar, much-used, city street set.

Passer eases directly into a real New York in his film, which is less about individual character than about coping nowhere else but in New York City.

The earlier films most literally dropped into their stories, which were set in mythical Big Town, U.S.A. The Big Town could as easily be Chicago or Detroit or Kansas City as New York. I doubt whether the oldtime studio filmmakers consciously denatured locations to obtain this kind of universality. It was more likely the automatic result of working in a studio. The lack of emphasis on geography produced a quite different kind of movie from what we're getting today. . . .

(Canby, 1974, p. 19)

Although these symbols are engaging, easy to manipulate, and essential to everyday communication, their validity is disputed. Is it really possible to encapsulate the essence of an incredibly complex, changing entity such as a city? An editorial in *The Los Angeles Times* asserts that it is not:

Writers from out of town have a hard time trying to get Los Angeles down on paper. Photographers have it even harder. Whatever it is that gives Los Angeles its character, it can't be verbalized or photographed.

New York has its skyline; San Francisco its bridge; Paris its Arc de Triomphe. The only two pictures I can think of offhand that instantly identify Los Angeles are the City Hall and Grauman's Chinese Theater, and they don't give us a lot of character.

(*The Los Angeles Times*, April 16, 1972)

Although cynics might argue that Los Angeles just doesn't *have* any distinctive character, there is an important point to this argument. Symbols are highly abstracted, frequently generalized. At best they can reflect but part of one's experience of any spatial environment. Perhaps an irate letter to the editor sums it up best:

Hell, to even attempt to characterize a whole metropolitan area with one big, hairy generalization should make any thinking reader think twice.

(*The New York Times Magazine*, Sunday, Nov. 18, 1973, p. 30)

Even Henry James, an archetypal thinking man, would have agreed with the letter writer. Writing shortly after his arrival in London, James claimed

. . . up to this time I have been crushed under a sense of the mere magnitude of London—its inconceivable immensity—in such a way as to paralyze my mind for any appreciation of details.

Later he recovered sufficiently to argue

> ... one has not the alternative of speaking of London as a whole, for the simple reason that there is no such thing as the whole of it. ... Rather it is a collection of many wholes, and of which of them is it most important to speak? Inevitably there must be a choice, and I know of none more scientific than to leave out what we may have to apologize for.
>
> (Quoted in White and White, 1962, p. 81 and p. 85)

Constructing representative symbols is at best a difficult task, one which deals with only part of the truth. Although James was not left speechless in the end, he blotted out "what we may have to apologize for," a technique resembling the "out of sight, out of mind" philosophy that we discussed earlier.

However, symbols need not reflect "real worlds." Many venerable symbols refer to such mythical places at El Dorado, Atlantis, Paradise, and the Garden of Eden. Such symbols have led to geographic equivalents of the search for the Holy Grail. People believed in their existence and sought them out: the Northwest Passage, the Jeffersonian river in the Great Plains, and the westerly passage to the spice islands of the Indies.

To this point, we have shown that cognitive structures, or maps, serve as a frame of reference, a basis for interpretation, a source of behavioral predictions, and as a means of shorthand expression and communication. Our emphasis on the *process* of cognitive mapping stresses its essential characteristics. Spatial information is processed (selected and organized) in such a way that it continues to be retrievable and manipulatable at any time in accordance with our plans for utilizing that information. In this sense, it answers our need for a spatial problem-solving ability that is fast, simple, reliable, and flexible. We need to be able to *rotate* environmental information in space, as in planning routes *to* and *from* a place. We must be able to *translate* it through time so that we can recall our childhood hometown or *imagine* what a place must have been like (London in the time of Sherlock Holmes or Boston in 1776). We want to *view* information from different perspectives: a bird's eye view of Washington, D.C., or Paris through the eyes of a tourist. One perspective all-too-frequently forgotten is that of the child! It is essential that we can *add* or *subtract* elements at will: We find a new restaurant, a street becomes one-way, an inner-city area is urban-renewed. Flexibility also requires that we can switch scales. We can have an understanding of the spatial layout of our house, which is in turn part of our neighborhood, which is part of our home town, and so on. Cognitive mapping is a process of both *analysis* and *synthesis*. We must be prepared to change the mode of expressing the information as the situation requires. If our attempt to give a stranger verbal directions does not work, we may have to draw a sketch map for him.

From this brief list of examples, the power and the pervasiveness of cognitive mapping is clear, and its second-nature disguise is stripped away. Yet there is one other role of cognitive mapping that is important. Having processed and reprocessed environmental information, having adopted an existing organization scheme or imposed one of our own, we are ready to go another step further: to associate *nonspatial* information with a well-known cognitive map. Several famous orators have described how they remembered the ordering of key points to be made in a long speech by associating the points with a well-known pattern of spatial locations. The association is usually achieved via a graphic visual image linking the point and the location. If, for example, the pattern of locations uses rooms in a house, then a mental walk around the house is sufficient to trigger, or cue, points in the appropriate sequence. This "method of loci" is termed a *spatial mnemonic,* an aid to memory.

The best-documented user of this mnemonic was a Russian, S., whose amazing talents were recorded and studied by Luria (1968). Luria (1968, pp. 31–33) describes S.'s strategy:

> When S. read through a long series of words, each word would elicit a graphic image. And since the series was fairly long, he had to find some way of distributing these images of his in a mental row or sequence. Most often (and this habit persisted throughout his life), he would "distribute" them along some roadway or street he visualized in his mind. Sometimes this was a street in his hometown, which would also include the yard attached to the house he had lived in as a child and which he recalled vividly. On the other hand, he might also select a street in Moscow. Frequently, he would take a mental walk along that street—Gorky Street in Moscow—beginning at Mayakovsky Square, and slowly make his way down, "distributing" his images at houses, gates, and store windows . . .
>
> This technique of converting a series of words into a series of graphic images explains why S. could so readily reproduce a series from start to finish or in reverse order; how he could rapidly name the word that preceded or followed one I'd select from the series. To do this, he would simply begin his walk, either from the beginning or from the end of the street, find the image of the object I had named, and "take a look at" whatever happened to be situated on either side of it.

S.'s capacity for memorization was so great that he could recall complex lists as much as 16 years after their original presentation. Yet even S. made mistakes, although these errors were errors of perception rather than errors of memory, as this explanation by S. indicates:

> I put the image of the *pencil* near a fence . . . the one down the street, you know. But what happened was that the image fused with that of the

fence and I walked right on past without noticing it. The same thing happened with the word egg. I had put it up against a white wall and it blended in with the background. How could I possibly spot a white egg against a white wall? Now take the word *blimp*. That's something gray, so it blended in with the gray of the pavement . . . *Banner*, of course, means the Red Banner. But, you know, the building which houses the Moscow City Soviet of Workers' Deputies is also red, and since I'd put the banner close to one of the walls of the building I just walked on without seeing it . . . Then there's the word *putamen*. I don't know what this means, but it's such a dark word that I couldn't see it . . . and, besides, the street lamp was quite a distance away . . .

(Luria, 1968, p. 36)

Our capacities as mnemonists may not be as developed as those of S., who could remember useless test information over many years. But we do share essentially identical cognitive mapping abilities and they do play a crucial role in our *everyday* lives. This idea is at the heart of this book, and our argument is a step-by-step attempt to isolate the characteristics of cognitive mapping. Thus far, we have equated cognitive mapping with spatial problem solving, and have explained the meaning of both "cognitive" and "mapping." The next chapter will show how the cognitive mapping process deals with specific instances of whatness, whereness, and whenness information.

Chapter 4

THE WORLD
IN THE HEAD

INTRODUCTION

In exploring the world in the head, we identified a key process, cognitive mapping, and looked at why the process exists and how it works. Now we turn to the outcome of the process and focus on the world as people believe it to be. We begin the discussion with two obvious questions. How *accurate* are cognitive maps? How *similar* are cognitive maps? Accuracy involves comparing maps with the "real world" while similarity involves comparing maps of the same environment produced by different people. The next sections expand on the ideas of the content (or vocabulary) and organization (or grammar) of cognitive representations. First, we consider the contents as identity and equivalence categories that cope with the whatness and whenness attributes of our spatial environment. Second, we discuss organization or grammar as a way of generating frames of reference, the most important of which are those incorporating whereness information.

THE ACCURACY AND SIMILARITY OF COGNITIVE MAPS

ARE COGNITIVE MAPS ACCURATE?

This is the most obvious and most frequently asked question. It is also one of the most difficult to answer. The problem is, what do we mean by accuracy? If by accuracy we mean a total *identity* between the attributes and arrangements of the spatial environment and the attributes and arrangements of cognitive representations, then the question is absurd. Such identity is impossible. One function of cognitive mapping is to cope with the staggering *volume* of spatial information. We have neither the processing nor the storage capacity to allow perfect identity between representations and the spatial environment. Cognitive mapping is of necessity selective. There is no one-to-one correspondence between the spatial environment and its cognitive representation. Indeed, if one were capable of entering into the head of a person, one would discover a cognitive representation the likes of which are only found in the realm of science fiction. Shapes and sizes are distorted; spatial relationships are altered; in some areas, detail is impoverished while in others it is augmented. C. S. Lewis (1957) describes Shoddy Land, a fantasy based on entering the world in a person's head while Edwin Abbott's (1963) Flatland attempts to convey a sense of what a two-dimensional world would be like in the experience of its inhabitants. Although both of these fantasy worlds are engaging and credible, they are *not* accurate.

If by accuracy we are asking whether there is a *correspondence* between the results of this selective process and the "real world" on which it was operating, the question poses two insuperable difficulties. Just what is the real world against which we compare a cognitive map? Ignoring the fundamentally philosophical debates over the meaning of the concept of a real world, we face a pragmatic problem of finding a suitable replica of the real world. Suppose, for example, we are interested in college student's cognitive representations of the U.S.A. What could we use as an expression of the "real life" U.S.A.? a cartographic map? a satellite photograph? the 1970 Census Bureau results? the United Airlines map (Figure 1.12)? The list of possible replicas is almost infinite. The degree of correspondence would depend on which replica was selected. However, assume that we have overcome this first difficulty by requesting from our students an external representation (sketch map) showing the location of cities, rivers, and mountains, and we will compare these sketch maps with a standard cartographic map of the same features.

The second difficulty in measuring accuracy as correspondence comes from the translation problem, or the student's attempts to communicate internal cognitive representations to us in a concrete, external form from which we can take measurements. We have asked the students to produce external representations as sketch maps. Can we judge similarity by comparing data taken from the sketch maps with similar data from the cartographic map? If this is an attempt to resolve the accuracy question, the answer is no. People vary widely in simple graphic abilities. Age affects basic manual skills involving eye-hand coordination. Both the young and the very old differ from our college students. Even discounting this age factor, we have the problem of differential training in both the rationale for and manual reproduction of sketch maps. Some people, notably artists, architects, and geographers, are trained in technical graphic skills. One would expect that the mechanical production and accuracy of the sketch maps would reflect this training.

Perhaps the most telling evidence with respect to the accuracy of sketch maps comes if we consider geography students. Given their training, one would expect them to produce the *most* accurate sketch maps. However, in one case study a *blind* graduate student drew a more accurate outline map of the U.S.A. than several *sighted* geography graduate students! This is no reflection on the sighted student's competence; rather, it emphasizes the constraints of the map-sketching task. The blind student acquired and learned (encoded) the cognitive representation through muscle feedback from touching a Braille outline map of the U.S.A. The sketching (decoding) employs a similar pattern of motor behavior, involving touch and muscle feedback. The sighted students acquired a representation using an entirely different mode, visual inspection, and verbal coding, and lacked the direct *interactive* experience of the blind student. Therefore, should we conclude that the sighted student's cognitive representations are less accurate because of their "handicap"? The answer is obvious. We cannot treat accuracy as the correspondence of representations to the real world because, to adapt Marshall McLuhan's phrase, the medium (or signature) is part of the message. The medium of translating from an internal or cognitive to an external or physical representation has a major effect on the *form* of the representation. People vary in their ability to make this translation. Hence, we cannot phrase our accuracy question in terms of the correspondence between two *external* representations, in this case a sketch map and a cartographic map.

The accuracy question is only meaningful if we ask, Does a person possess the spatial information and problem-solving strategies necessary to live successfully in a particular spatial environment? Are the cognitive maps that he generates useful for everyday spatial behavior (i.e., are they functional)? Can he use the cognitive map as a basis for spatial thinking? Does it help him to communicate his understanding to other people? Does it help him to interpret the world? Therefore, neither precision nor necessarily completeness of representation is important, but utility is. The world in the head is constructed as it is for a simple reason. We represent the environment as we do because it pays us to do so in terms of spatial thinking and behavior. Our objective is not accuracy but making the best use of our limited capacities for storing and handling information. The young school girl, blind from birth, who drew a near-perfect sketch map of her house, but omitted the windows, was not being inaccurate (Shemyakin, 1962). The friend who maps a route to his house, which ignores bends in the road and even distorts real distance, is not inaccurate. We cannot conclude that the entire population in Medieval times was inaccurate for believing that the earth was flat *and* the center of the universe. Their geocentric beliefs were supported by the theological and political system, which rejected Copernicus' heliocentric views as heretical (i.e., inaccurate).

As a consequence of these arguments, we can see that the obvious question concerning the accuracy of cognitive maps is misleading. It is only when accuracy is taken to mean useful that we can answer the question. This raises major problems for research into cognitive mapping since it suggests that the only criterion against which we can contrast a cognitive map is spatial behavior or spatial problem solving. Unfortunately, measures of behavior and problem solving are less readily available than are external representations such as photographs, cartographic maps, and so on. We can conclude, however, that success in dealing with everyday spatial problems is sufficient testimony to the accuracy of cognitive maps.

ARE COGNITIVE MAPS SIMILAR?

Just as the question of accuracy was obvious and yet difficult to answer, so too are there problems in resolving the question of the similarity of cognitive maps. However, the problem does not lie in the meaning of the question. We want to know if two people would produce similar cognitive maps of the same spatial environment. The difficulty lies in the many apparently contradictory answers that we can give.

We know, for example, that if the two people differ in age, their representations will differ as a result of manual skills (in map drawing) or vocabulary and verbal competence (in descriptions). If one were an adult and the other a child, then the differing levels of intellectual development would result in dissimilar maps (see Chapter 6). It is also true that experience with the environment would dramatically affect both the arrangement and the contents of the representation. Paris through the eyes of a tourist and Paris through the eyes of a life-time resident are two different places. Styles of training and thinking affect representations, even if both people are the same age and have the same experience of the environment. Gittins (1969) took scientists and writers on a walking tour of an unfamiliar city and asked them to describe and draw the city. The two groups adopted very different processes of cognitively structuring the city. These resulted in essentially different types of representation. The writers began with an intuitive structure that was gradually organized into a "comprehensive integrated conception." This conception combined insights into a concrete, sensuous impression. In contrast, the scientists neither began with an intuitive structure nor was organization present until midway through the tour. At this point they generated a clear, articulate, abstract, formula-like structure, which applied to cities in general and which was only slightly modified to incorporate experiences from the second part of the tour.

Even if we control for the effects of age, experience, skill, and training, the question of the similarity of cognitive maps cannot be answered definitively. The nearest that we can come to such a goal is as follows: Parts of our cognitive maps are common to all or most members of a large group of people, parts are common to a subgroup of people, while still other parts are unique to each person. These variations in similarity result from three interlocking variables: (1) the scale of the spatial environment, (2) the source of the information about that environment, and (3) the location of the person doing the representing.

Those cognitive maps, which are similar for most members of a large group, involve representations of large-scale environments such as nation states or continents. We share stereotyped representations of other nations, stereotypes that encapsulate our beliefs about the types of people and landscapes that are found in a particular country. We agree that "Russia is a place where . . ." The ideas following the "where" statement are a series of whatness and whereness attributes that together give Russia its characteristic identity. These shared cognitive maps are a pot pourri of fact and fiction, truth and distortion, broadminded views and prejudice. They form part of the common currency of expression in a culture and lie at the heart of much popular written and verbal communication. As one reflection of the anthropologist's idea of ethnocentricism, they portray the world as seen through the eyes of one national group. If we express the cognitive map of the world using a graphic signature, the impact of a stereotyped perspective is readily apparent. College students from the United States, Argentina, Fiji, India, and New Zealand were asked to sketch a map of the world, including as much detail as possible in ten minutes. For each national group, their own country was located in the center of the map and was drawn disproportionately large. Other countries were more likely to be included if they were close and/or important. Wittaker and Wittaker (1972) refer to this viewpoint as geocentrism (see also Figures 1.2 and 1.3).

Two factors ensure that most people share these geocentric stereotypes. First, these cognitive maps are rarely based on direct, firsthand experience. Instead, they result from carefully filtered, predigested information gained in our schools and colleges, in the press and from television. Second, they are self-perpetuating systems, almost self-fulfilling prophecies that reinforce themselves. Movies portray other countries and nationalities by means of prevailing national stereotypes; newspapers and advertisements draw upon these stock, one-dimensional images and phrases for their immediate expressive impact. Both the users and the used become the unwilling victims of conventionality. This is not to argue that such similarity is necessarily bad in all contexts nor that uniformity of viewpoint is absolute. Nevertheless, in a sample of cognitive maps of other countries we are more impressed by similarities than by differences.

However, if we consider cognitive maps of environments at a smaller scale, the general consensus breaks down. Whether we focus on large regions, such as the North or South in the U.S.A., states such as Pennsylvania or Alabama (see also Figures 1.10 and 1.15), or even urban neighborhoods, there are distinct subgroup viewpoints. Residence in an area, shared local interests and communications media, and shared activity patterns result in regional loyalty, a parochialism and pride of place, which generates a shared viewpoint different from that of people living in another area:

> Connie was accustomed to Kensington or the Scotch hills or the Sussex downs: that was her England. With the stoicism of the young she took in the utter, soulless ugliness of the coal-and-iron Midlands at a glance, and left it at what it was: unbelievable and not to be thought about.
>
> (Lawrence, 1959, p. 13)

The same basic processes are operating as in the development of national stereotypes, but the result is a mosaic of different viewpoints. The key difference is that for one group of people their experience of the environment is direct and highly personal. We are able to take a step backwards and recognize the effect of familiarity. As part of the ongoing debate over the relative safety of the East Side and the West Side in New York City, *The New York Times* (November 15, 1974, p. 23) carried a story with the following conclusion:

> Ultimately, familiarity may be as much of a criteria for the judgement of safety as crime rates.
>
> As Edith Fisher said, "I feel safer on the East Side because I live on it, but I would feel the same way about the West Side if I lived there. It's the unknown that's the most fearful."

A person subscribes to many regional viewpoints: He or she can have the views of a northerner, a Pennsylvanian, a Philadelphian, and so on. Each viewpoint is shared by a decreasing number of people, and is disputed by an increasing number. The answer to the question of the similarity of cognitive maps thus depends upon the size of the area: the smaller the area, the fewer who would produce similar maps.

Although we can expect parts of cognitive maps to be similar, we must not forget that representations are constructed to reflect the personal nature of experience and the meaning attributed to this experience. The "fine" structure of organization and the detailed contents of maps are expressions of individuality, which are superimposed on the common skeleton provided by similar cognitive capabilities and shared activity patterns. To expect too much similarity is to misunderstand the nature of the cognitive mapping process. The environment and our behavior within it offer but the raw material from which we assemble our representations. Cognitive mapping does not duplicate but selects, constructs, and organizes. Florence Ladd (1970) showed this in a study of Black youths in Roxbury (Boston). They were asked to draw a map of their neighborhood; the results indicate just how dissimilar representations can be. Anthony (age 12) and his brother Jerome (age 15) had lived on Normandy Street for almost four years. Their maps are shown in Figures 4.1 and 4.2. Their residences are marked in Figure 4.1 by an "X" and the phrase, "my house," and in Figure 4.2 by an "X." Only the Normandy signpost tells us that Anthony and Jerome are representing the same physical area; all other characteristics of the maps are different. Such dramatic differences are *not* just an artifact of this study. Terence Lee (1964, p. 16) asked people in Cambridge (England) to represent their neighborhood by drawing a line around it on a large scale map:

> These neighborhood maps showed a good deal of variation, and in order to confirm a growing conviction that although neighborhoods are salient, they are also highly individualistic, I sampled a terrace row of corporation houses, eight of them within about 100 yards. When their outlines

Figure 4.1. A map of Normandy Street drawn by Anthony, a schoolchild in Roxbury, Massachusetts.

Figure 4.2. Jerome's map: The same area is represented as in Figure 4.1, but the cartographer is different.

were superimposed they showed almost no coincidence. This was in spite of the fact that I had chosen an area labelled as a "neighborhood" on most people's lips and on the front of buses, and which in fact comprised an old village that had become assimilated into the edge of the city.

There is no *one* answer to the question: Are cognitive maps similar? They are similar enough to permit us to share and communicate our understanding of the spatial environment. They are personal enough to accommodate unique experiences. They are both similar and dissimilar. Above all, they are the outcome of a process that can cope with both social requirements and individual needs.

WHATNESS AND WHENNESS

What? When? Where? These are a trio of interlocking questions that people must answer in order to solve everyday spatial problems. They are also the three dimensions along which we can consider the nature of the world in the head since cognitive maps are constructed to answer what, when, and where questions. The contents of cognitive maps are representations of whatness and whenness information, ways of coping with and expressing the significant attributes of things and places in the spatial environment. In this section, we will focus on the repertoire of categories used for handling whatness and whenness, a repertoire that consists of a mixed vocabulary of equivalence and identity categories.

WHATNESS CATEGORIES

We can treat the spatial environment in one of two ways: as consisting of innumerable *particular* (and hence unique) places or as consisting of a limited number of *general types* of places and objects. These choices are not mutually exclusive nor are they forced on us by the nature of the world around us. Cognitive maps are a blend of knowledge of the particular and the general.

The particular is remembered through an identity category that consolidates the salient features of our direct and indirect experience of a place. Although my identity category for San Francisco is based solely on indirect experience, it encompasses a rich, though somewhat bizarre, assortment of ideas. Included are rough conceptions of its geographical location and layout; such characteristic symbols as the Golden Gate Bridge and the trolley cars on Telegraph Hill; miscellaneous oddments such as the BART mass transit system and the Giants baseball team; a garbled remembrance of the song, "I Left My Heart in San Francisco"; and a vague recollection of photographs of the city skyline. Taken together, these ideas encapsulate my representation of the particular place. Given these ideas, I can generate a series of representations of San Francisco using different cognitive signatures. In addition to a written description, I can conjure up a sequence of cartographic-like maps, a bird's-eye view of the city skyline, a montage of familiar graphic symbols, and a sound portrait of music, cable car bells, and sea gulls. These cognitive representations are alternative reflections of the particular and distinctive character that I ascribe to and identify with San Francisco.

In contrast, the general is treated as an equivalence category. Attention is focussed on the limited set of shared characteristics that we have abstracted and generalized from repeated experiences with different instances of a type of place or object. We emphasize characteristics that typify, that allow us to group together places, and that allow us to say that this is an example of . . . Thus, we think in terms of the *typical* characteristics of a country village: It is usually a small and compact place; with a few stores; a couple of taverns; a peaceful, bucolic atmosphere reminiscent of the "good old days"; and full of people with a tolerant but conservative attitude to life. My somewhat stereotyped and unrealistic representation is a composite, which synthesizes those salient characteristics that I have repeatedly encountered in real and fictional villages. No matter which signature that I use to express these ideas, the emphasis is on the shared characteristics that I normally expect to find in a village.

To speak of whatness demands a sense of place, the ability to relate to and identify with a particular place. Such identifications with places range from the shallow to the profound. On the one hand, some places are literally "known by name only," as jokes (Podunk, Peoria, or Timbuctoo) or as legends and myths (Atlantis, the Bermuda Triangle, or the Garden of Eden). They are shadowy, one-dimensional places, which have a meagre substance to them and which mean very little to us personally. Home represents the other extreme. Thomas Wolfe and Snoopy, an odd couple, both express the depths of emotional feeling that are attached to the place called home (see Chapter 1 and Figure 1.1). But what makes a place a place? Where is a place? Unfortunately, the world is not neatly divided into a series of places that can be clearly and immediately distinguished from all other places. There is no single, objective characteristic called "placeness." Most of the important dimensions through which we construe the world do not display sharp breaks or discontinuities. We live in a world of grays and gradations. Where, for example, do suburbs begin and the inner city end; suburbs end and the countryside begin? Where does a neighborhood end? When cities sprawl together, as in Southern California or around London, where does one end and the next begin?

Place is the consequence of an identity category that a group of people agree upon and make use of in their everyday life. Sometimes the agreement is reached easily; name and place and representation are indelibly fused together in a striking expression. Winston Churchill's memorable phrase, the Iron Curtain, has graphically imprinted the East-West demarcation in our minds, a demarcation that has been given additional visual reality by the Berlin Wall. Everyone in a town knows where the wrong side of the tracks are and shares the common knowledge of the good and bad places to live. Pablo Neruda (1974, pp. 33–35), the Chilean Nobel Prize winner, writes that "I come from a dark region, from a land separated from all others by the steep contours of its geography." But other agreements are more contentious. The physical environment is less generous in offering the abrupt separations that demarcate places. This uncertainty of place is reflected in Willa Cather's (1913, p. 19) description of the location of homesteads on the Nebraska plains:

> The Bergson homestead was easier to find than many another, because it overlooked Norway Creek, a shallow, muddy stream that sometimes flowed, and sometimes stood still, at the bottom of a winding ravine with steep, shelving sides overgrown with brush and cottonwoods and dwarf ash. This creek gave a sort of identity to the farms that bordered upon it. Of all the bewildering things about a new country, the absence of human landmarks is one of the most depressing and disheartening.

The Boundary Waters Canoe Area in Minnesota is equally lacking in the imprints of human landmarks, and Robert Lucas (1963) found several interpretations of the areal extent of the place. The two major types of visitor had different views of the extent of the wilderness area, views that did not coincide with those of the wilderness administrators. Paddle canoeists, seeking a place untouched by human hand, adopted the most restricted areal definition, while motorboatists, more tolerant of such human intrusions as logging, roads, and even people, espoused a more extensive definition of the place. Whatness and identity are given (or attributed) to a place; they are created, not found. Identity is in the eye and mind of the beholder.

The key to an identity category is *uniqueness*: the differentiation of a place from all other places such that there is nowhere else on earth like it. Uniqueness means distinctiveness, and, hopefully, with distinctiveness the quality of being well known and instantly recognizable. As an advertisement announcing the opening of a new Macy's department store on Staten Island argued:

> If Staten Island is the borough you've never been to, you're missing a lot. Because Staten Island is special. Staten Island is unique. It's like no other part of the city.

The advertisement provided a list of seventeen ". . . (f)ascinating things that make Staten Island special . . . these and more" (*The New*

York Times, October 4, 1972, p. 7). In a parallel effort to convey identity (and hence uniqueness), the Virginia State Travel Service constructed a collage of place names and graphic symbols (see Figure 4.3).

As these two examples suggest, the deliberate characterization of a place to convey identity and uniqueness is a major pursuit of the advertising industry. The motives behind such efforts are clear:

> The selling of a city as a major tourist attraction is a subtle, long-range operation, sometimes done at such a distance from the city and in such a low key that potential travelers do not realize they are being sold or where the sales pitch originated. New York City is one of the world's major tourist attractions but it has suffered from a tarnished image in domestic and international media [see Figure 1.8] and from an especially bad pounding by television comics and late-night talk shows about street crime. So in recent years its tourism leaders have been trying to sell the city back to the American tourist as an exciting, entertaining and safe place to visit.

*   *   *

> Why should a metropolis like New York want to sell itself? Well, tourism continues to rank as the city's second largest industry, second only to the fashion and garment industry.
>
> (*The New York Times*, October 14, 1973, Section 10, p. 33)

Unfortunately, New York's efforts to sell itself as a tourist attraction have not been blessed with a single-mindedness of will or purpose. April of 1975 saw the appointment of the "Committee in the Public Interest," a volunteer group charged by the mayor with "extolling the assets of the city and creating and stimulating the kind of confidence in New York City that it deserves." Its heroic task was not made easier by the firemen's and policemen's unions who, during the city's fiscal crisis in June of 1975, printed a pamphlet, "Welcome to Fear City." In this "Survival Guide for Visitors to the City of New York," tourists were advised to stay indoors after 6 P.M., to avoid public transportation, and to stay away from the city until things change. Despite these contradictions in the selling of New York, we can learn something from advertisements that attempt to create and convey identity. Not only can we emphasize the role of advertising in molding cognitive maps, we can also get some insights into the cognitive processes that people use for generating identity categories.

The most basic (and hackneyed) strategy for creating identity involves associating a series of desirable attributes with a place (see Figure 4.4). The appeal in this advertisement for South Carolina rests on the juxtaposition of the stereotyped images representing two widely endorsed but apparently conflicting value systems: that of unspoiled natural beauty with that of active economic development. The reconciliation and resolution lies in achieving the best of both worlds in one place: South Carolina. Sometimes the appeal is less subtle, as in the highway sign outside Galesville, a small town in Wisconsin:

WELCOME TO GALESVILLE

The Garden of Eden
Industry Invited

The result is an amusing, mixed metaphor: Factories have replaced apples and the innocent are tempting fate.

A second strategy for creating a distinctive identity for a place ac-

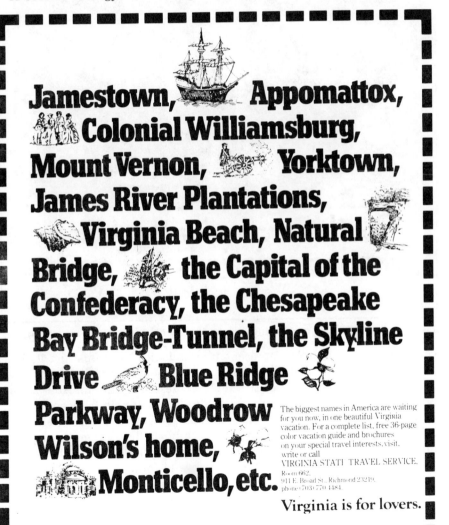

Figure 4.3. The cognitive geography of love: exploring romantic Colonial America.

South Carolina

South Carolina is a throbbing, pulsating, major industrial market.
We just don't look it.

Figure 4.4. Juxtaposing conflicting images: the appeal of (and by) South Carolina.

cepts the current popular representation and tries to reconstruct it. The popular conception of Indiana is that it is somewhere between New York and California, a belief strikingly expressed by the unusual juxtaposition of the cartographic maps of the three states in a recent advertisement. Middle America is dismissed as something that separates the East Coast from the West Coast, something to be driven through or flown across, a place that is, figuratively, *overlooked*. Yet, as the text of the advertisement points out, there *is more to* Indiana than we appreciate. The motif of the best of both worlds reappears; being somewhere *between* New York and California is converted into an unrealized advantage and not just an unfortunate expression of geographical isolation.

The saga of Metropolis (Illinois) shows how identity (and favorable publicity) can be generated by taking advantage of a fortunate accident, the town's name! The association between Superman, the comic book hero, and the fictional city of Metropolis is the key:

> So why not, reasoned the real Metropolis's fathers, capitalize on the town's name and give out a Superman of Metropolis Award. It would create good will and perhaps put the nation's only real Metropolis on the map.

*   *   *

> "Before Superman came, . . . Metropolis was a dying town. Now almost overnight there's a spark, a contagious enthusiasm and a boom like I've never seen in all my years."

*   *   *

> "This project is unique," said Mr. Smith, "there has never been one like it built around someone from another world. It's exciting and a lot of fun. But it's no joke for us. Not when you're dealing with the economic life of a community."
>
> (The New York Times, Aug. 8, 1972, p. 29)

A town in New Mexico has the unforgettable name of Truth or Consequences, although it was formerly known by the commonplace name, Hot Springs. However, as a result of one of those quirks of popular culture, it received so many plugs on the radio show, "Truth or Consequences," that it became known as "that town on the radio," and, capitalizing on this image, changed its name. Even if renaming is not possible, a town can resort to another sign of distinction: It can bask in the reflected glory of the name of a famous son. "The birthplace of" scale ranges from Presidents to popular musicians. Yet, as John Steinbeck (1962) wryly observes in Travels with Charley, these attention-getting signs are most frequently used by places with the shortest histories and the least world-shaking events.

Identity can even be achieved by making a virtue out of obscurity! A recent advertisement by the Toledo Edison Company began:

Toledo.

> The best kept secret in the midwest. Until now that is . . . but no-one can keep the lid on one of the nation's most dynamic and valuable entities . . . and that is exactly what Toledo is.
>
> (The New York Times, June 19, 1973, p. 54)

Like Indiana, Toledo is now a place to be reckoned with, a place that should appear on our cognitive maps. You can't keep a good place hidden forever.

A final advertising strategy for establishing the identity of a place uses the "but" technique. Place X is like place Y but ... We use a well-known place as a starting point of reference and then work on the "similar but different" principle:

Poconos.

The near country. It looks like Switzerland but look what the Swiss are missing. It's got the Pennsylvania Dutch, Indian lakes and waterfalls. Summer stock, auto races and trout-stocked streams. Grand golf and great bikini scenery. Wild game farms and wilder nightlife. It's every sport under the summer sun. And some that aren't. (Even ice skating!) It's mountains of fun. Next to home but no place like it.

(*The New York Times*, July 22, 1973, Section 10, p. 8)

All of these advertising strategies for establishing identity are mirrored in the *cognitive* mapping of whatness information. The motivating force for the collection and storage of whatness information is the need to evaluate, compare, and choose between places. The world in the head is differentiated along dimensions of desirability: good and bad places to live, to walk, to shop, to visit, and so on. The result is analogous to the renowned Michelin guides, the red ones for restaurants and hotels, and the green ones for tourist places. The latter are graded by stars with three stars signifying that a place is worth a journey, two stars worth a detour, while a lone star is just interesting but not worth going out of your way for. Our cognitive maps may lack the organization and encyclopaedic character of the Michelin guides, but they do enable us to cope with the world around us. The dual questions of what a place is good for, or conversely, what places are good for a particular activity, are central to everyday spatial problems. It is essential that we have the information at our mental fingertips to solve these problems promptly and accurately. Identity categories are the major source of this information. We associate a clear representation of the characteristics of a place with a convenient label (the place name) or graphic symbol. Representations are continually updated with additional information. Places can be put on cognitive maps; familiar places are reevaluated. In describing and discussing a place, we may use the "but" technique to emphasize distinctiveness. If a friend had visited Rome, we might say that Athens is like Rome but ... We have established a reference point from which to develop an image of Athens' identity.

However, another person may totally disagree with our characterization of Athens. Disagreement, while not necessarily healthy, is inevitable; there is no universally accepted way of describing a place. Cognitive maps are not identical because identity is in the eye of the beholder and we should not expect to see eye to eye about places, especially those that are metaphorically larger than life. Texas springs to mind as an example and John Steinbeck (1962) suggests:

> By its nature and size Texas invites generalities, and the generalities usually end up as paradox—the "little ol' country boy" at a symphony, the booted and blue-jeaned ranchman in Neiman-Marcus, buying Chinese jades. (p. 205)
>
> The word Texas becomes a symbol to everyone in the world. There's no question that this Texas-of-the-mind fable is often synthetic, sometimes untruthful, and frequently romantic, but that in no way diminishes its strength as a symbol. (p. 206)

Nowhere are the paradoxes of symbols more revealing than in the answers to the question, What is New Jersey? Its car license plates proclaim it to be the Garden State, yet a brief drive along the northern part of the New Jersey Turnpike disabuses one of that belief. Gardens and the petrochemical industry are incompatible. The inherent contradictions in the images of New Jersey are counterpointed in the following advertisement by Midatlantic Banks Inc.:

> **The great open spaces of New Jersey**
>
> What is New Jersey? Part of the megalopolis that stretches from Boston to Washington? Right. One of the most populous states in the U.S.A.? Right. And superhighways? Deep-water docks? Busy airports? More railroad tracks per square mile than any other state in the nation? Right. Right. Right. Right.
>
> But don't get the idea that New Jersey is wall-to-wall people. Three-quarters of the state is still farmland and forests. And it isn't mountainous, inaccessible land. The highest point in the state doesn't even reach 2,000' and most of it rolls gently along at under 300'.
>
> (*The New York Times*, April 16, 1973, Section 3, p. 2)

In contrast, consider this less euphoric viewpoint:

> **Guess what state's initials are N.J.?**
>
> New Jersey does not have earthquakes. Its weather is mainly left over from Ontario and the Gulf of Mexico. It is a state custom to reelect the Governor to a second term because the people are only getting used to his name by then. It is never clear which party he belongs to. Most of the residents are from Illinois, Maryland and Buffalo.

*   *   *

New Jersey has never been considered—by the rest of the nation—a valid place to come from. When asked where they are from, out-of-state New Jerseyans have to give the relative distance of their home from New York and Philadelphia. You make people uncomfortable when you tell them you're from New Jersey. They are inclined to respond with "Oh!" or "Why?" Unlike the New England states, the South, etc., New Jersey has no indigenous cultural warts for an outsider to hang his cliché on. The New Jerseyan defies general analysis.

(The New York Times, Feb. 21, 1973, p. 39)

Unfortunately, we have reached the position where every single fact is true and yet the total picture that they generate is false and distorted. By judicious and selective reshuffling, we can construct a diametrically opposed representation of the same place. It is perhaps even more unfortunate that many places are characterized by identity categories, which are powerful stereotypes, firmly entrenched in popular wisdom. They spring to mind when a place is mentioned; they *are* the place. Where do stereotypes come from? How are they kept alive?

The Appalachian mountaineer is a poverty-stricken, uneducated, backward hillbilly who tries to scratch a living from a non-productive mine or farm. Who or what is to blame for one-dimensional views of Appalachia? Is it the comic strips, the movies, television or a lack of attention to the region on the part of our schools? How does one measure the impact of Snuffy Smith or the sexually perverse mountaineers portrayed in the movie *Deliverance*, not to mention Nashville's hillbilly *Hee-Haw*?

(Symanski, Harman, and Swift, 1973, p. 21)

Without answers to these questions, it is difficult to modify stereotypes so that they become representative, true in both detail and totality.

Richard Jackson (1972) has traced the genealogy of an important stereotype, which was neither true in detail nor totality. In 1847, Brigham Young was leading the Mormons in search of their promised land. He came to believe that the region north of the Salt Lake Valley was too cold for agriculture whereas the region to the south was suited to agriculture. These beliefs guided Mormon settlement in a southerly direction. Such a spatial pattern runs counter to environmental logic. The south was arid and barren. Settlers, on being told to go there, claimed, "Why it is like sending me out of the world." (This cry had a twentieth-century reverse in South Vietnam where signs at airports instructed U.S. servicemen on procedures for *returning* to the world.) Young's beliefs did not come from direct, personal experience but from two, indirect sources: a meeting with a traveller, and the reading of a propaganda volume—an emigrant guide book—which extolled the virtues of California over Oregon and Utah. Oregon and Utah were delib-

erately misrepresented in this guide book. Once Young's mistaken belief was established, it was tenaciously perpetuated in Mormon teaching
and preaching. Jackson (1972, p. 38) argues:

> ... the existence of the agricultural villages in marginal locations in
> southern Utah is largely the result of Young's misconception of the envi-
> ronment north of the Salt Lake Valley. In order to encourage settlement of
> these marginal areas, the leaders either consciously or unconsciously
> transformed the history of the Mormon experience with the environment.
> These transformations were effective in motivating the people to go
> south, but they were also accepted as fact by historians and other writers
> and continue to dominate histories of the west and the Mormons even to-
> day.

It is rare that we can document the history of a stereotyped identity.
Although much of our spatial information is encapsulated in a similar
form, we know surprisingly little about the origins, maintenance, use,
or even number of identity categories. Unfortunately, there are no cognitive gazetteers for reference. To counterbalance this rather sombre
discussion of identity and stereotypes, perhaps the last comment
should go to John Steinbeck (1962, p. 122):

> From my earliest memory, if it was a cold day, Fargo was the coldest
> place on the continent. If heat was the subject, then at that time the pa-
> pers listed Fargo as hotter than any place else, or wetter or drier, or
> deeper in snow. ... I must admit that when I passed through Moorhead,
> Minnesota, and rattled across the Red River into Fargo on the other side,
> it was a golden autumn day. ... It's bad to have one's myth shaken up
> like that ... [Later] I found with joy that the fact of Fargo had in no way
> disturbed my mind's picture of it. I could still think of Fargo as I always
> had — blizzard-riven, heat-blasted, dust-raddled. I am happy to report that
> in the war between reality and romance, reality is not the stronger.

In contrast to identity categories that represent specific places,
equivalence categories are built around the similarities between places
or objects commonly found in the spatial environment. The aim is to
classify places and objects, grouping them together on the basis of
shared characteristics: X is like Y and Z, and no buts! Of course, we
know that this is not true. There are always differences if we choose to
look for them. But this choice is a luxury that we cannot afford to make.
If we were to treat every place as unique, then the goal of using the past,
in the present, to solve the future would be an impossible one. In some
situations, we must ignore the differences in favor of the similarities.
    An equivalence category employs a set of key, defining character-
istics that allow us to recognize that this is an example of an ... Thus

skyscrapers are tall, slender office buildings, which huddle in the downtown of a large city, and row houses are strings of two-story, brick houses, which typically carpet large areas of the inner city. In a sense, we construct a cognitive representation of a typical member, which acts as a model or a template for an equivalence category. In *Main Street*, Sinclair Lewis (1920, n.p.) captures the essence of a small town, an essence that symbolizes America:

> This is America—a town of a few thousand, in a region of wheat and corn and dairies and little groves.
>
> The town is, in our tale, called "Gopher Prairie, Minnesota." But its Main Street is the continuation of Main Streets everywhere. The story would be the same in Ohio or Montana, in Kansas or Kentucky or Illinois, and not very differently would it be told Up York State or in the Carolina hills.

To Will Kennicott, Gopher Prairie is "a darn pretty town," distinctive, exceptional. To his wife Carol, "Only to the eyes of a Kennicott was it exceptional." Carol saw it as the end of the world, as typifying *all* small towns. Where her husband identified distinctiveness, she saw only universal similarity:

> Nine-tenths of the American towns are so alike that it is completest boredom to wander from one to another. Always, west of Pittsburg, and often, east of it, there is the same lumber yard, the same railroad station, the same Ford garage, the same creamery, the same box-like houses and two-story shops. The new, more conscious houses are alike in their very attempts at diversity: the same bungalows, the same square houses of stucco or tapestry brick. The shops show the same standardized, nationally advertised wares; the newspapers of sections three thousand miles apart have the same "syndicated features"; the boy in Arkansas displays just such a flamboyant ready-made suit as is found on just such a boy in Delaware, both of them iterate the same slang phrases from the same sporting-pages, and if one of them is in college and the other is a barber, no one may surmise which is which.
>
> If Kennicott were snatched from Gopher Prairie and instantly conveyed to a town leagues away, he would not realize it. He would go down apparently the same Main Street (almost certainly it would be called Main Street).
>
> (Lewis, 1920, p. 268)

Equivalence categories are linked together so that they can handle a range of places and objects. For example, we rely on a four-fold classification of land use: urban, suburban, rural, and wilderness. We array settlements along a size continuum: megalopolis, city, town, village, and hamlet. Since the categories are generated by people and not "given" by the environment, we have contrasting alternatives. Land use can also be viewed as industrial, commercial, residential, and agricultural.

We can tie together equivalence categories in another way, by subdivision. Suburbs can be classified as street car, commuter railroad, or automobile. The key defining characteristics are technology and historical development. Although we are dissecting the spatial environment into pieces or categories, we can reassemble the pieces into many alternative cognitive mappings, each one useful in a specific problem context. The pieces themselves are not fixed and immutable. As the spatial environment changes so do the equivalence categories necessary to represent it. The post-World War Two impact of the automobile on urban patterns has spawned a new spatial vocabulary: freeways, interchanges, drive-ins, sprawl, slurbs, strip developments, and so on. For each of these categories we have a typical cognitive representation, usually a highly stereotyped visual image, which is cannibalized from bits and pieces of experience.

In many ways, equivalence categories of whatness are more useful than identity categories. Identity expresses the particular, equivalence reflects the general. Much personal (and thus private) experience is encapsulated in identity categories, blending specific memories of places, people, and times. The communication of private experience is hesitant and difficult. Most of us do not have the verbal or graphic fluency that we need to express ourselves to others. The highly personal remains locked in our memory. But we do share common denominators in the form of equivalence categories. The categories may be broad clichés, lacking in rich personal detail; nevertheless, they are an effective currency of communication. Many of the advertisements in this book achieve differentiation of place (and hence identity) from a common base of equivalence categories. Taken together, identity and equivalence categories give us a vocabulary for representing the whatness of the spatial environment. The categories are flexible and changing; they cover the particular and the general. Above all, they form one essential part of the raw material of cognitive mapping.

WHENNESS CATEGORIES

Philosophers argue that space and time are the two fundamental dimensions of human experience. It is not surprising therefore that cognitive maps can be organized to account for both dimensions, either singly or together. Representations incorporate knowledge of the complex interrelationships between places and time. Information linking time and space plays a dual role in everyday spatial behavior—as a basis for *interpretation* and as a source of *predictions*.

Interpretation depends on a frame of reference that structures experience and that focuses on the major dimensions of that experience. One obvious dimension for ordering experience is within the context of a temporal sequence, viewed in either a relative or an absolute sense.

The most common conceptual frameworks based on *relative time* are models of structural change. They are extremely simple, consisting of an ordered set of equivalence categories for classifying and describing places. One very familiar model considers the sequence of socioeconomic development in an area. We speak of countries as being developed, underdeveloped, or undeveloped, associating with these categories a stereotyped set of attributes describing the "normal" patterns of population, resources, and spatial organization. A second and equally familiar model expresses the generalized temporal sequence of urbanization, the so-called "cornfields-to-suburbs" transformation of areas inundated by the spreading city:

> Actually Union Place is a part of metropolitan Toronto; a large suburb which has wandered east of the city along the lakefront and then northward to meet the Macdonald-Cartier Freeway. It's much like the environs of any modern city: flat farmland which has been paved over and seeded with trim brick bungalows, small factories and office buildings, service stations and shopping plazas, all of it since 1950.
>
> (Wright, 1970, p. 8)

In this capsule biography of Union Place, Wright blends together a set of characteristic images, which typify the essence of unbanization — rapid and yet almost whimsical construction, the patternless repetition of stock buildings. The process of spread is seen as biological: Farmland is seeded with a crop of suburbia. However, Anselm Strauss (1961) has identified within American thinking and writing a series of images of the process of urban change. These encompass growth (simple additive increases in physical and population size), development (a biological or organic metaphor of youth to senility), discontinuity (a major, qualitative shift in urban structure), and no change (the belief in some enduring and essential, almost Platonic, city character). As a warning, Strauss (1961, pp. 24–25) cautions

> ... anyone who makes temporal statements about a city necessarily is ordering a tremendous mass of events into a complex symbolic system. He will be highlighting what he takes to be very significant civic happenings and ignoring or failing to perceive others because they seem unimportant. He will even conveniently, or unwittingly, forget other happenings — even eras — that previously seemed important to people who lived through them. Certain events are conceived as momentous for the city's character and are so remembered and celebrated in myth and ceremony (Chicago's fire), or they are remembered as turning points in the city's transforma-

tion (the saga of the Texas oil wells), or as marking the end of an era and the beginning of a new one (Chicago's Columbian Exposition or San Diego's World War II boom). What seemed to be a radical disjuncture to an earlier generation may now be viewed as a number of sequential steps in the city's march towards its present condition.

By making these temporal statements about specific cities such as Chicago or San Diego, we are ordering events on an *absolute* scale. We are responding to a sense of history by developing models of historical change, by switching attention from the general (as in relative time models) to the particular. The product is an ordered sequence of identity categories that describe the significant patterns of change in an area. For example, American school children are taught an idealized model of the spread of settlement in the U.S.A. From an initial colonization of the East Coast, settlement takes place in a series of spatial leaps, which can be visualized as progressively filling in an outline map: the crossing of the Appalachians, the opening of the Midwest, the scattered inroads on the West Coast, and so on. Each step is a distinctive merger of time and place, of pioneer figures and new towns, of economic opportunities and new routes. Related to this model, both in structure and purpose, are the numerous city histories. They range in style from year-by-year recitations of happenings to Chamber of Commerce boosterisms to imaginative interpretations that interweave time and place. Reyner Banham's (1971) architectural exploration of Los Angeles exemplifies the latter style. He identifies four ecologies (Surfurbia, Foothills, the Plains of Id, and Autopia), which display distinctive mixes of topography, land use, historical development, and built forms.

Relative and absolute time models are cognitive structures that allow us to carry the past forward as a way to interpret the present situation. Interpretation alone, however, is not sufficient. We must be able to look ahead in both space *and* time. *Prediction* requires a set of concepts and cognitive strategies for coping with a common type of spatial problem: knowing what will happen or is likely to happen where. Once we have generated reasonable expectations that relate time to space, we can make appropriate decisions about spatial behavior.

The most obvious use of prediction is in hunting, an activity that provided a basic source of food and raw materials for early man. The ability to know where animals would be found at certain times, either throughout the day or on a seasonal basis, was an essential survival mechanism. One plausible explanation for the development of cognitive mapping has viewed it as an adaptive response to the spatial problems confronting early man (see Stephen Kaplan, 1973). Today, groups such as the Lapps, following reindeer herds, and the Eskimos, tracking seals and fish, still depend upon the predictive powers of cognitive mapping.

This predictive capacity is neither defunct in modern man, nor has it atrophied. We still make constant use of it although the immediate survival value is less apparent than in the example of hunting. From the simplest forecasts of tomorrow's weather, or the likelihood of a government office being open, to the complex planning estimates of urban spread, people are trying to foresee what will happen where and when. And the range of predictions and explanations and rationalizations is amazing. For example, Robert Adams (1973) has suggested that weather forecasts are mentally revised to bring them into line with planned behavior, in this case trips to the beaches of New England. People with a strong commitment to go to the beach interpret weather forecasts as favorable, as suggesting merely a chance of showers, even if the forecasts predict a high probability of rain. Those with a weak commitment perform a reverse feat of mental gymnastics: They interpret the chance of rain as greater than the forecast suggests. Adams' study is one product of a long-running, extensive research program, which is now called the Collaborative Research on Natural Hazards. The underlying theme is the human reaction to the threat of natural hazard. How do people cope with the spatial and temporal uncertainty of unpredictable events? Ian Burton and Robert Kates have produced a typology of some strategies by which people hope to make the unknowable knowable (see Table 4.1). Rationality with respect to environmental predictions is suspect to say the least. Paradoxes abound: As flood protection structures increase in number, so does the amount of damage sustained after serious flooding. The dams and levees encourage people to build on flood plains in the mistaken belief that "it" can't happen to them. Despite the salutary warning administered by the 1971 earthquake in California, building on

Table 4.1   COMMON RESPONSES TO THE UNCERTAINTY OF NATURAL HAZARDS

Eliminate the Hazard		Eliminate the Uncertainty	
Deny or Denigrate Its Existence	Deny or Denigrate Its Recurrence	Make it Determinate and Knowable	Transfer Uncertainty to a Higher Power
"We have no floods here, only high water."	"Lightning never strikes twice in the same place."	"Seven years of great plenty. After them seven years of famine."	"It's in the hands of God."
"It can't happen here."	"It's a freak of nature."	"Floods come every five years."	"The government is taking care of it."

(Taken from Ian Burton, and Robert W. Kates (1964) "The perception of natural hazards in resource management." *Natural Resources Journal,* **3,** pp. 412–441, Table 5.)

or near the lines of the San Andreas fault system continues unabated. In many situtations, people do not *want* to look ahead; the predictive component of our cognitive mapping ability is not so much defunct as disregarded.

WHERENESS

Our everyday experience with the world around us reflects its scale and complexity. The physical area that we can perceive directly at any moment is restricted by the spatial range of our senses and the information sources and barriers that surround us. In comparison to the earth's surface, this perceived area is minute. And what we experience within this area is limited. We can only pay attention to a few things at a time. Of course, we compensate for these restrictions and limitations in many ways. Movement allows us to experience or sample a wider area. Tall buildings and hills give us a panoramic view. Photographs, maps, and verbal descriptions are invaluable substitutes for direct, personal experience. But, if we think of experience as sampling the spatial environment, then our sampling design is unsystematic and biased. Some places are experienced many times daily, others once every blue moon; some are seen but not heard, others read about but not visited.

The obvious problem is one of synthesizing these incomplete, unrelated, and often contradictory bits and pieces of information into a useful (i.e., comprehensible) cognitive representation. Since the bits and pieces are not parts of an already structured jigsaw puzzle that we can patiently assemble, we must develop cognitive strategies for relating things, for *making sense out of the world*. The crucial idea is *relationship*. Without a strategy for connecting together and condensing the stream of experience, we could not solve spatial problems. The use of the past, in the present, to solve the future would be impossible because there would be no past, only a transitory present. Given our capability for information storage and retrieval, which although impressive is nevertheless limited, the idea of a past demands the simplification and structuring of experience.

Our cognitive mapping ability uses three constructive strategies for coping with spatial experience: (1) We can focus on the essential similarity between places or objects in our environment. This allows us to classify and order experience according to shared characteristics, and results in the identity and equivalence categories for whatness that we have just discussed. (2) We can organize information according to spatial relationships. In this case we represent the spatial organization of places in the "real world" by cognitively generating *spatial frames of reference*. (3) We can incorporate both similarity and spatial relationship in a *regionalization* process; a common result of this process is a set of stereotypes (see Chapter 3).

SPATIAL FRAMES OF REFERENCE

At the heart of the constant effort after spatial meaning is the ever-present problem of *wayfinding*, of purposive movement over the surface of the earth. Wayfinding is a necessary prerequisite for human survival at all spatial scales: within a room, house, neighborhood, city, and so on. If we can understand the process of wayfinding, then we can also understand the structure and development of spatial frames of reference. The spatial behavior patterns that result from wayfinding are the experiential skeleton for knowledge of the world around us.

Although wayfinding is as basic to everyday life as eating or sleeping, our ignorance about how the process works is almost total. We probably know more about wayfinding in birds such as pigeons (see Keeton, 1974) than we do about how people get to and from the local supermarket. Ironically, much of what we believe about wayfinding is wrong! The most common misconception about wayfinding is that it is a mysterious, innate ability that some groups of people possess and others have just as mysteriously lost. The belief that "primitive" man is blessed with an innate ability to find his way around is simply not true (see Box 4.1). Nor is it true that this ability has atrophied and withered away in "civilized" man. While it remains a mystery, there is nothing innate about the ability that allows a Tuareg to cross the Sahara or Aborigine tribes to travel in northern Australia or Polynesian sailors to find minute coral atolls in the Pacific Ocean (see Chapter 5). Nor is the cherished myth true that men are better at wayfinding than women. Whatever the detailed procedures of wayfinding, they are *learned* and *taught*, not innate and inherited. Although we speak of some people as having a good sense of direction and others as not knowing where they are, there is no innate, special *sense* that guides wayfinding. If some people are better at wayfinding than others, then it is the result of superior learning strategies. These strategies *all* rely on the same basic cognitive mapping ability applied to a specific spatial problem and environmental context.

THE PROCESS OF WAYFINDING

Wayfinding describes the process of solving one class of spatial problems, the movement of a person from one location on the earth's surface to another. For convenience of discussion, we can break the process into four sequential and interrelated steps: (1) orientation, (2) the choice of route, (3) keeping on the right track, and (4) the discovery of the objective.

The first step in wayfinding, *orientation*, is the key one. We must know where we are in relation to some selected places on the earth's surface. Without such knowledge we are lost. Being lost does not mean that wayfinding is impossible; one obvious coping strategy is to seek help. Help may be forthcoming in a city, but it is unlikely in either the Sahara or the Pacific. Knowing where we are, therefore, means being able to tie together our cognitive map and the surrounding environment, being able to say, "If I am here, then that means X is over there to the right and Y is directly behind me." The tie between cognitive map and perceived environment comes from selected places that act as landmarks. We can mentally work out our position relative to these landmarks and fix our present location.

BOX 4.1

THE MYTHICAL "SENSE OF DIRECTION"

Many people subscribe to the time-honored myth that man is blessed with an innate "sense of direction." The origin of this myth is unknown, and the evidence that supports it is suspect. A Russian psychologist, F. N. Shemyakin, has recently severed one of the roots of this myth, a root that was nurtured by, of all people, Charles Darwin. Both Darwin's memory and his scientific thinking were at fault:

> In one of his articles on instincts Charles Darwin . . . had reference, as he himself wrote "from memory," to F. Vrangel, the well-known Russian explorer, from which it appears that the Siberian "savages" could with remarkable accuracy maintain a definite course, "travelling long distances between ice-hummocks, continously changing directions without being guided by any landmarks in the sky or on the frozen land." Commenting on this reference, Ch. Darwin remarked that, in his opinion, this "sense of direction" was the property of not the "savages" alone but in some degree or other of all men . . . Turning to the F. Vrangel text . . . we find, first of all, that the man described who possessed a remarkable "sense of direction" was not a "savage" at all but Tatarin the Cossack sotnik (junior officer). Secondly, F. Vrangel describes in detail those landmarks which Tatarin used as guideposts, and remarking on his ability in this respect points out that these were guideposts for all "the inhabitants of the Siberian tundra." Such landmarks are, first of all, snow drifts formed by winds blowing in one direction, and second — the shadows formed by the hummocks. In order not to deviate from the course when changes in direction are made, it is necessary mentally to project a straight line which will intersect the shadow from the hummocks or the drifts at a definite angle. For this, Vrangel wrote: "It is necessary to possess a special knack of noting the general direction of the course." This means that Vrangel did not speak about a "sense of direction" which had no need of any "guiding landmarks in the sky or on the frozen earth."
>
> (Shemyakin, 1962, p. 194)

We need more than landmarks and cognitive maps to orientate ourselves. We also need a "language" for tying map to environment, a way of expressing spatial relationship. In the example above we used here and there. We can also point to the location of the landmarks. But an immediate reaction of people, when confronted with the problem of spatial relationship and hence direction, is to think in terms of cardinal directions: north, east, south, and west. In the terminology of Chapter 2, cardinal directions are based on a coordinate system and lead to a *state* description of location. If we can give a state description, we can also give a *process* description: "If I am here, then that means that if I follow that road and then take the second left turn, I will get to X." We can express relative location using either mode of description.

However, there are major problems with using cardinal directions as a language system for tying cognitive maps to the perceived environment. To begin with, most people have difficulty in determining which way is north; confusion reigns when watches and the sun are compared to work out direction. And cartographic maps only add to the confusion: Literacy in map reading is not widespread. Such language and translation problems are compounded by place names. For example, in State College, Pennsylvania, the real world and compass directions are out of alignment. North and South Atherton Street run approximately west to east, while naturally East and West College Avenue run north to south. Such local orientation systems are all too frequent (see Chapter 2).

Not only do we find local orientation systems, but also local language systems for expressing spatial relationship and direction. Einar Haugen (1957) has analyzed an intriguing language system commonly used in Iceland. Since the ninth century, Icelanders have known the true (or magnetic) cardinal directions. In the absence of a compass, however, these can only be determined by celestial observation. Consequently, cardinal directions are useful at sea or when referring to the weather, itself a celestial phenomenon. Such usages are easy to understand. On land, the language system for expressing orientation and direction is highly confusing. A traveller may speak of going north when he is actually travelling south or east in compass terms. How can we account for this peculiar expression?

Haugen distinguishes between two systems of orientation, both in everyday use in Iceland. The first, *proximate* orientation, refers to celestial observations of directional relations between places in one's immediate neighborhood. These observations are visual judgments and lead to statements such as Thor's farm is to the north of the church. The second system, *ultimate* orientation, is based on social practices developed to aid land travel. At the time that the system of expression was established, travel was by horseback along winding coastal trails, which connected the thin line of settlements ringing the Icelandic coast.

Travel across the uninhabited, mountainous interior was impossible. The meandering trails did not even approximate straight lines and so celestial orientation was meaningless. Iceland itself was divided, by common agreement, into four quarters: North, East, South, and West (see Figure 4.5). The trail led around the island, connecting each quarter. Anyone travelling along the trail would say that they were going in the direction of the next quarter; therefore, going east means going to Eastern Iceland, although the compass direction of travel may be due north. The key to the language system is in terms of destination name, not compass direction of travel. There is an underlying logic to this system for tying cognitive map and environment, and the logic emerges from a combination of local environmental conditions and patterns of travel.

Many other systems for expressing orientation have been developed to cope with a particular environment. The Yurok and Karok Indian tribes of northwestern California orientated themselves not by the apparent motion of the sun (or cardinal directions), but by the direction of river flow (Bright and Bright, 1965). This system is built around four cardinal terms: upriver, downriver, towards the river, and away from the river. Figure 4.6 is a representation of the world view, or cosmography, of the Yurok tribe. (For similar examples, see Appendix II in Kevin Lynch's (1960) book.) Even so-called "civilized" societies use noncompass-based orientation systems for expressing spatial relation-

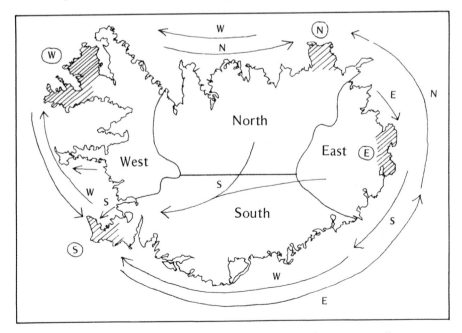

Figure 4.5. Icelandic orientation: another "pivot of the four quarters."

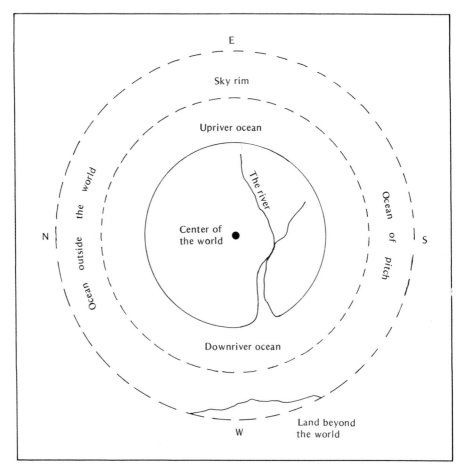

Figure 4.6. Yurok orientation: "as long as the rivers shall run."

ship. People speak of the Near East, the Middle East, and the Far East: Thomas Saarinen has suggested that this indicates the degree of removal from Europe, the assumed center of civilization! In the U.S.A., places are out West, back East, down South, or up North. New Yorkers go uptown or downtown. In England, London is the cognitive peak to which people go up and from which they come down. Oxbridge University students go up at the beginning of term and come down at the end. It is reasonable to speak of going up to seats of *higher* learning, but what is up in New York? Where is down? How do such language systems develop?

Richard Howell (1969) answered these questions in an exploration of the vertical dimension of cognitive maps of Staten Island, New York. Figure 4.7 maps responses to the question addressed to local residents, Which parts of the Island are "up" and which are "down"? The dis-

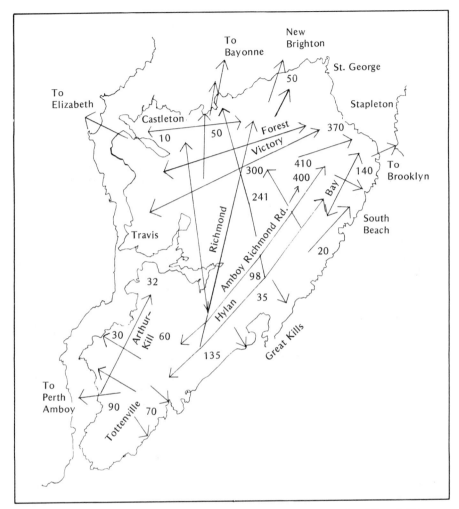

Figure 4.7. Richmond (Staten Island, N.Y.) orientation: "up-island" and "down-island." (Numbers indicate approximate elevation in feet.)

tinction between proximate and ultimate systems of orientation is essential for understanding the subtleties of cognitive ups and downs:

> ... when one is speaking of the immediate neighborhood (proximate orientation), one is governed by physical features. Thus if one goes down locally, it is usually because one is going downhill to some extent.
>
> (Howell, 1969, p. 52)

Ultimate orientation depends upon less obvious considerations: traditions which stem from the difference between heavily populated areas (and their importance for shopping) and sparsely populated areas ("the sticks," with limited facilities); very general topographical features ... , in the same sector of the Island and to some extent separating the North and East Shores from the rest of the Island; and, finally, and perhaps most important, the communication network in which all public transportation facilities converge at St. George (the main exit to the City, into which one goes).

(Howell, 1969, p. 56)

The logic and language for expressing orientation and spatial relationship varies. There is no universal, "natural" system used throughout the world. Instead, the systems are tailored to the nature of the physical environment and form part of the larger culture. However, lost is lost no matter who or where you are. According to Clifford Geertz (1972, p. 35):

Balinese regard the exact maintenance of spatial orientation ("not to know where north is" is to be crazy), balance, decorum, status relationships and so forth, as fundamental to ordered life. . . .

Although Western society may not accord such prominence to spatial orientation, directional expressions (see Table 3.1) play a major role in language systems and imagery. No one likes environments that are confusing and in which one can become disoriented. And disorientation may have strange and disconcerting effects, as Box 4.2 suggests.

Although we have stressed the importance of orientation, the other three steps in the wayfinding process must also be executed successfully. The choice of a route requires that a person make a cognitive connection between his current location and that of the desired destination. To be useful, this connection must be converted into a plan of action, usually by a sequence of directed movements, which hinge upon a series of landmarks. Each landmark represents a decision point: Turn left at the corner, take the third right, and look out for the grey and orange house. A plan is a complex hierarchy of actions that will get a person from A to B. In the future, however, this part of the wayfinding process may be simplified:

"A good hotel, please."

The Supervisor was unimpressed, "They're all good. Name one."

Gaal said, desperately, "The nearest one, please."

The Supervisor touched a button. A thin line of light formed along the floor, twisting among others which brightened and dimmed in different colors and shades. A ticket was shoved into Gaal's hands. It glowed faintly. The Supervisor said, "One point twelve." Gaal fumbled for the coins. He said, "Where do I go?" "Follow the light. The ticket will keep glowing as long as you're pointed in the right direction." Gaal looked up and began walking. There were hundreds creeping across the vast floor, following their individual trails, sifting and straining themselves through intersection points to arrive at their respective destinations. His own trail ended.

(Asimov, 1951, pp. 7–8)

BOX 4.2

A GHASTLY DISORIENTATION

Shirley Jackson's *The Haunting of Hill House* first came to public attention when it was released as a movie, retitled *The Haunting*. The film, since then rerun many times on late-night TV, has entertained millions with its superb recreation of many unforgettable episodes in the novel. What escaped the film makers, however, was the extraordinary explanation, advanced by the professorial leader of the explorers of Hill House, for its strange and frightening powers over those who dwelt within. It was *disorientation,* which *might* have resulted in the illusion of supernatural manifestations. Given the supernatural and paranormal experiences reported in the popular press, one might ask whether explanations similar to that advanced below may sometimes be put forth:

"One of the peculiar traits of Hill House is its design—"

"Crazy house at the carnival."

"Precisely. Have you not wondered at our *extreme* difficulty in finding our way around? An ordinary house would not have had the four of us in such confusion for so long, and yet time after time we choose the wrong doors, the room we want eludes us. Even I have had my troubles." He sighed and nodded. "I daresay," he went on, "that old Hugh Crain expected that someday Hill House might become a showplace, like the Winchester House in California or the many octagon houses; he designed Hill House himself, remember, and, I have told you before, he was a strange man. Every angle"—and the doctor gestured toward the doorway— "every angle is slightly wrong. Hugh Crain must have detested other people and their sensible squared-away houses, because he made his house to suit his mind. Angles which you assume are the right angles you are accustomed to, and have every right to expect are true, are actually a fraction of a degree off in one direction or another. I am sure, for instance, that you believe that the stairs you are sitting on are level, because you are not prepared for stairs which are not level—"

They moved uneasily, and Theodora put out a quick hand to take hold of the balustrade, as though she felt she might be falling.

"—are actually on a very slight slant toward the central shaft; the doorways are all a very little bit off center—that may be, by the way, the reason the doors swing shut unless they are held; I wondered this morning whether the approaching footsteps of you two ladies upset the delicate balance of the doors. Of course the result of all these tiny aberrations of measurement adds up to a fairly large distortion in the house as a whole. Theodora cannot see the tower from her bedroom window because the tower actually stands at the corner of the house. From Theodora's bedroom window it is completely invisible, although from here it seems to be directly outside her room. The window of Theodora's room is actually fifteen feet to the left of where we are now."

Theodora spread her hands helplessly. "Golly," she said.

"I see," Eleanor said. "The veranda roof is what misleads us. I can look outside my window and see the veranda roof and because I came directly into the house and up the stairs I assumed that the front door was right below, although really—"

"You see only the veranda roof," the doctor said. "The front door is far away; it and the tower are visible from the nursery, which is the big room at the end of the hallway; we will see it later today. It is"—and his voice was saddened—"a masterpiece of architectural misdirection. The double stairway at Chambord—"

"Then everything is a little bit off center?" Theodora asked uncertainly. "That's why it all feels so disjointed."

"What happens when you go back to a real house?" Eleanor asked. "I mean—a—well—a *real* house?"

"It must be like coming off shipboard," Luke said. "After being here for a while your sense of balance could be so distorted that it would take you a while to lose your sea legs, or your Hill House legs. Could it be," he asked the doctor, "that what people have been assuming were supernatural manifestations were really only the result of a slight loss of balance in the people who live here? The inner ear," he told Theodora wisely.

"It must certainly affect people in some way," the doctor said. "We have grown to trust blindly in our senses of balance and reason, and I can see where the mind might fight wildly to preserve its own familiar stable patterns against all evidence that it was leaning sideways."

(Jackson, 1959, pp. 106–107)

The final word in such spatial omniscience may be Mike, a sapient but science-fictional computer, whose wayfinding capacity is almost limitless:

How Mike knew a phone was outside that hall is hard to say, since "space" could not mean to him what means (sic) to us. But he carried in storage a "map"—structured relations—of Luna City's engineering, and could almost always fit what we said to what he knew as Luna City; he hardly ever got lost.

(Heinlein, 1966, pp. 88–89)

For mere mortals, the choice of a route is not as simple. Marion Marchand (1975) found that even asking for directions may not ease the burden of choice. In Greece, people tried to determine just what route the questioner really preferred. Their answers were tailored to satisfy the traveler's wishes, and led to "appalling prodigies of mis-information." If only we were as fortunate as Dorothy in the *Wizard of Oz*, who simply had to follow the yellow brick road.

The third step in the process, *keeping on the right track*, monitors the execution of the route plan. This part of wayfinding was largely re-sponsible for giving rise to the belief that wayfinding was an innate process (see Box 4.1). Nothing could be further from the truth. Keeping on the right track is achieved by *keeping* our cognitive map tied to the perceived environment, by making and taking appropriate actions at each decision point. As check-off points on the route up the Berrens River from the mouth at Lake Winnipeg to Grand Rapids (100 miles away), the Saulteaux Indians make use of 50 named rapids. By follow-ing the known sequence, the Saulteaux Indians maintain a constant sense of position and can anticipate what will come next (Hallowell, 1967, p. 196).

Monitoring is not only necessary to give reassurance that we are on the right track; it is also vital because of the human tendency to stray off the straight and narrow. In the case of walking, Gatty (1958, pp. 261–68) reports on studies of the human tendency to walk in circles. Without the aid of guiding landmarks (as in forests or on featureless terrain), most people complete a full circle in about a half an hour. This circling tendency is not connected with handedness since 55 per-cent circle to the right and 45 percent to the left. The explanation seems to lie in the physical assymetries of leg length. Yet even the need for the reassurance of being on the right track is rejected by some people:

> There are map people whose joy is to lavish more attention on the sheets of colored paper than on the colored land rolling by. I have listened to accounts by such travellers in which every road number was remem-bered, every mileage recalled, and every little countryside discovered. An-other kind of traveller requires to know in terms of maps exactly where he is pinpointed every moment, as though there were some kind of safety in black and red lines, in dotted indications and squirming blue of lakes and the shadings that indicate mountains. It is not so with me. I was born lost and take no pleasure in being found, nor much identification from

shapes which symbolize continents and states. Besides, roads change, increase, are widened or abandoned so often in our country that one must buy road maps like daily newspapers.

(Steinbeck, 1962, p. 62)

Not all features on the face of the earth are as transitory as roads, and this allowed the ability to tie cognitive maps and the perceived environment together to reach an unsurpassed peak in the person of William Buckland, a nineteenth century Dean of Westminster:

> . . . the stories about Buckland were legion. . . . It was claimed that his field geology was so profound that when lost one day on a horseback journey from Oxford to London, he dismounted, scooped up a handful of earth and remarked: "Ah, yes, as I guessed, Ealing."

(Millar, 1972, p. 25)

The environment is something that we learn to read for its informational value in wayfinding. Consequently, one goal of environmental design is to build legible clues into the structure of the physical environment (see also Chapter 8):

> People as well as packages can travel without knowing any of the conventional languages. For instance, a foreigner in certain air and rail terminals can locate an information desk or pickup point for lost children, if he looks around for these signs. "I got off the plane in Moscow some years ago," Dreyfuss remembers, "and I was able to find my way to my baggage, customs, the bank at the airport, a taxi and the hotel, and I don't speak a word of Russian—all by symbols."

(Time, April 13, 1972, p. 47)

Other designs are less successful in conveying a sense of location. Given the symbol that the Watergate complex in Washington has become, there is an amusing irony in these plaintive comments by Mary McCarthy (1973, p. 5):

> The sense of being in a high-security castellated fort or series of forts is added to by lower-level passages, know as Malls, which constitute a labyrinth. The whole place, in fact, is a maze, marked here and there by highly misleading signs directing you to *"Les Champs," "Mall," "Restaurant," "Arcade."* When you try to follow them, you either go round in circles or end up against a blank, no-entry wall. It is as if there were a war on, and the red, green, and blue directional arrows had been turned to point the wrong way in order to confuse the enemy expected to invade at sunrise. Every day, so far, I have got lost in this eerie complex, hoping to

find an Espresso bar that was rumored to exist somewhere in the vicinity of "*Les Champs*." Once I found myself in "Peacock Alley," and another time standing on the verge of the forbidden swimming pool. Yesterday, though, I reached the goal, following the instructions of a porter: "You just keep goin' around."

Mary McCarthy only paid for her failure to keep on the right track with bemused frustration. Sometimes the experience can be more frightening (see Box 4.3).

Assuming that one has, like Theseus, mastered the environmental maze, one faces the final step, the *discovery of the objective*. You must recognize that you have got to where you are going. Again, this recognition depends upon linking a cognitive map with the perceived environment, a linkage that usually brings profound relief. On occasion, the discovery may be anticlimatic: as Gertrude Stein lamented about Oakland, "When you get there, there isn't any there there."

FRAMES OF REFERENCE AND LEARNING

Each time that we solve a particular wayfinding problem, we exercise part of our cognitive mapping ability. Each solution can be viewed as a performance, and each performance results in learning. We learn the appropriate plan of spatial behavior to get from place A to place B. The plan itself is reinforced by repeated performances of the same journey and eventually becomes a *sequential route map*. Two locations are mentally joined by a path that is punctuated by a sequence of landmarks. The landmarks are the means of linking cognitive map and the perceived environment. They allow us to monitor our spatial progress and to keep on the right track. As we argued in Chapter 3, we may not be consciously aware of this ongoing process; sequential route maps underlie the feeling that we can make a journey blindfolded because we know a place like the back of our hand.

BOX 4.3

THE WORLD OF THE STRAIGHT AND NARROW

Making a wrong turn can be a costly mistake. It can bring both annoyance and fear. It can bring us face-to-face with parts of the world that are different and that have been hidden beyond the bounds of our normal everyday experience. In the Harlem bus trip (discussed in Chapter 3), the trip is likened to a stagecoach ride through hostile Apache country. Earlier in the same chapter, Spreiregen suggested concealing "gray areas" of the city so that travellers would be spared even fleeting glimpses of a world that taxes our patience. Caryl Rivers' experience is a graphic accounting of the taxing costs of straying from the straight and narrow:

> The world of black Washington might as well have been on Mars, for all we knew of it. We drove through it, peering from behind locked car doors at dark people sitting on the stoops of redbrick row houses. We felt insulated on the other side of the District line, but we understood how things were. I remember one of the jokes we used to tell:
>
> A white Washingtonian picks up a black hitchhiker in Alabama. The man is shuffling, servile. "Please, sir, can I have a ride, sir?"
>
> In Atlanta, the white man opens the door and says: "Get out, boy."
>
> "Oh, please, sir, let me ride a little further, sir."
>
> This goes on through the major cities of the South until the driver crosses Memorial Bridge from Virginia into Washington. He opens the door again and says: "Get out now, boy."
>
> The black man grabs him, pulls a knife and snarls: "Who you calling 'boy,' white man?"
>
> Implicit in the joke was a concept of territory we all accepted without really understanding it. I first became aware of it in more than a subliminal way when I was driving through Southeast Washington one night with some of my highschool friends. We were coming home from a Chesapeake Bay beach (white, gentiles only). We made a wrong turn, and at the same instant everyone in the car realized that outside there were nothing but black people for miles and miles and miles. We were all suddenly and irrationally afraid. No one had looked at us in a hostile way; few people even noticed us. But I felt, for the first time in my life, that I was not on my own ground. I had assumed, I suppose, that every place in the United States of America was "my turf." I had a glimpse, in those few nervous moments, of what it must be like so often to be black in white America.
>
> (Rivers, 1972, 95–96)

We can also learn from individual performances in a second way. We can gradually integrate several sequential route maps. The integration follows from shared end points and landmarks, and we develop a *spatial route map*. Although spatial learning forms the substance of Chapter 7, the important point for our current argument is that, through spatial route maps, experiences are woven together. They are no longer disjointed and unrelated bits and pieces. The result of the mental weaving process is something approximating a traditional cartographic map, something that can be added to and ammended as both needs and the spatial environment change. These cognitive representations of spatial relationship overcome the unsystematic way in which we get to know the world around us. Obviously, spatial route maps offer flexibility in problem solving. We can find alternative ways of connecting locations. We can link together places to produce a plan for a route between places never before visited in that spatial sequence. These maps are the spatial frames of reference, which are both the consequence of and basis for wayfinding. The skeleton of these frames of reference results from spatial experiences produced by wayfinding.

Although the total amount of research into cognitive mapping has not been great, the bulk of it has centered on spatial frames of reference. Two topics have been prominent: the structural elements, which make up the frames, and the metrics (or cognitive distance) of the spatial relationships, which comprise the frames. We turn to these next.

THE STRUCTURE OF FRAMES OF REFERENCE

In applying the dictum of Occam's razor, we seek simplicity wherever possible in explanations. We know that cognitive mapping simplifies and organizes spatial experience. It would be pleasant to report that such simplicity is reflected in the structure of frames of reference, and that there are a few common principles of organization and a few cognitive building blocks. At present, such a report is not possible. Despite a series of empirical studies, the case for a few building blocks, although suggestive, is not proven.

The search began with the pioneering work of Kevin Lynch (1960) on images of three cities: Boston, Jersey City, and Los Angeles. Lynch claimed that the contents of these images could be classified into five element classes: paths, edges, landmarks, nodes, and districts. Many people uncritically accepted these findings (and their underlying methodology) as proof of the existence of cognitive building blocks, an acceptance that was fostered by a flood of replications of Lynch's approach.

Before we consider this and other evidence of simplicity, we must recall the major obstacle to *all* research into cognitive mapping. There is no assurance of similarity between the cognitive signatures used for storing spatial information and the signatures used for decoding or mapmaking. The particular signature chosen for the decoding process can have major effects on the structure of the cognitive map that is generated. For example, there are limits both to what can be expressed in a pencil sketch and how the selected ideas are conveyed. Alternatively, the request to draw a map of an area encourages people to try to decode information via the signature of a cartographic map. Although Lynch used map sketching and verbal descriptions to generate city images, many others have restricted respondents only to map sketching. Moreover, Lynch (1960, p. 46) claimed:

> This analysis limits itself to the effects of physical, perceptible objects. There are other influences on imageability, such as the social meaning of

an area, its function, its history, or even its name. These will be glossed over, since the objective here is to uncover the role of form itself.

Bearing these qualifications in mind, Lynch's elements do suggest that cognitive maps are constructed from common building blocks. Paths, nodes, and landmarks are essential to plans for wayfinding and it is logical that the world in the head is organized accordingly. Lynch argues that other environmental elements are arranged along and related to the basic path structure. The spatial route maps developed from wayfinding provide a skeleton for organizing experience.

The tendency to separate the world into discrete units is reflected in the idea of edges, linear breaks in continuity. The intimate connection between place, territory, and edges is seen in this comment by Richard Burton (1973, p. 15) on his boyhood home in Wales:

> We went to the meeting ground of our part of the village. It was called "the end." It was a vacant stretch of stony ground between two rows of cottages—Inkerman and Balaclava. Both the Inkerman people and the Balaclava people called it "the end." Insularity, I realize now, streetophobia—to each street it was "the end." It should have been called "the middle."

Districts are two-dimensional areas, which a person "mentally enters inside of," and which have common identifying characteristics. We have discussed these as identity categories for handling whatness.

But spatial frames of reference contain more than a knowledge of physical, perceptible forms. We endow space with *meaning*, on both a personal and a cosmic level. There are many anthropological accounts of the way in which environment, religion, and mythology are intertwined. To some Aborigine tribes in Australia, the landscape is interwoven with tracks followed by legendary heroes, while some places (or landmarks) are the homes of spirits and ancestors. The people of Puluwat (see Chapter 5) learn the mythical sea life of the surrounding Pacific Ocean. For other peoples, cardinal directions represent supernatural forces, mountains are the homes of ancestral spirits, weather is an expression of the mood of the gods: A *symmetry* and *comprehensibility* is given to the confusion of spatial experience. There is harmony between the form and arrangement of the earth and the forces that control and shape it. Yi-Fu Tuan (1974) discusses these cosmographies in his study of what he calls *topophilia*, the affective bond between man and place.

Such efforts after spatial meaning also lend organization and simplicity to the world just as much as Lynch's elements do. Ethnocentric stereotypes bring an oversimplified order out of chaos. As you see, it is impossible for us to bring order out of the chaos of evidence. While we are certain that spatial frames of reference simplify the world and make it comprehensible, our grasp of this simplicity is tenuous. We believe that a few organizing principles exist, but this belief is at best an act of faith. The world in the head is still *terra incognita*.

COGNITIVE DISTANCE

For many affluent people in the developed nations, Figure 4.8 draws on an image of the world that represents part reality, part wishful thinking, and fantasy. In a cognitive sense, the world is being reduced to a handful of places that are next door to each other. Cognitive space is collapsing and being concentrated into this striking panorama of urban symbols. Distance and direction are being negated; the great cities of the world are being offered in instant access by telephone and airline companies. Yet, underlying this fantasy image is a reality, which is experienced by more than the affluent jet set. For most people, the world is being pulled together and distance is shrinking. Technological advances are diminishing the separating effects of location on the earth's

Figure 4.8. The annihilation of distance.

surface. Spatial problems still exist, but they are of a different order of magnitude from those that confronted even the previous generation. If cognitive maps both reflect spatial experience *and* are the basis for future decisions, how do we represent the distance relationships between places? Such a question is important because people are supposed to be sensitive to the costs of overcoming distance. If people are the distance minimizers that geographers believe them to be, their understanding of distance will affect spatial problem solving. How is spatial separation reflected in cognitive mapping?

Before we can answer this question, we must make an important distinction between *perceived* and *cognitive* distance. Perceived distance refers to judgments of the relative distance between a *visible* object and the person making the judgments. The focus of interest is on the properties of visual space and the factors that affect it: monocular versus binocular vision, depth cues, and familiarity with the object. However, most spatial problems are not perceptual: We cannot see the places that we are concerned with. Cognitive distance refers to judgments and beliefs made or held in the *absence* of the object. The basis for making such judgments is the spatial information stored in cognitive maps.

How do we generate cognitive distance estimates? The key word in this question is *generate*. It is inconceivable that cognitive maps are organized like those road maps that contain an exhaustive table of distances between important places. It is likely that the constructive nature of cognitive mapping manipulates stored information to make distance estimates.

Ronald Briggs (1973) offers five possible mechanisms for generating cognitive distance estimates:

1. motory response: the amount of energy expended in moving between two places;
2. time and velocity: the knowledge of the relationships between time, velocity, and distance;
3. perception: the addition of all of the perceived distances between places (or landmarks) on the route from A to B;
4. the use of patterns in the structure of the physical environment: counting city blocks or traffic lights;
5. symbolic representations: a reliance on maps, roadsigns, and so on.

Although Briggs favors the third mechanism, the answer probably lies in a combination of all of them. Each reflects a part of our experience with the spatial environment. All mechanisms are not feasible in all environments for all groups of people. For example, in societies where cars have not replaced legs, the physical effort involved in walking (mechanism one) is a key source of information (see the comments by Elizabeth Bowen in Chapter 2). Patterns only exist in regular, manmade environments (mechanism four). Symbolic representations are the only basis for making judgments about places never before visited (mechanism five). Thus I can "guesstimate" the Moscow-to-Peking distance, although I have never travelled between them. However, the daily journey to work makes us keenly aware of time and velocity (mechanism two). The use of several mechanisms for distance estimation recalls the flexible, organizing nature of the cognitive mapping process.

Given these generating mechanisms, what is the relationship between cognitive distance and "real" distance in the spatial environment? Unfortunately, there is no definitive answer to this question. Current research findings are often contradictory and lacking in plausible explanations. In part, the contradictions stem from the diverse ways in which research has been undertaken. For example, studies have asked about route distances and "as the crow flies" distances. People have been asked to make direct estimates of distance (e.g., A to B is so many miles) or relative estimates (e.g., if A to X is 10 units along this line, mark how far A to B is in the same units). Estimates have dealt with distances involving hundreds of yards or hundreds of miles. These variations in methodology make the task of generalizing about cognitive distance highly speculative.

Cognitive distance estimates reflect much more than the simple geographical separation between places on the earth's surface. They are one result of the attempt by cognitive mapping to synthesize a variety of spatial experiences. Information derived from personal travel, conversation, maps, and highway signs is drawn upon to build a cognitive representation of spatial relationship. Implicit in this building process is not only the need to reconcile driving time with road mileage signs or walking time with the number of city blocks covered, but also the need for a richness of language and a flexibility of expression. There is no universal yardstick for expressing a sense of distance. We can generate different types of cognitive distance estimates to cope with a range of spatial problems within the same physical area. Probably the simplest system is that of near-far, a system that dichotomizes spatial relationships. For finer discriminations, we can replace near-far judgments with estimates of travel time. These allow us to speak of degrees of proximity or relative distance. In estimating travel times, we can make allowance for traffic conditions at various times of the day or seasons of the year. All of these expressions of distance are based on the human scale of experience. They calibrate distances according to the human expenditure of effort that is needed to overcome the separation between places: Man is the measure. Thus the Saulteaux Indians speak of how many times they have slept or will sleep (Hallowell, 1967, p. 206), a yardstick that parallels our usage of the number of nights on the road. Polynesian sailors use canoe-days for the same purpose (Gatty, 1958, p. 47). However, even this simple system of expression has its quirks.

While the Yoruba of West Africa speak of days on a journey, their days are in fact double: One day is equivalent to one day of travel plus one day of rest.

No matter what type of yardstick we use to express our sense of cognitive distance, the resultant estimates express a complex of feelings about the places themselves as much as they represent a human scaling of simple geographical distance. The geometric properties of geographical space are not necessarily reproduced in the cognitive structure of our frames of reference. Although the geographical distance between two places is the same no matter whether we measure from A to B, or vice versa, the same invariance does not always hold true for the world in the head. The distance from home to somewhere always seems to be greater than the return distance from the same somewhere to home. There is nothing like returning home, and home is an anchor point that dominates our cognitive sense of spatial relationship. The homeward-bound theme, a recurrent motif in popular music, expresses the pulling power of home. As Sir Julian Huxley (1973, p. 166) writes in his autobiography:

> All too soon we were airborne in a plane well-named *Argonaut*, the map of the world below narrowing to the pinpoint of home and all that it represented.

The kinds of people at a place affect distance estimates. The people in Elizabeth Bowen's novel (see Chapter 2) used near and far to indicate an amalgam between physical and social distance. If you like someone, they live nearby, while the home of a disliked person is pushed into the mental distance, far away. A group of Swedish psychologists have related distance estimates to capital cities to a person's emotional involvement with those cities: the higher the emotional involvement, the more accurate the subjective distance estimates (Lundberg, 1973). Emotional involvement is easily translated into geopolitics, as this letter to the editor of *Newsweek* points out:

Giant step

In its foreign-policy cover story (INTERNATIONAL, Dec. 14), *Newsweek* reports that a "Marxist has taken over on the U.S.A.'s doorstep in Chile."

Have any of your comrades looked at an air-distance chart lately? Santiago is over 5,100 miles from New York. Or, if you prefer, Moscow is over 400 miles *closer* to New York than Santiago. Ultimately, we may have reasons to be bugged by developments in Chile, but proximity surely won't be one of them.

DONALD KLEIN

New York City   (*Newsweek*, 1971, January 18, p. 4)

Why is Chile thought to be on the U.S.A.'s doorstep? Why do Americans see the world this way? Their cognitive maps have been sculptured and shaped by history (the Monroe Doctrine of spheres of influence), by geopolitics (the Organization of American States), by place names (the nomenclatural affinity of North and South America), and by atlases, which include North and South America on the same map while Europe and Asia are torn off at the Bering Straits to be mapped on a separate page. We are at the mercy of influential cartographic conventions and need to be reminded of their biasses.

Cognitive distance estimates are a function of the particular cognitive mapping signature that we use to generate a representation. They depend upon the scale of the signature; that is, the ratio between distances in the representation and real world distances. This functional relationship between cognitive and real distance is not simple. We do not consistently over- or underestimate distance in all spatial situations. At first sight, some of the findings are contradictory. Terence Lee (1970) has shown that people overestimate distances to places that are away from the city center (in this case, Dundee, Scotland). In contrast, Golledge and Zannaras (1973) found that in Columbus, Ohio, people tend to underestimate distances away from downtown and that distances into town were viewed as relatively longer than distances out of it. Lee explains his findings in terms of the greater desirability of the downtown destination as compared with the desirability of peripheral destinations. While Lee believes that the differential feelings for places affect cognitive distance, Golledge and Zannaras see the experience of the journey itself as affecting distance estimates. As you go downtown, travel times are slowed by traffic conditions and signals. However, there is general agreement that familiarity breeds accuracy: the more familiar the places or the longer the time of residence in an area, the less that we over- or underestimate distances.

How can we resolve these findings? Canter and Tagg (1975) offer a plausible resolution. They argue that accuracy of estimation is related to the imageability or legibility of a particular city. In order to cope with everyday urban life, people try to fit their spatial experience into some simple cognitive structure that serves as a ready basis for the storage and manipulation of information. The structure is built around the road and rail systems, general topography, and major geographical features. The more readily a city lends itself to developing a simple cognitive structure, the more accurate are the distance estimates that its inhabitants generate. Golledge and Zannaras studied distance estimates along a major road in essentially featureless country, and hence, the emphasis on the experience of the journey. The places in Lee's study were structured by the hills and the river in the city of Dundee.

Despite the plausibility of this argument, we are still groping to understand a complex psychological process that is subject to many influences: the attractiveness of places, the legibility of the environment, the source of information, the length of residence, and the frequency of travel. All of these influences shape the structure of our spatial frames of reference. The world in the head is a warped and twisted model of the real world. Distance estimates give a feel for the degree of twisting and warping, a feel that is difficult to convey. Perhaps one of the most insightful comments is that of Sir Francis Galton, written in 1872 (pp. 292–293).

> It is difficult to estimate, by recollection only, the true distances between different points in a road that has been once travelled over. There are many circumstances which may mislead, such as the accidental tedium of one part, or the pleasure of another; but besides these, there is always the fact, that, in a long day's journey, a man's faculties of observation are more fresh and active on starting than later in the day, when, from the effect of weariness, even peculiar objects will fail to arrest his attention. Now, as a man's recollection of an interval of time is, as we all know, mainly derived from the number of impressions that his memory has received while it was passing, it follows that, . . . , the earlier part of his day's journey will always seem to have been disproportionately long compared to the latter. It is remarkable, on taking a long half-day's walk, and subsequently returning, after resting some hours, how long a time the earlier part of the return journey seems to occupy, and how rapidly different well-remembered points seem to succeed each other, as the traveller draws homeward. In this case, the same cause acts in opposite directions in the two journeys.

CONCLUSION

In looking at the world in the head in terms of whatness, whenness, and whereness, we are in danger of losing sight of the wood for the trees. We have tried to get inside this world by breaking it into pieces and partial explanations. Yet, cognitive mapping itself is an organizing, synthesizing process, which works in the opposite direction. It allows people to come to grips with the world as a whole, to build a *gestalt*. To counterbalance the analytic approach of the book so far, Chapter 5 will present the tale of two places, chosen to reflect different facets of cognitive mapping.

The first place, Puluwat, is a tiny island in Micronesia that is the home of a group of people for whom it can be said that cognitive mapping is central to their way of life. The personal, social, and religious worlds of the Puluwatans are built around long sea voyages and the art of navigation. Through rote memorization on land and practical apprenticeship at sea, Puluwatans absorb a traditional navigation system that is entirely dependent on the world in the head, on accurate cognitive maps, on wayfinding strategies, and on the ability to "read" the natural environment. This represents cognitive mapping in its most basic role of spatial problem solving. The second place, Boston, is seen through two contrasting viewpoints. The first is an amalgam of the academic research on Boston's distinctive character, on its legibility, on its neighborhoods and symbolic places. Boston is the home of cognitive mapping research, and we have learned to see it through the eyes of these researchers. But cognitive mapping is also a highly personal means of coming to grips with the world. Boston is a place where one of us has lived for a considerable period of time. So our second viewpoint is that of an inhabitant. We try to convey a sense of one person's cognitive map, an impression of the flavor of life in Boston. This reflects cognitive mapping in its highly personal role as a coathanger for our memories and as a basis for our personal sense of place in the world.

Chapter 5

A TALE OF
TWO PLACES

PULUWAT: THE ART OF NAVIGATION

For most people, the South Pacific is a blank area on their cognitive map of the world, a vast blue-shaded expanse with very little whatness in a large chunk of "nowhereness." In a cognitive gazetteer, the next places after Hawaii are New Zealand and Australia. Whatever fragments of knowledge we possess concerning the intervening ocean are likely to be a curious residual amalgam of ideas gleaned from movies such as *South Pacific* and *Mutiny on the Bounty,* vague memories of Captain Cook's voyages of discovery and the Kon Tiki expedition, and unpleasant associations from the campaigns of the Second World War and the more recent nuclear bomb tests on deserted atolls.

Such stereotypes unjustly overlook many remarkable peoples and places in Polynesia and Micronesia. One of the unique achievements of these people is the pattern of the interisland sailing, which, although less prevalent than it used to be, is still an amazing feat of human skill and endurance. We will look at one representative group of people, less than 400 strong, who live on the U.S.-administered island of Puluwat in the Caroline Islands of Micronesia (see Figure 5.1), and who continue to practice the art of navigation.

Our discussion is primarily based on two superb books, Thomas Gladwin's *East Is A Big Bird* (1970) and David Lewis' *We, The Navigators* (1972). Both men learnt much of the art of navigation from Hipour, an initiated Puluwatan navigator or *ppalu*. Gladwin's ultimate interest was in understanding the intelligence and cognitive styles of the Pu-

146

luwatans. Lewis was concerned with the limits and effectiveness of oceanic navigation, particularly as it related to the competing theories of accidental or deliberate settlement of Micronesia and Polynesia. We will reinterpret their work in the light of our own ideas on cognitive mapping. As we see it, Puluwatan navigation is a classic example of how cognitive mapping is tailored to spatial problem solving in a specific environmental context.

Many of the island peoples in the South Pacific made long, intentional sea voyages between the scattered island groups. The Puluwatans maintain this tradition. For example, they sail from Puluwat to Kapingamarangi, a distance of 465 sea miles (see Figure 5.1), Puluwat to Truk (135 miles), Puluwat to Satawal (130 miles), and Saipan to Pikelot (450 miles). Although these are long distances, such voyages do not seem remarkable *until* we appreciate the following. First, voyages are made in small, outrigger sailing canoes, approximately 26 feet by 3 feet, which hold only six people, and have no mechanical power. Second, most voyages cover long distances out of sight of land and head for very small destinations. Third, the Puluwatans use *no* navigational instruments or charts. (This characteristic is changing since some canoes now carry a magnetic compass as an added safety precaution.) Fourth, neither the Puluwatans nor any other inhabitants of the South Pacific are blessed with a special sixth sense of navigation. Taken in combination, these characteristics suggest the magnitude of the achievements of these island voyagers.

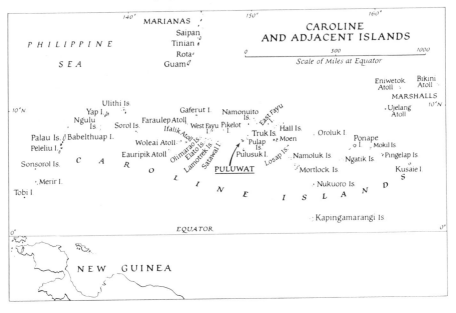

Figure 5.1. The Puluwat Atoll, Caroline Islands, Micronesia.

Instead of a mysterious sixth sense, Puluwatans rely on their memory and the acutely trained powers of their five senses. The art of navigation is built around an orally transmitted tradition, which is learned and committed to memory during a lengthy and exacting process of teaching and apprenticeship. The oral tradition is a closed system capable of coping with every forseeable situation encountered during wayfinding. The culmination of trial and error learning, it is a classic example of using the past, in the present, to solve for the future. Instruction includes demonstrations and rote learning on land, and direct, interactive experience at sea. Given the magnitude of the learning task, not all Puluwatans try to become one of the select group of *ppala*, nor do all who try succeed. Nevertheless, because of the role of seafaring within the culture, even the uninitiated possess navigation skills that would impress a Western-trained navigator.

Although Puluwat has two schools of navigation, *Warieng* and *Fanur*, which differ in some esoteric detail of mythical sea-life and terminology, the schools are identical in their practical outcome. Training in either equips a navigator with an immense store of practical information and spatial problem-solving strategies. The system is complex, efficient (the last deaths, five, occurred in a 1945 typhoon), rational, and, in all major respects, non-Western in principle and organization. It enables the Puluwatans to undertake long journeys with a complete and justified self-confidence. They literally stake their lives on the accuracy of this art of navigation, although such an observation would be meaningless to them. In their eyes, the ocean is a safe highway, which *connects*, not separates, the islands. It is not an amorphous mass of water, but a well-known, mentally charted landscape that can be crossed with safety.

Why do they continue to make these voyages? There is no simple answer to this question. Above all, there are no rational, economic reasons for the voyages. The necessary interisland trade and administration is accomplished by intermittent visits from ships run by the island trading companies, which bring essential supplies and export copra, the main product of Puluwat. Although trade in goods, ideas, and marriage partners was a major reason in earlier periods, as were interisland raids, warfare, and conquest, the current rationale for the voyages stems from the central role of seafaring in the Puluwatan cultural heritage. Surprising as it may seem, the canoes and sailing are more important to the people of Puluwat than the automobile is to the average American:

> We say the automobile has become a part of our way of life and we do not want to give it up. If this be so, on Puluwat the sailing canoe is not merely a part of their way of life, it is the very heart of it. To suggest that the Puluwatans should beach their canoes and retire their navigators would be to foretell disaster.
>
> (Gladwin, 1970, p. 36)

Accentuating this role is a sense of adventure and curiosity, which impels the Puluwatans to take to sea. Sometimes the impetus for a voyage is trivial: trips to Satawal (135 miles) or to Truk (130 miles) just to get a particular brand of tobacco (Gladwin, 1970, p. 37). Puluwatan crews even start trips to Pikelot (100 miles) when they are drunk (Gladwin, 1970, p. 43). Lest these last two reasons should make sailing seem frivolous and the sailors irresponsible, we must stress that sailing is central to their way of life. It is an activity that underlies social structures (extra family units are organized around canoe houses), life styles, mythology, personal ambitions (everyone goes on at least one voyage in his lifetime), prestige, and, above all else, self-respect. Voyages are never undertaken recklessly (despite the occasional drunken forays to Pikelot). The Puluwatans know and understand the sea around them; they also respect it. It is this respectful knowledge that is essential for interisland voyages, and we must try to link knowledge and cognitive mapping. How do the Puluwatans find their way in the Pacific?

In essence, the navigation problem can be stated simply. The navigator must guide a sailing canoe over many miles for several days to an island objective, which is sometimes no more than 500 yards in width. This spatial problem must be solved without the aid of a magnetic compass, chart, sextant, chronometer, and signposts (as we know them). The only information comes from the memory of the navigator and from the spatial environment surrounding him. In explaining this problem solving, we will use some distinctions and concepts introduced in our discussion of wayfinding in Chapter 4. We will commence with the linked problems of choosing a route and keeping on the right track. The second stage of the navigation process depends on discovering the objective.

CHOOSING A ROUTE AND KEEPING ON THE RIGHT TRACK

The key to Puluwatan navigation is the concept of a *star course*. The Puluwatans use selected stars, which are low and near the horizon of the night sky, to maintain direction at sea. The stars are chosen for their position, not their magnitude, and are mentally organized into a star (or sideral) compass (see Figure 5.2). There are 32 star positions, based on the rising and setting positions of 16 stars. Unlike the Western compass, these star positions are irregularly distributed around the circumference of the compass. One disputed explanation of the relative clustering of east-west star positions argues that they reflect the greater need for sailing directions in the predominantly east-west orientation of the island groups. Altair, the Big Bird, is the cardinal point of the compass. However, except for teaching models used on land, the compass has no physical existence; it is purely a mental reference framework.

The star course is a memorized list of steering directions, which connect a pair of islands. (It is a sequential route map, which provides a

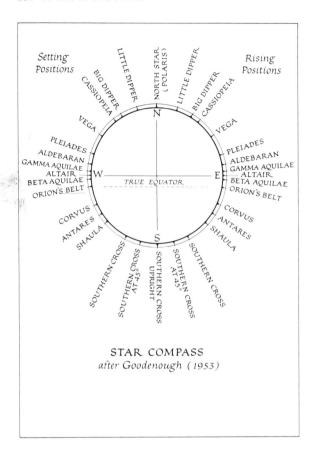

STAR COMPASS
after Goodenough (1953)

Figure 5.2. Star compass (see text).

process description of the location of the destination.) The island that is the destination of the voyage is said to lie under a particular star in the star compass. This star serves as both the initial heading to be followed and the name to describe that course. However, during the night, the stars move up and across the sky from east to west. Consequently, the initial star is only useful for direction maintenance when it is low in the sky. After a while it is replaced by another rising (or setting) star, which also serves for a limited period of time. A series is established for a single night's sailing, a series that may be up to ten stars in length. Not only are these series memorized, but so are alternative star courses, which take into account the time of the year, since weather, currents, and the visibility of stars vary throughout the year. Even in an obscured sky, a single glimpse of a star is sufficient for the navigator to keep on the right track. The navigators know the sky and they steer by the "shape of the sky" and not towards a single point of light. They work from a representation of the overall star pattern as it relates to the rigging of the canoe and to the direction of the destination.

The memorized star courses serve as a reservoir of prepackaged plans for solving spatial problems. Part of the arduous learning process involves memorizing star courses between all pairs of islands that are commonly visited. In this way, the navigator constructs a spatial route map of the area, and the system as a whole achieves generality and flexibility through built-in knowledge:

> ... the sideral compass and related systems ... are flexible concepts that allow for the mental recording of a great deal of information in an easily applicable form. Nevertheless, the volume of information a navigator still has to memorize is formidable.
>
> (Lewis, 1972, p. 69)

The memorization task is eased somewhat by the use of myth. The Puluwatans have interwoven myths and stories with the star courses. Stars take on the roles of people and animals. Objects and events are built into the structure of the star course. In this way, Puluwatan cosmography is preserved in a functional system of knowledge that is part of their everyday life.

Although steering by the stars forms the heart of the Puluwatan navigation system, the memorized star courses are "mental coathangers" for additional information, which allows other spatial cues to assist in wayfinding. During the day, the sun is used to maintain approximate direction, although it is not as accurate a guide as the stars in the night sky. Two other sources of information reinforce and back up the sun or star course. The effect of the ocean swell systems on the motion of the canoe is vital. The sensation is one of feel, not sight. The Puluwatan tries to disentangle the cumulative effects of three swell systems, one each from the north, east, and south, to indicate the canoe's heading through the water. Lewis (1971a, p. 86) shows how navigators from another area of the Pacific select different swells as cues:

> It follows that every island navigator must select those swells that he considers most significant and reliable, and though there are patterns that are generally recognized throughout each navigational area, there can also be a personal element in this selectivity. In the Gilberts, for instance, it was certainly not due to confusion and ignorance that Iotiebata described the most important swell as coming from the east, while the equally accomplished Abera drew a diagram that showed it to come from the south and Rewi asserted that the main swell was easterly but with a less prominent southerly component.

As a final check on direction, the wind can be used, but this is the least accurate and least desirable source of information.

The Puluwatan navigation system has built-in redundancy; there are backup systems that can both check the sense of direction and can be used in their own right, if necessary. Not only do they improve the efficiency of the system as a whole, but they also provide a measure of safety. The system is designed to cope with as many contingencies as possible. For example, there is a procedure for coping with such emergencies as gales, which may blow for days and obliterate all of the wayfinding systems that we have discussed. Because of the manner in which the canoe drifts, outrigger downwind, and the counter-clockwise nature of storm circulation systems, the navigator makes the reasonable assumption that he is located where he was when the storm began. He calculates where the nearest land or "landmark" (which may be a submerged reef) ought to be, and sails towards it. The low death rate attests to the success of this procedure. Wherever possible, the navigator is provided with a solution to the wayfinding problem.

All of these bits of locational information—stars, sun, swells, and wind—are continuously *integrated* by the navigator to maintain a cognitive representation of his position at sea. This integration forms the basis of a *dead reckoning* system for establishing location (or orientation) and direction. Dead reckoning—dead being a corruption of the abbreviation for deduced (Oatley, 1974, p. 864)—uses estimates of the distance covered and the course made good in order to maintain an idea of the canoe's location. (The course made good expresses the course ac-

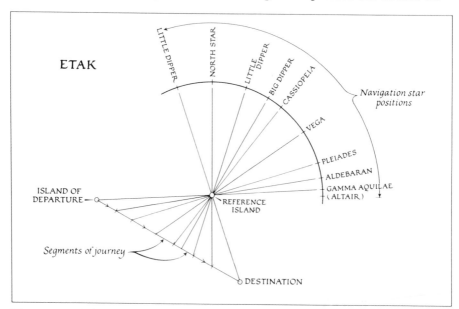

Figure 5.3. *Etak:* a Puluwatan framework for integrating navigational knowledge.

tually travelled by the canoe as compared with the course steered. These differ as the result of three cumulative effects: ocean currents, leeway, and gale drift.) As the name suggests, dead reckoning has one major flaw. A sense of position must be maintained continuously; otherwise the canoe is lost.

In order to integrate the wayfinding information and to visualize position, the Puluwatans have developed a system of thinking called *etak* (see Figure 5.3). The essence of this complex system is best expressed in the words of the two Westerners most familiar with its operation:

> A voyage is conceived of as being divided into stages or segments with reference to an island lying away to one side of the course. The canoe is regarded as being stationary and the islands mobile. Thus the destination "moves" nearer to the vessel and the reference (*etak*) island "moves" back from beneath one star point to the next. Each star point the reference island "moves" corresponds to the completion of one *etak* stage of the journey . . . this is a purely mental concept that allows the navigator to visualize his position; the islanders are, of course, perfectly aware that the islands do, in fact, remain stationary.
>
> (Lewis, 1971b, p. 445)

> . . . the contribution of etak is not to generate new primary information, but to provide a framework into which the navigator's knowledge of rate, time, geography, and astronomy can be integrated to provide a conveniently expressed and comprehended statement of distance travelled. It also helps keep his attention focused on these key variables which are central to the entire navigation process. It is a useful and deliberate logical tool for bringing together raw information and converting it into the solution of an essential navigational question: "How far away is our destination?"
>
> (Gladwin, 1970, p. 186)

Etak offers us a glimpse into the ongoing process of cognitive mapping as it is engaged in spatial problem solving. The system builds a cognitive representation that allows the navigator to monitor the canoe's progress along the chosen star course. Etak stages provide a language for expressing the distance travelled.

THE DISCOVERY OF THE OBJECTIVE

In developing strategies for discovering the objective and making a successful landfall, the Puluwatans rely on the inferential powers of cognitive mapping. They seek out a wide range of circumstantial evidence as early warning indicators of the presence of land. Five types of information may suggest both the presence and, more importantly, the direction of land while it is beyond the visual range of the canoe. (Most land is visible from sea level for up to 10 miles.) Used either separately or more effectively in combination, birds, clouds, swell patterns, phosphorescence, and deep reefs extend this range in a cognitive sense. Lewis refers to this process of extension as the idea of the *expanded target* while the Puluwatans view these expanded targets as a "screen to catch the canoe." The ability to expand the target is fundamental to the success of the Puluwatan art of navigation. There is a basic trade-off between the size of the target and the level of navigational accuracy that the navigator must maintain. The larger the target, the less the demands on the navigator in terms of steering an accurate course. Over very long voyages the demands for accuracy may be impossible to meet and so the navigator adopts an alternative strategy. He steers for a large target that is near the destination, and on arrival, makes a short voyage to the actual destination. This is another instance of the built-in safety features of Puluwatan navigation.

To expand the target, the crew of the canoe are on the lookout for specific bits of information. Land-based birds are valuable indicators that signal the direction of land during their early morning flight out to fishing grounds and on their return in the evening. Since species forage over different spatial ranges, they also provide an estimate of the maximum distance of land from the canoe: terns up to 20 miles from land, noddies 25 miles, boobies 30 miles, and frigate-birds 75 miles. The shape of cloud formations and cloud color (because of reflections from the land surface and the lagoons) indicate the location of land. A pale shimmering column—the loom of land—is caused by the sand and the lagoon reflecting the tropical sun glare. The swell patterns, which are used for keeping on the right track, are reflected and refracted by land barriers. One of the arts of the navigator is in reading these reflected and refracted swell patterns. Islands produce characteristic patterns, which can be recognized by the navigator and can be used to suggest his position relative to the land. As a teaching device for use on land, the older navigators build *mattang*: theoretical models made out of coconut palms, which show the expected wave deformation patterns (Gatty, 1958, pp. 165–166). Phosphorescence is unexplained underwater "lightning," which alledgedly points to the direction of land and which can be seen about 50 miles out from the island itself. Many parts of the ocean contain submerged coral reefs, which affect both water color and wave patterns. These reef signs are used as signals for the location of land and as landmarks for keeping on the right track.

The navigators piece together these signs to suggest the location of the destination:

> When the ship had eventually been snugged down for the night Hippour
> proceeded to explain his deductions about our position. The birds had

flown towards the Southern Cross angled 45° sinking, the bearing called *Majemeledo* (190°), so Pikelot must lie in that direction. It was between 10 and 20 miles off; if it had been less than 10 we should have seen it; if more than 20 there would have been few birds or none. The large size of the flocks suggested that the islet was nearer 10 than 20 miles away.

(Lewis, 1972, p. 222)

In place of direct perceptual cues from the objective itself, the navigator uses a cognitive inferential process. He reads the spatial environment, and interprets the information in the light of preexisting cognitive representations. Again we have an instance of using the past, in the present, to solve the future; in this case, the range at which the objective can be discovered is expanded.

SUMMARY

The complex system of Puluwatan navigation is but lightly sketched in our discussion. Some of the details of the art have been lost due to the decline in the number of voyages undertaken. Much of it is impossible to describe because it operates in terms and concepts that are alien to Western styles of thinking (e.g., the logic of the *etak* system for dead reckoning). Some parts are deliberately hidden since they constitute a secret cultural heritage, which can be known only by the initiated navigators (e.g., some of the myths associated with the star courses). Unfortunately, other parts are being contaminated and destroyed by the infiltration of Western technology and navigational techniques, especially by the magnetic compass and sailing charts.

Nevertheless, we can see the practical workings of cognitive mapping in a context where there is an ultimate test of effectiveness: survival at sea. Even this light sketch of Puluwatan navigation conveys a sense of the impressive skills and achievements of the *ppalu*. They inherit and pass on a body of navigational theory that is effective, accurate, full of built-in checks and safety devices, and designed to solve all conceivable wayfinding problems. Part of the strength of the system depends on it being tailor-made to the particular environment. The Puluwatans have learned to read and to understand a section of the Pacific Ocean. This strength is also a limitation of the system: given its use of specific sky and sea features, the system will only work in the specific locality. Only the fundamental principles can be generalized to apply to another area. An extension of the system would demand the rote memorization of a mass of new star courses and environmental information. Despite this reservation, if you need reassurance that cognitive mapping is more than just another academic abstraction, then the navigators of Puluwat present eloquent testimony. Cognitive mapping lives, and it works.

TWO VIEWS OF BOSTON

Boston through academic eyes

The city is both liberal and reactionary at the same time and not one to fit into a convenient descriptive phrase. European visitors often prefer Boston to any other United States city.

Pan Am's Boston and Cambridge City Map, published for
foreign visitors to the U.S.A. by Pan American World Airways

Today, the remark that "American cities have no character" is so widespread and commonplace that it counts as a cliché. But even the perpetrators of this cliché agree that there are a few exceptions that stand out from the backdrop of urban monotony — cities such as San Francisco and New Orleans, which they view as atypical and as worthy of special note and mention. For many people, the city of Boston is the first among these exceptions, a distinction that is one reason for our choice of Boston as an exemplar of the many facets of cognitive mapping discussed in the preceding chapters.

The other reason is the extensive work done on cognitive mapping in Boston by a variety of investigators from a variety of disciplinary backgrounds. As one indicant of this focus on Boston, over half the issues of *Environment and Behavior* published in the five years ending in 1973 contained articles on research in Boston. Whether this reflects a great general interest in Boston's problems and prospects, the inherent suitability of the site for research into cognitive mapping, or a disproportionately large number of researchers living in Boston, we do not know. What comes down to us is a mass of data and ideas concerning the character of a unique American city.

Boston was not the birth place of environmental cognitive mapping. The honor probably belongs to that other Cambridge in England, and to the 1954 doctoral dissertation of a British psychologist, Terence Lee (see Lee, 1963–1964), or even perhaps to much earlier work in geography and psychology (Binet, 1894; Claparède, 1903; Gulliver, 1908; Trowbridge, 1913). But Boston was the principal site for Kevin Lynch's (1960) influential study of urban imagery, still the most cited and widely read work on cognitive mapping. For many of us, this is where it all began, and we will always see Boston through Lynch's sketches and marginal drawings. *The Image of the City* is now so well known that even a brief review is probably superfluous. Suffice it to say that Lynch obtained sketch maps of Central Boston, verbal descriptions of parts of the city, and other survey responses from 30 respondents. With these he constructed a set of aggregate "image maps," using the five element classes: landmarks, paths, districts, nodes, and edges (see Figure 5.4). He identified those elements of Boston recognized by few or many inhabitants, and used his results to characterize "imageable" and

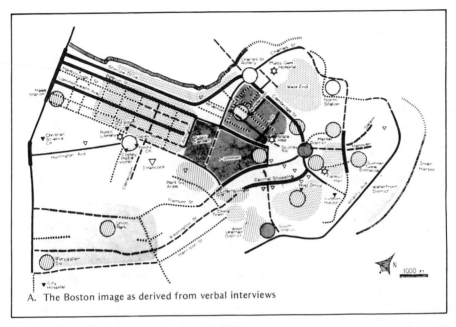

A. The Boston image as derived from verbal interviews

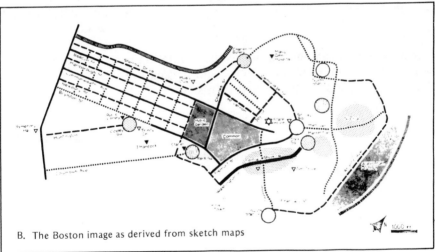

B. The Boston image as derived from sketch maps

Figure 5.4. Composite images of Boston derived from verbal interviews (above) and from sketch maps (below).

"legible" cities. Given his concern with physical design, the interpretations of imageability and legibility were largely based upon the relative *visual* potencies of the elements identified.

Appleyard, Lynch, and Myer (1964) built on Lynch's earlier work in developing a notational language system to communicate what people saw (and remembered) on repeated trips along expressways in Boston and three other major cities. Such trips are a central unit of experience in constructing a general representation of the whatness and whereness of a city, and Appleyard, Lynch, and Myer made recommendations for the provision of appropriate visual stimulation along a proposed expressway.

Other investigators have questioned whether visual potency per se is the only contributor to urban imagery. Carr and Kurilko (1964) used an eye-movement camera and a film simulation of an expressway trip into Boston to develop hypotheses concerning ". . . the way in which people achieve, organize, and transform these sequential perceptions in forming a representation of such an experience" (Carr and Schissler, 1969, p. 9). Carr and Schissler adapted a similar technique for field use, recording eye movements and memory (the latter via free recall, graphic recall, and detailed description) for trips along Boston's Northeast and Southeast Expressways. They concluded

> . . . both perception and memory of the city as seen from a highway seem to be determined by the form of the environment itself. Whether analyzed in terms of eye fixations, head orientation, or the number of mentions in memory reports, it is clear that it is the structure of what is out there to be seen which largely determines what *is* seen by a diversity of subjects.
>
> (Carr and Schissler, 1969, pp. 31–32)

Nevertheless, once a person leaves the insulating cocoon of a car, other sensory inputs do contribute to a cognitive map of Boston. As Michael Southworth (1969, p. 49) argued in his study of the sonic environment of Boston:

> Today's city dweller is bombarded by a continuous stream of invisible but highly attention-demanding sounds, smells, and micro-climates. His experience of the city is a crazy quilt of sense impressions, each of which contributes to the total picture.

The contribution of sound to the total picture made

> . . . city experience more intense by building up contrasts and by increasing sense of involvement and of the flow and rhythm of events, particularly if the sounds related to the scenes, and if the scenes were animated. Settings were more dominant when the sounds correlated with activity that was visible and spatial form that had identity.
>
> (Southworth, 1969, pp. 64–65)

Carl Steinitz (1968) had previously shown that the meaning of certain parts of Boston depended on the person's ability to perceive congruence between visual form and activity patterns.

In the foregoing studies, Appleyard, Carr, and their co-workers have been primarily concerned with the cognitive effects of the passing scene on the highway traveller's representation of the city. Reversing the perspective, others have been involved in the permanent effects of Boston's highways upon the city and its residents. As a popular protest slogan pointed out, "Cambridge is a City, Not a Highway" (Goodman, 1971, p. 18). Lamartine Street, for example, in Boston's Jamaica Plain area (ironically known as Ground Zero of the Federal Interstate Highway Program) consists mostly of white Catholics

> ... who make up the bulk of Boston's population. Ask them where they live, and they'll as likely tell you the parish before the name of the street. And if you're not familiar with the parish, they'll think it strange. You'll call their neighborhood parochial, and some will call it colorful. Whatever you call it, those who plan, design, and construct America's highways call it a rite-of-way.
>
> (Lupo, Colcord, and Fowler, 1971, p. 9)

Protest and social commentary have made us aware of those people who are in the path of a rite-of-way and who are forcibly displaced from their homes. Fellman and Brandt (1970, 1971) remind us about another group of residents whose lives are disturbed by highway construction, the "survivors":

> In a higher-status area, the survivors are those living directly adjacent to a newly built expressway, who may receive some financial compensation for the inconvenience of the traffic, with its accompanying noise, fumes, and vibrations. In a working-class area like Brookline-Elm, however, the survivors include the people on adjoining streets and blocks whose friends and relatives had to move away or whose work places, businesses, churches, and other community facilities were destroyed by construction of the road. . . .
>
> (Fellman and Brandt, 1970, p. 297)

> Herbert Gans (1962), in his study of Boston's West End, called people like those studied here "urban villagers," a highly appropriate term. For, like rural villagers, they are tied to their locations by friends and family, work and recreation, background and general life style.
>
> (Fellman and Brandt, 1970, p. 298)

The human extent of the "ties to location" referred to by Fellman and Brandt has been fully realized only since the early 1960s. Again, studies of Boston played a prime role in that realization. Previously, it had been assumed by most planners that urban renewal and its stepchild urban rehabilitation were universal goods, that social benefits would always accrue to the former residents of the slums and physical benefits to the city as a whole. This conventional (and convenient) wisdom was challenged by Herbert Gans (1962), and by Jane Jacobs (1961) in her book, *The Death and Life of Great American Cities*. Walter Firey (1947) had previously analyzed the meaning of Beacon Hill, a district with a resident aristocracy who saw an intertwining of family inheritance, tradition, and class pride with their houses and streets. Gans, Jacobs, and others saw that this same *sense of place*, of spatial identity, was felt by the displaced victims of highway expansion. In a pair of landmark articles concerned with Boston's West End, Fried and Gleicher (1961, 1963) identified several dimensions of residential "belonging":

> ... For more than half the people, their West End homes formed a ... central feature of their total life space ... the West End occupied a unique status, beyond any of the specific attributes one could list and point to concretely. This sense of uniqueness, of home, was not simply a function of social relationships, for *the place in itself* was the object of strong positive feelings.
>
> (Fried and Gleicher, 1961, p. 308, italics added)

The extent of this locational attachment was so strong that many residents forced by renewal to leave the West End responded with grief akin only to the sort one feels at the death of a loved one. A sense of place provides a sense of security, which blends together past and future.

The blend of past and present, of death and life, is of great significance in Boston, and the historic *symbols* of death are part of the cognitive maps of Bostonians. The Japanese refuse to acknowledge the presence of one monumental tomb (see Chapter 3); Bostonians revere their cemeteries almost as much as other historic landmarks:

> ... the colonial burying-grounds of Boston have become invested with a moral significance which renders them almost inviolable. Not only is there the usual sanctity which attaches to all cemeteries, but in those of Boston there is an added sacredness growing out of the age of the grounds and the fact that the forebears of many of New England's distinguished families as well as a number of colonial and Revolutionary leaders lie buried in these cemeteries. There is thus a manifold symbolism to these old burying grounds, pertaining to family lineage, early nationhood, civic origins, and the like, all of which have strong sentimental associations.
>
> (Firey, 1945, pp. 145–146)

Each of these academic studies examines one aspect of the flavor of Boston. Put together, they give some idea of the city's uniqueness, and of its commonality with other cities as well. Some of what they say, and much of what they do not say, is reflected in the experience of one of the authors, who lived in Boston for three years, and from which many of the following comments have been drawn.

BOSTON THROUGH AN INHABITANT'S EYES

Boston is like all other cities and yet unlike any other city. It has rich, middle class, and poor areas; mushrooming suburbs; problems of inner-city decay and urban renewal; traffic and transit problems; racial conflict; crime; violence and more salutary forms of excitement; waterways; freeways; and tollways—in short, it has what other American cities have. But other aspects of its physical and social morphology are distinctive. Physically, it has more in common with the cities of the Old World than with many of the New. Its irregular, winding, narrow streets are more like those of an English town than of most major cities in North America. Ironically, New England was originally called New England because of the origin of most of its *people*; after generations of extensive polyglot immigration, it still deserves the name because of its *physical* appearance. But its present image is richer than this. Boston is renowned as the center of higher education. It matters not that its most famous institution is actually in Cambridge, or whether it really has more institutions of higher education or more students enrolled in these institutions than any other American city of comparable size; people regard Boston as the pinnacle of higher learning (see Figure 5.5). Boston is famed as a center of history. What other city typifies the Puritan America of the seventeenth century? It is famed as a medical center and as a fountain of architectural innovation.

Boston is "down East" from the once distant but now (by rail and air) neighboring cities of the old South and Southwest: Newport, New Haven, New York, Baltimore, and Washington. The phrase "down East" has always been confusing, since on a typical cartographic map, Boston is "up" in relation to the cities mentioned. But "down East" is a nautical term, employed by mariners of the last century, who leisurely sailed *down*wind from more southerly points on the Atlantic Seaboard to Boston and more northerly ports beyond.

Examined in detail, Boston reveals additional distinctive features, and even more strange paradoxes. As a problem in navigation, for example, it is fascinating. Approaching Boston from a distance, especially from the south, a stranger is prone to wonder if New England's isolationism (another stereotype) is responsible for apparent attempts to confuse the traveller, to prevent him or her from reaching the goal at all (see Figure 2.6). We know that concepts of near and far distances vary greatly from one part of the United States to another, with the shortest concepts of far perhaps being those of New Englanders. The horse and carriage of colonial times could not travel many miles in a single day,

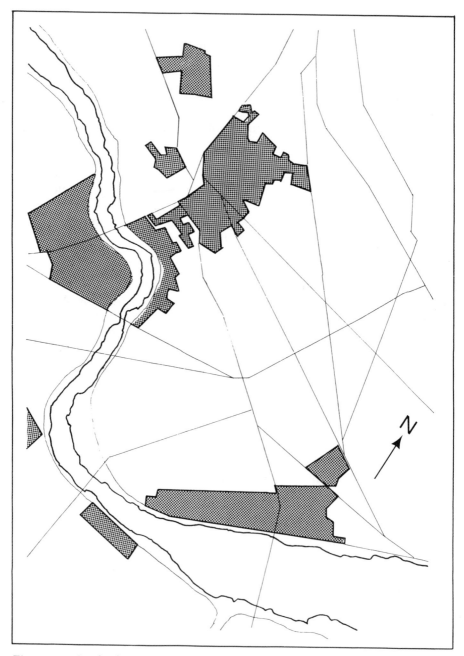

Figure 5.5. Cambridge, Massachusetts, north of the Charles River, and its in-
    stitutions of higher learning (shaded areas).

and signs announcing approaches to major cities, even today, often do
not appear until one is less than ten miles away. One Pakistani planner
suggested a few years ago, half in jest, that New England's Puritan past

is reflected in the construction of its present-day expressways and interstate highways. He explained the design principles in terms of Puritanical concepts of virtue and sin. You are *supposed* to know where you are: that is virtue. Not knowing where you are is a sin. Sin is to be punished. Hence, interchanges on interstate highways are placed as far apart as possible, in case one misses one's exit. Signs indicating exits are placed as close to the exits as possible, or even beyond them, and so on. To make matters worse, the countryside surrounding Boston is just rolling enough to conceal most of the central city from view until one is literally on top of it. All but one of Boston's hills were leveled in the nineteenth century to provide land fill, the only remaining prominent one being aristocratic Beacon Hill. But even Beacon Hill is not visible from afar, and neither is the old downtown adjacent to it. Moreover, Beacon Hill is no longer the highest point in Boston. What *is* visible to the traveller is a *new* center, now marked by the Prudential Tower near one end and the new but ill-fated John Hancock Building at the other. Some architects have damned the Prudential Tower for its lack of aesthetic appeal. Be this as it may, the Tower does perform one vital function: It tells the traveller where Boston is. And the man-made "Pru" is higher than nature's Beacon Hill.

The Prudential Center is a mile or so from Boston's traditional center, but once at the Pru, you are well into the "funnel." Boston's shape is much like a funnel in cross-section, bounded by the Charles River and Boston Inner Harbor. "Inbound," as used on the transit system, means towards the apex of the funnel (downtown), while "outbound" is towards its mouth. Compare this cognitive structure with "uptown" and "downtown" in Manhattan, "North Shore" and "South Shore" in Chicago, and "Left Bank" and "Right Bank" in Paris as a model for aiding the wayfinding process. The funnel and the areas surrounding it are laced with streets that go "every which way." Traditional compass coordinates are worse than useless as direction-giving devices. For those arriving from gridiron cities in the Midwest, getting around in Boston and New England can be a problem. In Chicago, one is told to "turn right"; in Boston, where few streets meet at right angles, you have to "bear right." The New Englander's remarkable sense of history complicates the wayfinding problem still further. Directions are often given in terms of names known only to locals and in terms of landmarks that have long since disappeared from the face of the earth, if not from the locals' cognitive maps. "Go straight along the street, bear right where the old fire house used to be, then proceed uphill." The straight may be a slow curve. This "uphill," in a gently varying landscape, may be all but imperceptible to visitors from more mountainous terrain. Equally puzzling is the Bostonian concept of a square. In many cities, a square is a plaza; in Philadelphia, it is a city block; in Boston, it is often a street intersection, the site of a memorial to a fallen hero in one or another World War. In most cities, street intersections are indicated by the names of the intersecting streets, which generally appear on crossed signs. One sign is a guide to direction change, indicating the consequences of such a change. The other provides reassuring feedback, telling the traveller which street he is on. Signposts in Boston generally contain *only* the first category of sign; once you have begun to travel on a street, you cannot find what street you are on! Squares provide an added bit of reassuring information on occasion.

The orientation problem extends to public transportation as well. New York's subway follows the surface street pattern; Boston's MTA does not, thus resembling London's Underground or the Paris Metro. The station names are street names in New York, place names (and hence orientation points) in London and Paris, but a confusing combination of the two in Boston. Thus, Boston has three essentially independent systems of communications, which meet at selected points: surface streets, expressways, and the MTA. In this sense, as in many others, Boston "is not a tree" (Alexander, 1965).

The irregularity of Boston's man-made morphology is deceptive in yet another way. Its street pattern is not the simple grid characteristic of Manhattan, nor the complex (and shifting) grid of Los Angeles, nor the radial system of Paris, nor even the awkward radial-and-grid combination displayed by Washington and Mexico City. Yet, it is not completely amorphous either, displaying considerably more regularity than the typical English town. But no single rule system, no simple set of orientational plans will enable the stranger to get around. Several residents of eastern Massachusetts have commented upon the relative difficulties of moving about New England cities. It is easier to get around the more irregular cities such as nearby Worcester, they contend, because one makes no assumption about regularities of shape, facing each navigational situation as a unique problem. Boston, they claim, is just predictable enough in certain limited areas that it lures the unwary traveller into making rash assumptions about other areas, often to his eventual discomfort, dismay, and even severe annoyance.

A case in point is the Boston Common. As Figure 5.6 indicates, the Common is a five-sided figure, an irregular pentagon. The nature of its irregularity is such that it contains one 90° turn and several near-90° turns (the latter allowed by the gentle curves on the bordering streets). Therefore, many people who walk around it for the first time cognize the Boston Common as a simple structure, either a square or a rectangle. A person operating under this belief and starting his or her circuit of the Common at the intersection of Boylston and Tremont Streets will, after making three turns at the corners, be surprised to find himself many blocks from his starting point. Starting at Beacon and Park yields similar disconcerting results, while beginning at Beacon and Charles yields the most disorienting result of all: finishing one's four-sided "rectangular" tour at the opposite side of the park from the point at which one began.

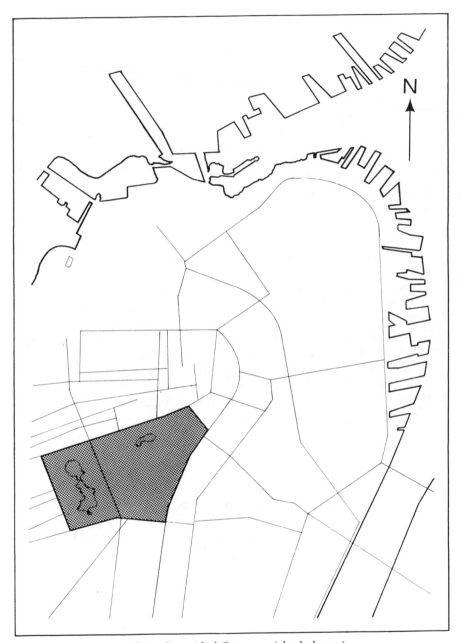

Figure 5.6. Boston, with its five-sided Common (shaded area).

If compass directions can be useless, or even misleading, in giving directions or describing how one gets about Boston, they have also be- guiled those who named the districts of the city. Among the names, one finds the North End, the South End, the West End, East Boston, and South Boston. If we take the Boston Common as the traditional center of the city, we find that East Boston is not really east, nor South Boston really south, but no matter. What *is* important is that each area has, over time, acquired its own flavor, its own set of distinctive attributes. Five districts—the North End, South End, Back Bay, Beacon Hill, and Roxbury—illustrate this objective and subjective distinctiveness, both in the physical form of the area and in the characteristics of the inhabitants. How different the cognitions of various groups can be is well illustrated by a study of nearby Worcester. Here, verbal and graphic cognitive maps were obtained from residents of adjacent Italian and Black ghettos, areas between which considerable hostility had existed for some time. The Black's map of the Italian ghetto bore almost no resemblance to the Italian's map of the Italian ghetto, and vice versa. Each group attributed nearly identical negative qualities to the neighboring area.

Unlike Mexico City's *colonias*, the boundaries of which are so clear that colonia names can be used interchangeably with postal zone numbers for addressing mail, the boundaries of Boston's districts are fuzzy, with many transition areas the precise spatial identity of which are unknown (see Figure 5.7). The *Back Bay*, a thoroughly planned area of Boston laid out during the nineteenth century by filling in part of the Charles River, is an exception. It is distinguished by a strict rectilinear grid system, with its north-south street names arranged in alphabetical order from east to west. To many people, Back Bay contains no outstanding landmarks; its cognized attributes are global ones such as neatness and affluence. It is bounded by commercial areas and con-

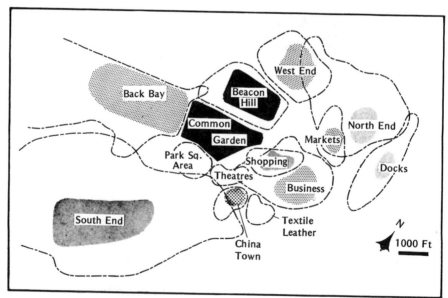

Figure 5.7. Cognized boundaries, 2: various Boston districts.

sequently, has only a few, rather small shops in its interior. The architectural control of the nineteenth century has led to the elegant and homogeneous row houses of today. It is judged a pretty area, not overly interesting to the architecturally uninvolved; its action, if there is any, is on the periphery. Because it is judged safe, people who have the means and who want a city dwelling are advised to choose the Back Bay. It has a lovely view of the Charles River from the highest rent apartments, few distinctive smells, and almost no subway noise (the MTA runs underground in the Back Bay).

Across the Common is *Beacon Hill*, bearing some physical resemblance to its upstart neighbor. This is the archetypal Boston. It is what most strangers think of when they think of Boston; it is the prime source of the charm that foreign visitors find in the city. It is the symbol of Boston. The architectural homogeneity of the row house is present on some streets, but the narrow streets themselves, many quaintly cobbled, are in strong contrast to the broad avenues of its neighboring district. It has its distinctive landmarks, such as world-famous Louisburg Square and the golden dome of the State House. The lively commercial area along Charles Street, which cuts through the west side of "The Hill," acts as a linear node, Students like it; that, combined with some drug traffic during the 1960s, has caused Beacon Hill to be judged less safe but more interesting and exciting than the Back Bay. The action is there or nearby, and pleasant smells along Charles Street are occasionally complemented by music coming out of open windows in clement weather.

As you recross the Back Bay through a transition area on your way to the *South End*, the music is even more evident if your path passes between the Conservatory of Music and Symphony Hall. The street names take advantage of an unusual opportunity, and the corner of Symphony Road and Opera Place is a highly desired location for people in certain occupational groups. Unlike Back Bay and Beacon Hill, the area has a mixture of groups, principally Anglos, Spanish-speaking peoples from the Caribbean, and Blacks. Several more ethnic and linguistic groups are stirred into the mixture by the time one reaches the South End. It seems probable that the South End was the prototype for the Back Bay: Its streets and midnineteenth-century row houses display order and homogeneity. But the architectural homogeneity is not matched by a homogeneous population. The area centering about Union Square (once as fashionable as Louisburg Square is now) until recently housed one of the most varied populations of any contiguous area in any American city. At one time, it was possible to walk around a single block and hear a half-dozen or more languages spoken, none of them English. It was a district of shops and shopkeepers; of political activism; of Greeks, Syrians, Lebanese, Chinese, Japanese, Africans, and Caribbeans of all hues and many languages. Its underground newspaper in the late

1960s was published in a single trilingual format—in English, Spanish, and Chinese.

Union Park was opened once a year for the annual multinational street fair. Black Muslims and Black Panthers vied with each other for poster space on the brick walls. People's parks and people's art (such as three-story-high murals on blank building walls) were everywhere. On hot summer nights, musical groups arrived on a street in large trucks, and within minutes a street dance would grow. It was "unsafe," of course, but the action was everywhere. Visual stimuli were all around and judgments of prettiness or ugliness seemed irrelevant (and perhaps irreverent). Smells abounded, and the elevated MTA made certain that things would never be *too* quiet.

The South End has been rediscovered by the affluent, for whose rental the old buildings have been bought up and renovated. Minority groups cannot afford the new rents. Much of the people's art and many of the people's parks are gone. Perhaps it will soon be judged safe and pretty; it will probably be quieter, but the nodal meeting point of Boston's many nationalities will be gone forever from cognitive maps of the city.

At its southwestern extreme, the South End fades into *Roxbury*, Boston's largest Black ghetto. Travelling to the southeast and crossing the estuary known as the "Inner Harbor" brings one into *South Boston*, in large part an Irish ghetto. Cognitive maps label Roxbury unsafe because it is Black and South Boston (Southie) uninteresting because it is Irish. Tourists do not visit either place, and these districts constitute blank areas for the casual visitor or the uninvolved resident. The interests of the tourist who wants to go slumming center instead on the *North End*. This Italian ghetto is at the apex of the Boston funnel, neatly cut off, both physically and cognitively, from the rest of the peninsula by an elevated expressway, and elsewhere bounded by the waterfront. Only the Northenders, among Boston's school children, are not surprised to learn that Boston is a seaport; it is only to them that its harbor functions are visible and obvious. Tourists expect to find outstanding seafood and Italian restaurants in the North End; they usually do not expect to find many of the landmarks of colonial New England as well. For the little buildings and narrow streets are as ancient as any in New England, their landmark value only recently rediscovered by the planners whose understandable first tendency is to classify anything old that is occupied by poor people as a slum. So cognitive maps of Boston are changing. The North and South Ends are no longer slums; they have been relabeled as "historical areas of interest."

But much of historic *Cambridge* is a slum. The urge to consider Cambridge a district of Boston is almost irresistable, even though the two are separate political entities. It may stem in part from the desire to imagine the great Cantabridgian educational institutions—Harvard, Radcliffe, and the Massachusetts Institute of Technology—as part of Boston. This institutional real estate covers much of the Charles River waterfront on the Cambridge side. And Harvard Square is the most famous academic crossroad in North America, if not in the world. It is said that if a professor stands long enough on one corner or another of The Square, he will sooner or later meet everyone he has ever known or will ever need to know.

The college-town image is deceiving. Behind the waterfront university facade is a vast area inhabited largely by poor people, people whose children have little hope of entering the neighboring institutions of learning. They are the invisible inhabitants of another blank area. To them, the schools revered so much by the middle class are simply ravenous monsters waiting for opportunities to gobble up the real estate on which their homes are located. Perhaps nowhere in the Boston area are the cognitive maps of the resident and the tourist quite so discrepant.

This is one man's view of an American city (see Figure 5.8). Clearly, much has been omitted. We have said nothing, for example, about the vast difference between the winterscape and summerscape along the Charles River, or about the many bridges that cross it (the Harvard Bridge goes to M.I.T. for example). Some elements of the human scene, Jane Jacobs (1961) "street ballet," are omitted as well. The first sign of the *real* Spring is the blossoming of many sunbathing bodies, fresh from quasi-hiberna-

Figure 5.8. Mentally "looking" east along Commonwealth Avenue ("inbound"): a sketch from memory.

tion, alongside — where else? — the Charles River. Along the Charles somewhat later in Spring come the singles seeking to become doubles, each with a dog on leash. Strange people are reticent about establishing contact, but strange dogs have no such compunctions. Nowhere is this so evident as in thawing Boston. The thaw, climatic and human, extends itself, reaching even the sterile Prudential Center, and the inhabitants of the city know that the short, hot, humid Boston summer is close at hand. "We were lucky last year," a few of them say. "Spring came on Sunday."

Chapter 6

THE GENESIS OF COGNITIVE MAPPING

Two bands of apes stand facing each other. The apes bare their teeth, mouth threat noises, and gesture to their opponents. Individuals and small groups break out of the pack, advance towards the opposing band, and then retreat. This alternating, to-and-fro movement continues for a time, whereafter both sides retire. Later, one of the apes happens upon the dismembered skeleton of an animal. He seizes a particularly interesting bone, which he examines meticulously, turning it this way and that. Suddenly, he brings the bone down with force upon the remainder of the skeleton, striking it again and again until the other bones are scattered and jumbled. Later, he carries the bone into another confrontation between his band and a neighboring band of apes, striking and disabling one of the opposing apes in the ensuing threat display. He has converted a found object into a tool, and in so doing, created the first weapon.

*   *   *

A few million years later, a little girl is busily constructing two towers from wooden building blocks. One tower is considerably taller than the other, but because she has built the towers in different parts of the room, it is difficult for her to compare sizes. Being as inquisitive as small children always are, however, she wants to know just how much bigger one tower is than the other. She searches about for a tool to help her, and she decides to use her own body. After placing one of her hands at the base of the smaller structure and the other at the apex, she moves across the room, maintaining what she believes to be the same separation between her hands, until she

171

reaches the larger tower. Only later will she spontaneously seize upon a wooden dowel rod as a more objective measuring instrument, and even later make use of that graduated tool we adults term a ruler, or scale.

INTRODUCTION

The first of these vignettes will be familiar to most moviegoers; it is an excerpt from the prologue to the motion picture, *2001: A Space Odyssey*. Blending plausible hypothesis with artistic license, it is concerned with *phylogeny*, or *evolutionary development*. The second vignette is perhaps less familiar; it is a hopefully excusable condensation of an observation by the renowned developmental psychologist, Jean Piaget. It blends our academic license with an actual example of *ontogeny*, or *individual development*. These vignettes share two characteristics. First, both are examples of development. Second, both involve changes in cognition. The ape's cognition or understanding of the bone changed with its appreciation of a new and possibly needed application. If there was such a thing as a representation in the ape's brain, one would say that something had been added, another whatness attribute, which converted the bone into a functional weapon as well as an intriguing but essentially useless object. The example of the ape's response to the bone, although as exaggerated as it is clichéd, illustrates a hypothetical "aha" experience in the evolutionary development of behavior, a process that has extended over millions of generations. In the second, more realistic example, cognitive development occurs in the little girl within a small portion of just one generation.

Both of these vignettes involve cognitive development, but neither refers to cognitive *mapping* in quite the sense of the earlier chapters. However, they do suggest a series of questions that relate to our specific interests. What are the phylogenetic or evolutionary origins of cognitive mapping? (Recall the parallels drawn in Chapter 2 among the behaviors of the bees, the wasps, and the rats.) In the infant, in the infant developing into a child, and in the child developing into an adolescent, *when* (according to the Brunerian school of thought) or *at what stage* (according to the Piagetian school) does cognitive mapping appear? How is such cognitive mapping manifested? Does cognitive mapping of environments at the geographical or large scale take place before or after cognitive mapping of environments at the perceptual or small scale? *How* do we know *what* is happening *when*? What constitutes normal and abnormal development in cognitive mapping? How can one characterize mental dysfunction in terms of spatial thinking and problem solving?

The term development can be, and has been, applied both to ontogeny and to phylogeny. One view of development suggests that the unfolding sequence of ontogeny (individual development) recapitulates or mirrors the sequence of phylogeny (evolutionary development). While we do not subscribe uncritically to this view, we do hold that mobile higher organisms *develop* the capacity for cognitive mapping, that such development is *not* restricted to human beings, and that such development is a necessary prerequisite for survival in the face of the continual spatial problem-solving demands posed by life on a large-scale, two-dimensional surface. These ideas underpin the fundamental argument of this chapter. In developing this argument, we are in some respects starting from scratch and proceeding along our own road. The theoretical positions of such major developmental thinkers as Jean Piaget and Jerome Bruner are represented in the Boxes that are interspersed throughout the main body of the text. However, it is our contention that these theorists have given comparatively little attention to the problems of spatial cognition at the *geographical* or large scale. (For an alternative view, see Hart and Moore, 1973.) Our account of the development of cognitive mapping must therefore proceed along somewhat different, though by no means necessarily contradictory, lines. It would be presumptuous for us to claim that we can fully answer all of the obvious questions in a single book, let alone in a single chapter. Some answers find much support in the empirical record; others are frankly speculative. We have neither a party line nor a totally encompassing theoretical position to offer, but merely—at this stage—ideas towards the latter.

The ideas begin with an interpretation of some recent neurophysiological evidence, proceed to the evolutionary record, review studies of the childhood development of geographical learning, and finally, lead to our integrated overview of the development of cognitive mapping. The search for the physical bases of mental processes in many ways resembles the search for the intellectual philosopher's stone. We would have to agree with Howard Gardner (1975) that the gap remains enormous between most work in neurophysiology and the comprehension of our own mental ability to comprehend. Despite this sobering assessment, some recent evidence, although fragmentary and occasionally wildly speculative, is too provocative to be ignored. In particular, a currently emerging theory of brain function, which assigns two rather different forms of cognition to the two hemispheres of the brain, throws light on the nature of the spatial problem-solving process, and gives us a sense of the physical locus and functional role of the mysterious spatial ability that is the concern of this book. Following this exploratory foray, we make an even more speculative excursion into the evolutionary record. We argue that cognitive mapping, which we have presented as a general property of mobile organisms (see Chapter 2), is an evolutionary adaptive mechanism necessary for spatial survival. The third step in our argument proposes that the cognitive mechanisms and processes necessary for the development of the ability for spatial learning are acquired very early in life. This step is more securely grounded in the empirical record; here, we discuss some of our own research, which suggests the early emergence in human childhood of the ability to cognize large-scale spaces.

A final question inevitably arises at this point: What is the relationship between development, the subject of this chapter, and learning, the subject of the next? In its simplest terms, adequate, or normal, development is a necessary (but *not* sufficient) precondition for learning. In our view, cognitive development is the development of the capacity for learning. The two proceed hand-in-hand; obviously, it is not necessary for development to be *complete* before any learning can take place. A somewhat more technical distinction has been offered by Hart and Moore (1973, p. 250):

> *Learning* involves quantitative changes in the reception and retention of information or subject matter. It refers to the situation in which information is presented to the individual who changes through reacting to it and corrects initial attempts in response to indications about his prior successes. . . . On the other hand, *development* implies qualitative changes in the organization of behavior. Most often it refers to the situation where the individual changes as a function of interaction between current organization and discrepancy with the environment . . .

Thus, the newborn human can perceive a number of things, but the signals have not been sorted out or differentiated in the newly formed brain. We do not know exactly how the newborn interprets the sights, smells, and temperatures it apprehends. William James likened the child's world to a "blooming, buzzing confusion," and perhaps it is. We do know, however, that a newborn infant has a very limited repertory of motor responses: It can cry, kick out a bit, and move its arms, but it cannot walk, crawl, or even turn over. It cannot manipulate anything successfully with its hands. It is from this cognitive and behavioral baseline that we can assess the course of ontological development. Specifically, we are concerned with the maturational processes that affect a child's ability to cognitively map the spatial environment and to engage in spatial problem solving.

COGNITIVE MAPPING AND THE FUNCTIONING OF THE BRAIN

There are two different but related approaches to understanding the functioning of the brain: The more familiar is *neurophysiology*, and we will use Howard Gardner's term, *neuropsychology*, to characterize the second approach. Operating at the microscale of brain morphology, neurophysiology is concerned with the biochemical and bioelectrical functioning of the 10 billion neurons that make up the essential physical matter of our brain. To our knowledge, only Stephen Kaplan (1973) has attempted to relate cognitive mapping to neurophysiology. This surprising absence of even speculative accounts is not simply a consequence of the unbridged chasm between the understanding of physiological and psychological functioning. Of the researchers currently exploring the *terra incognita* of cognitive mapping, few are equipped with a thorough knowledge of both sides of the chasm: Kaplan is one of the few, and his work draws heavily upon the neural net hypotheses of D. O. Hebb (1949). Kaplan suggests a physiological mechanism whereby cognitive representations of the spatial environment are formed. Repeated experiences with places and objects lead to a correspondence between the essential attributes of these experiences and an assemblage of associated neurons. In Kaplan's terms, these neurons are "on," or active, when the appearance of an attribute in the immediate vicinity of the person is promptly followed by the neuron in question going "on." In this sense, the neurons are data-processing units. Associations of neurons form a representation of the place or object, reflecting its distinctive characteristics. These representations are in turn associated with many other representations to form complex neural networks. Such complex networks are the cognitive maps that underlie spatial problem solving. For example, we can interpret the wayfinding process in the light of Kaplan's mechanism: At any point along a journey, cues from the spatial environment can trigger, or activate, a set of associated neurons that allow us to identify our current location. If we are on the lookout for a crucial decision point, fewer cues are necessary to make the identification. Associated with this currently active representation are representations of other places and the alternative routes that lead to them. Thus we can choose the appropriate route, and the same mechanism will allow us to keep on the right track and to identify our objective. This provocative and plausible foray into the microlevel of neurophysiology provides us with some ideas; but, apart from this, we are forced to interpret cognitive mapping from the perspective of the neuropsychological approach to brain functioning.

Many neuropsychologists adopt a macrolevel viewpoint, seeking links between the gross morphology of the brain and the normal range of mental and behavioral abilities. The rapid advance and increasing volume of imaginative research in this burgeoning area render current accounts obsolete soon after publication. Undoubtedly this brief survey of one set of links, those between brain structure and cognitive mapping, will suffer the same fate. Nevertheless, the ideas are so important that they deserve at least an interim account. They derive from a question that would have seemed naive and essentially unanswerable only a few years ago. Why is the brain divided into two parts? Why does it have two hemispheres? Recent research indicates that the two structurally symmetrical parts of the brain reflect a fundamental functional asymmetry, with each part specializing in particular functions and modes of thinking. Of these two parts, the right hemisphere of the brain (right-brain) appears to be the principal locus of the skills and abilities that we have labelled cognitive mapping.

Before we discuss this brain structure-function link in detail, it is important to weigh the evidence on which the proposed link is based. Many of the findings are counterintuitive in that common sense relations between mental abilities are not supported by empirical evidence. Abilities that ought to go together do not, and vice versa. This causes some terminological confusion and makes interpretation difficult. The major evidence comes from some unanticipated consequences of a fairly novel and rarely performed operation in neurosurgery. The two hemispheres of the brain are linked by several bundles of transverse nerve fibers, or tracts, called commissures. The largest of these commissures, the *corpus callosum* (literally, "colossal body"), is held to be responsible for the transmission of vast quantities of information from one hemisphere to the other. A few people, however, have undergone surgical severance of the corpus callosum in order to reduce the spread of severe epileptic seizures. This operation, a step of last resort, renders the two halves of the brain more independent than they would otherwise be. Although successful in its intended purpose of controlling epilepsy, it has major and undesirable side effects, which have been an invaluable source of information on the nature of brain structure-function links. Additional supporting evidence comes from the vast literature documenting the effects of traumatic damage to specific areas of the brain. Localized lesions are accompanied by (and diagnosed by) the selective impairment or loss of basic mental and behavioral abilities. The problems of precise diagnosis are severe and the brain pathology literature is strewn with disagreements over the appropriate description of various syndromes (or presumed structure-function links). The temptation to produce "maps of the brain," which show the precise physical locations of mental and behavioral abilities, is irresistible, and we will succumb to the temptation later in this section. However, in assessing the evidence from brain pathology, we should bear in mind Howard and Templeton's (1966, p. 271) admonition:

> The clinical literature as a whole is characterized by a tendency to "symptom naming," which produces a welter of named disorders with little attempt at a theoretical or experimental analysis. The answers in this field are not simple; man's skills of geographical orientation are very complex and very idiosyncratic.

Accepting the qualified nature of the neuropsychological evidence, we can make two statements about the purpose and role of the two hemispheres. First, each hemisphere appears to dominate the control of a particular set of mental and behavioral abilities. Second, each hemisphere has its own characteristic way of storing information, handling information, and solving problems; that is, the two hemispheres have distinctive modes of "thinking." Michael Gazzaniga (1972, p. 312) provides an effective introduction to these differences in brain function and mode of thinking; after operations in which the corpus callosum is severed, it is found:

> ... The left hemisphere, because of its intact language and speech system, can fully communicate its thoughts and ideas; it seems to be normal and conscious. It is the right hemisphere's status that is both crucial and difficult to ascertain. It does not have a speech system and thus cannot tell about its experiences through speech ... (it is claimed), for example that the right hemisphere remembers faces in terms of a "gestalt" — of the actual pictorial and configuratory cues — while the left hemisphere is more analytical and tends to remember by analyzing specific features of a face. The idea here is that mind left is poet-like and mind right is the painter in us.

The basic differences in function that we are referring to here should *not* be confused with the relationship between the right-brain and the left side of the body, and that between the left-brain and the right side of the body. Thus the right-brain controls the motor functions, including vision, of the opposite, or left, side of the body: These are known as the contralateral functions. The functions of interest here are best illustrated by Figure 6.1. The left hemisphere is the locus for verbal language (which is largely responsible for its designation as the major hemisphere), difficult calculations, and the process of sequential, logical reasoning using verbal ideas. In contrast, the right, or minor, hemisphere is the locus for the appreciation of the arts, for emotion, and, of greatest importance to our argument, the spatial abilities. Included in this latter category are abilities to perceive spatial relations, to remember places and locations, to use spatial imagery, to wayfind, and to engage in geometrical thinking.

These basic differences in function correspond to differences in ways of achieving them, in modes of thinking. Bogen, Marsh, and TenHouten (1970) refer to left-brain functions as *propositional*, and right-brain functions as *appositional*. The terminology is perhaps an unfortunate choice, since it too easily allows an erroneous equation of propositional with "logical" and appositional with "nonlogical." Be this as it may, the distinction between the two modes of thinking can best be understood by the following:

> ... viewing propositional thought as reasoning through division or partition of phenomena (including time), and appositional thought as focusing

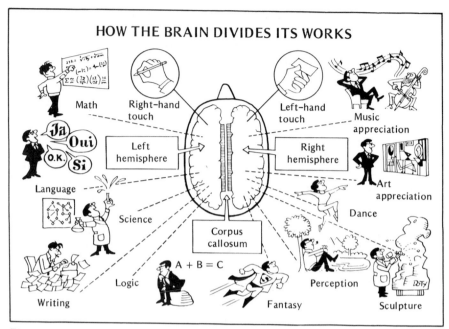

Figure 6.1. A Roy Doty cartoon illustrating the hypothesized division of cognitive functions between the left and right hemispheres of the brain.

on reasoning through integration and consideration of the totality of phenomena (including time).

(Bogen, Marsh, and TenHouten, 1970, p. 6)

The left-brain, propositional style is characterized by a focal representation, which emphasizes the analysis of details. According to Bogen,
Marsh, and TenHouten, it analyzes, orders, proves, and reasons through
fragmentation rather than through simultaneous consideration. It is particularly effective in integrating similar units of information and, as a
consequence, relates especially to such behaviors as manual skills and
speech, which require fine sensorimotor control. (For a more elaborate
discussion of many of the points in this section of the book, see Gardner (1975).) In contrast, the right-brain employs diffuse forms of representation, which are based on a process of synthesis. This permits the
integration of dissimilar units of information and allows a person to
grasp general outlines and to relate parts to wholes. The appositional
mode of thinking relates especially to behaviors demanding that the
person integrate information from diverse sources and modalities. And
nowhere are such demands greater and more pressing than in spatial
problem solving. The attempt to construct a useful cognitive map of an
area necessitates pulling together and organizing bits of information
from memory and from the surrounding environment. A sense of space

necessitates a flexible process of integration, synthesis, and unification: One product of cognitive mapping is a spatial frame of reference. We are continually forming and reforming general outlines of areas, relating the parts to various spatial wholes. As we have defined them, cognitive signatures are particular modes of appositional thinking.

Thus we can develop a sense of one set of brain structure-function links: We can apparently "localize" cognitive mapping within the right-brain. Spatial abilities are susceptible to right-brain lesions, and it has been shown that lesions in such specific areas as the parietal lobe or the angular gyrus lead to the selective impairment and loss of particular facets of spatial ability. Here, however, we are in danger of producing the poorly substantiated "maps of the brain" that we cautioned against earlier. Not only is the evidence for such maps imprecise and questionable, but the right-brain localization of cognitive mapping omits a major part of the story. As we argued in Chapters 3 and 4, a key characteristic of cognitive mapping is its flexibility: We can use a variety of cognitive signatures to solve spatial problems. Consequently, cognitive mapping is *not* exclusively concentrated in the right-brain because verbal language does play a significant role. For example, the inability to read text, known as alexia in adults (resulting from brain lesions) and as dyslexia in children (as a result of developmental reading problems), can prevent a person from reading maps and street signs. Given this handicap, wayfinding in an urban environment, in a subway, or on a freeway is thus rendered difficult. Aphasia, a speech impairment, may make it impossible for a person to describe his world using a verbal signature; nevertheless, he may be able to draw it, indicating that his wayfinding ability is not impaired.

The right-brain, left-brain roles in spatial thinking bring us back to the original question: Why is the brain divided into two highly specialized parts? Gardner (1975) reviews some provocative ideas suggested by Young (1962). These ideas *may* offer an answer to the above question, and, at the same time, give us some insights into the evolutionary development of cognitive mapping (a topic to be considered in the next section of this chapter). Animals other than man have a symmetrical brain with no apparent hemispheric differentiation in brain function beyond the normal contralateral pairing of the left side of the body with the right-brain and vice versa. This symmetry would appear to provide vital information about an extensive area of the spatial environment speedily and accurately, thus enhancing the animal's ability to construct accurate representations, or "topographic maps." (The two eyes and two hemispheres are necessary to provide a wide field of coverage.)

The human appears to be the only mammal with an asymmetric brain. Because of the development of language, human beings have been able to abandon total reliance on a topographical map of the environment, which is expressed in the form of visual, auditory, or tactile imagery. The left-brain language function permits an alternative mode of expressing spatial relationship. It permits abstract thinking, which is removed from or independent of actual objects present in the external world. Thus we can express orientation and wayfinding movements by means of linguistic statements. These are based on a very different cognitive signature from that used in generating either a sketch map, a visual image, or a nonvisual image. By adding another set of styles (or cognitive signatures) to right-brain styles of spatial problem solving, increased *power* and *flexibility* result. The best summary of this argument is provided by Young (1962, p. 24; quoted in Gardner, 1975, p. 388):

> ... perhaps it is the two together that serve to make the most truly useful representation of the world, partly map-like, partly abstract.

Not only does an attempt to localize cognitive mapping in the right-brain overlook the role of language in spatial problem solving, but it also ignores significant variations in the degree to which people emphasize either left-brain, propositional styles of thinking or right-brain, appositional thinking. It has been suggested that the right hemisphere is dominant in some individuals and the left hemisphere dominant in others. Whether this dominance is inherent at birth (genetic or congenital) or acquired thereafter is currently in question. However, there is sufficient evidence to suggest that to a certain extent dominance is acquired, and that there is a left-brain dominance in Western industrialized culture among the "in-power" group. Thus, white males are more likely to display left-brain dominance than all Blacks and white females. The explanation, should these tentative ideas be substantiated, seems to be primarily a question of who gets rewarded for exercising the forms of thought encouraged by the power groups in our society. Left-brain, propositional modes of thinking are those largely taught, emphasized, and encouraged in our schools. A reasonable interpretation, in the view of Bogen and his colleagues, is *not* that Blacks and other minority groups, who *are* denied access to much of what our education system stresses, learn to cognize *less*. Instead, *some may* learn to cognize *differently*. Perhaps the usual left-brain dominance shifts, leaving them in control of another less "linear" but more "spatial," or holistic, mode of cognizing the world around them:

> ... we have the impression that subdominant groups in a technological society are provided less access to propositioning and consequently must rely more often upon the alternative appositional strategy.
>
> (Bogen, De Zure, TenHouten, and Marsh, 1972, p. 50)

Recent results support this interpretation. Bogen, De Zure, TenHouten, and Marsh (1972) used a highly verbal test (the "Similarities" subtest of the Wechsler Adult Intelligence Scale) and a highly pictorial test ("Street") to investigate the relationship between propositional and appositional modes of thinking. Performance on the Street test (termed appositional, and presumably controlled by the right-brain) was compared with that on the Similarities test (termed propositional) via an appositional/propositional ratio (A/P). The higher the value of the ratio, the greater the presumed dominance (or lateralization) of the right-brain. The results of the study indicated

> . . . hemispheric disconnection has preferentially lowered the capacity for Street performance (in those patients with severed commissures). This strengthens the supposition that a normal person's Street performance draws upon the right hemisphere. This in turn is consistent with the notion that higher performance on Street by certain ethnic groups (such as the Hopi) may be attributed to relatively greater development of right hemisphere potential.
>
> The ethnic differences possibly can be explained on a genetic rather than an environmental basis. Against this is the finding of a higher (A/P) ratio in a white subculture of rural farmers. . . . In any case, the nature-nurture issue is peripheral to our main point. Either explanation is compatible with our suggestion that cultural differences can be interpreted in part as *a result of asymmetry in hemispheric utilization.*
>
> (Bogen, De Zure, TenHouten, and
> Marsh, 1972, p. 58, italics added)

Patients varied as to the age at which their commissures were severed, and the A/P ratios of the male patients with commissures severed at a later age were, in general, considerably lower than for other patients. This was taken as indicating a greater degree of lateralization, and a lesser degree of compensation through the left-brain "requisition" of an appositional mode of thinking. Put into simpler words, if the right-brain is responsible for appositional thinking and the left-brain for the verbal communication of that thinking, *some* connection between the two halves of the brain is required for the patient to talk about his right-brain experience! If he can still talk about appositional events even with severed commissures, it means that the left hemisphere has taken over some of the appositional mode of thinking normally carried on in the right hemisphere. The older the patient at the time of the operation, the *more* likely it is that complete lateralization has taken place. Thus, in our culture, where the left-brain's propositional mode of thinking has become fully dominant, the older commissurectomized patient is likely to experience more difficulty in compensating for the loss of hemispheric interconnection, especially where right hemisphere functions are involved.

Why have we gone into such detail to present these technical findings about the relationship among age, culture, and modes of thinking? First, the nature of the relationship raises such obvious and controversial issues that the underlying argument must be spelled out. Second, if we assume, as seems plausible, that lateralization or dominance is at least partly (and in our view, largely) *acquired* during early experience, *and* that there is a marked effect of age upon the degree of this acquired dominance, it would appear that development *induces* lateralization. It also suggests that the types of learning experience encountered in school can have a major effect on the level of spatial ability demonstrated by school children. Third, we are reminded once again that cognitive mapping is not just an interesting idea, but is something that is central to everyday existence and development. Finally, the idea that there are differences in the degree to which people are capable of thinking spatially provides a bridge to the next section of the chapter. The following passage relates an everyday phenomenon to the ideas discussed above, wherein those souls perhaps incapable of appositional thinking are referred to as "terrain-intelligence-defective":

> Living immediately adjacent to the Front Range of the Rockies, we read nearly every other day of the plight of people lost in the "wilderness" (usually only a few miles from a National Forest Service road). Children are especially vulnerable to getting lost in unfamiliar mountain settings. But it is possible that the losers of their way represent a terrain-intelligence-defective minority. No-one ever seems to have tested individuals who are prone to getting lost . . . they are not necessarily urbanites.
>
> (Gordon Hewes, personal correspondence)

THE EVOLUTIONARY RECORD

One of the most significant processes taking place in the growing juvenile member of *any* animal species is the ontogenetic development of the capacity to perceive and to learn. Our major contention is that some of the most important things learned are characteristics of the spatial environment, and that spatial learning requires the ontogenetic development of the capacity for cognitive mapping. Such a capacity is clearly related to basic spatial problem-solving behavior in animals: There is a continual need to find food, to avoid dangerous locations, to maintain contact with companions and mates, and to return to the home base or nest. The task associated with each of these behaviors has more than a whatness quality about it; it has a *whereness* as well, and often a *whenness*. To defend a territory, an animal must know not only the appropriate threat display, but also the spatial boundaries of its territory and how to reach these boundaries with dispatch whenever they are approached by a potentially hostile interloper.

How did cognitive mapping develop phylogenetically? What are the evolutionary connections between spatial problem-solving abilities in animals and in humans? Gordon Hewes, an anthropologist, has considered the environmental conditions encountered by our primate and subprimate ancestors, the spatial problems that they must have been forced to solve, and the fundamental evolutionary role of the development of a "sense of place." In a recent letter to James Blaut, Hewes offered an articulate statement of a basic position that is shared by many cultural and physical anthropologists (see Pfeiffer, 1969; Washburn and Lancaster, 1968; Laughlin, 1968):

> A "primitive sense of place" presumably could be demonstrated in most higher animals, since an ability to find one's way about within one's range, find food or prey, and return to nests, protected places, or whatever, would be a necessary condition for survival . . .
>   Avoidance of *getting lost* in a natural environment setting must have always had a highly positive selective effect on animal populations. Getting lost . . . means losing one's way back to other familiar members of one's family, social group, home base, or comparable social unit. Animals who manage to lose their way reduce their breeding potential, even if they can physically survive after breaking contact with their social reference groups. For most primate species, such losses are reduced by the strong cohesion in the group, the tendency to remain in eye-view, or at least in ear-shot. Some primates can enter strange groups of their own species, or even different species . . . although the latter situation normally precludes effective interbreeding.
>   . . . That modern chimpanzees apparently exchange environmental information in some fashion is indicated by current experiments by Dr. Emil Menzel, Jr., of the Delta Regional Primate Center, Covington, Louisiana. I was fortunate enough recently to witness some of these ususual experiments in a large outdoor enclosure (about 100 x 300 feet). The point is that chimpanzees can retain a "memory map" of such an area . . . If this ability is already present in rudimentary form in apes, it is not unreasonable to suppose that our early man-like ancestors had also developed certain terrain-intelligence processing skills.

Figures 6.2 and 6.3 show two of Menzel's (1973) experiments, which clearly demonstrate a sophisticated spatial problem-solving ability in the chimpanzee. Two questions usually arise in the context of such material. How did cognitive mapping begin? What was the first cognitive mapper like?

Unfortunately, we are often no better at discovering primal exemplars than we are at uncovering prime movers. We have no real idea of how far down the ladder of evolutionary development cognitive mapping extends. Are there one-celled cognitive mappers? Who knows, and, for that matter, is the answer to such a question important? The validity and utility of a concept are in no way always dependent upon

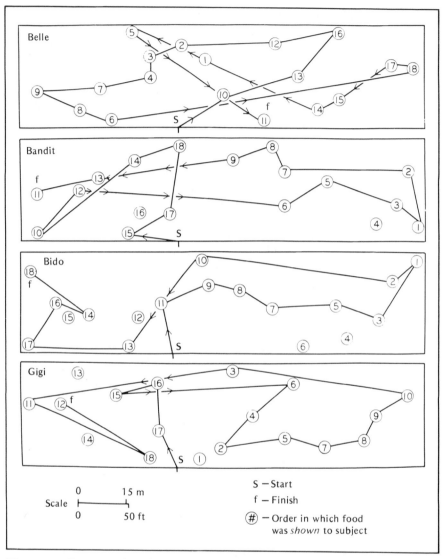

Figure 6.2. Some results of a recent experiment of Emil Menzel, subsequent to that reported by Hewes (see text). The maps show the best performances of four chimpanzees who had been carried about an outdoor field and shown 18 *randomly* placed (hidden) foods. Note that the apes remembered most of the hiding places and that the search pattern approximates an optimum routing, a clear indication of cognitive mapping in action.

pinpointing its ultimate source, either ideationally or evolutionarily. What *is* important is that students of experimental psychology who have forced rats to run through learning mazes know that rats can suc-

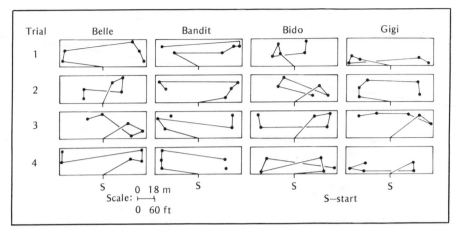

Figure 6.3. Another Menzel experiment, using the same four chimpanzees of Figure 6.2. Two pieces of food were hidden in one third of the outdoor enclosure and three pieces in the opposite third. On 13 of the 16 trials shown, the first area approached by the chimpanzees was the site containing the larger cluster of food. To the "least distance strategy" depicted in Figure 6.2, the apes added another cognitive mapping strategy to maximize the rate of food acquisition.

ceed in opening the hatch and gaining access to the forbidden top of the maze. The rat will then run straight to the goal, displaying the sort of spatial problem solving that the unfortunate student is forced to label as a "mistrial." Such mistrials as these probably led Edward Tolman (1948) to write his landmark paper putting forward the concept of a cognitive map. And yet a rat—especially a laboratory rat—is not a particularly advanced rodent, let alone one of the higher mammals. Even the bees and wasps that we discussed in Chapter 2 produced patterns of spatial behavior that *appear* to reflect the operation of a cognitive mapping process.

However, we cannot resolve the question of the evolutionary level at which cognitive mapping *first* appears. Even the attempt to trace the evolutionary development of cognitive mapping within early man is largely an exercise in intelligent speculation. Again, Hewes offers some plausible insights:

My feeling is that the rise of man was dependent on a much enhanced "sense of place," or rather, awareness of the "map" of an extended range, based mainly on visual cues or landmarks, to which was joined at perhaps an early date in the hominization process, a proto-language system for the further encoding of landscape cues, directions, and landscape information. Your findings as to the remarkable abilities of seemingly naive young children to decipher air-photo information, making the appropriate 90° spatial transpositions, realizing the notion of scale, etc., strengthens my hunches as to the great importance of this sense or ability.[1] As long as our primate ancestors occupied mainly arboreal habitats, consisting of relatively small tracts of forest or woodland, their cognitive mapping of their environments did not have to be very complicated. They were (even though olfactorily feeble) probably assisted by olfactory cues from trees and other vegetation in mapping their environment, as well as by sound (e.g., of noisy streams). Their social groups were such that individuals rarely strayed far from the main band, rarely beyond hearing distance of calls. They fed in groups, as monkeys and apes do still. With terrestrial expansion, some primates still do not make a very drastic shift. Baboon troops still tend to stick close together, and their ranges are still strikingly small compared say, to the enormous territories of predators like wolves.

But the advent of hunting and/or scavenging, even as a partial supplement to a vegetarian diet, must have transformed the territorial basis for early hominid existence (as has been suggested by a number of anthropologists). Effective early hominid hunters may have roamed over territories approximating the dimensions of those utilized by hunting dogs and wolves. Unlike them, they could not depend on an acute sense of smell to follow game, or to find their way home after pursuing prey. If, as most of us think, the advent of hunting behavior among early hominids was accompanied by a separation from females and young, and the males did most or all of the bigger game tracking, this trail-following ability would have been crucial for survival. Landmarks previously ignored by terrestrial monkeys, to say nothing of forest-bound apes, and tree-bound other primates, would become essential features of the environment, for effective ventures out after game (or predator-kill scavenging), existence in semi-arid grasslands or savannahs in the dry season when waterholes are widely scattered, and so on.

A greatly improved control (over) and processing of environmental information must have accompanied hominization, up until the relatively recent period when our ancestors became relatively sedentary once again, with the rise of agriculture, or inshore or river fishing. We must suppose that "geographic awareness" of the territories approximating the size of our larger countries in the United States was critical to hominids. For the effective utilization of larger territories, early hominids must have been able, in some fashion, to coordinate their movements and rendezvous activities, especially when the group was divided according to sex (if our reconstruction of the role of males in early hominid hunting and females in more territorially-constricted foraging is valid).

The risk of losing one's way for a far-ranging early hominid hunter must have been extreme. I was deeply impressed, a couple of years ago, in an African game reserve, by the incredibly complex pattern of criss-

---

[1] The work to which Hewes refers was performed over a three-year period by one of the present authors in collaboration with James Blaut. It is discussed in the next section of this chapter since it deals with the development of cognitive mapping in small children.

crossing game trails, and the repetitious character of the landscape. Although we were safely travelling in a Landrover, I felt that several times we had been driving in circles (perhaps we were), and that there were no worthwhile landmarks (the mostly dry creek beds seemed to offer no meaningful pattern of a drainage network). One actually feels more safely oriented in most deserts, where there are usually some distant hills on which to fix a bearing.

We know from ethnography that people like the Australian aborigines possess fabulous terrain lore, built up over generations or millenia, relating to waterholes, localities where this or that kind of wild food can be collected, and so on. Soil color, distant landmarks, directional hints from the drainage pattern, even when dry, etc. must all play an important role in keeping individuals in such groups from wandering off in the wrong direction, and losing all contact with the main body of their band. But these factors have rarely been systematically explored by anthropologists — partly because so little of the work has been done with genuine hunter-gatherers. Most of the world's ethnographic record deals with sedentary villagers, or with pastoralists whose flocks help them to find their way about. I suspect that one of the great advantages of domesticated dogs for hunters lay in the ability of dogs to overcome the olfactory dullness of man in finding the way home.

Experience in terrain obviously improves one's trail-finding abilities, but it must rest on something already built in, the "primitive sense of place" (and of direction, one might add), which must have functioned from very early on in keeping animals within their established territories, and from the tremendous risks of getting lost.

Hewes' arguments are a judicious blend of accepted scientific fact and plausible science fiction. We share his belief that the emergence of cognitive mapping has played a central role in human evolutionary development. Can we take the argument one step further and outline the process by which cognitive mapping develops during the lifetime of one human being?

THE DEVELOPMENT OF COGNITIVE MAPPING

COGNITIVE MAPPING IN SMALL CHILDREN

Good Heavens, what a tiny, hole-in-the-corner place it all seemed! Had it been like this all these years, with those little streets rising so steeply toward the town, so narrow and quaint between their gabled houses? . . . Occasionally during these thirteen years, when suffering from indigestion, he had dreamed he was at home again in the old, echoing house on the slanting street, and that his father was there again, too, indignantly upbraiding him for his degenerate way of life; and he had always felt that this was entirely as it should be. And he could in no way distinguish his present impressions from one of those delusive and compelling fabrications of the dreaming mind during which one asks oneself whether this is fantasy or reality and is driven firmly to the latter conclusion, only to end by waking up after all.

(Mann, 1970, p. 188)

This confusion of reality with fantasy is an example of a common adult recollection from childhood: the apparent change in scale of a place experienced early in life and revisited very much later. The scenes one remembers best are usually those experienced at an age between four and six, when a certain degree of independent spatial mobility has already been attained. But spatial experience begins at a very much earlier stage in life. It is surprising to learn how much we have developed and acquired after an extremely short span of life—even during the first few months of existence. For example, consider the following startling findings in the perceptual realm:

Contrary to (certain) widely held views . . . size and shape constancy do *not* emerge from a combination of prior and presumably more primitive perceptions . . . experiments by Thomas Bower (1966) at Harvard University have shown that six-week old infants already display size and shape constancy and that these constancy phenomena are dependent on parallax (seeing one object moving in front of another).

(Pribram, 1971, pp. 89–90)

One statement in this quotation is so very important that it deserves reemphasis: ". . . *size and shape constancy do not emerge from a combination of prior and presumably more primitive perceptions* . . ." (italics added). It seems to be an implicit, though rarely explicit, assumption of many developmental views that larger units must be built upon smaller units, that "atoms" of experience must generate the "molecules," and so on. Thus, it is almost universally assumed as being common sense that the cognition of small-scale spaces must inevitably precede the cognition of large-scale spaces. A child must fully comprehend his room before he can understand the surrounds of his house, and this spatial understanding must come before an understanding of his town, and so on. But there is comparatively little evidence to support this persuasive piece of conventional wisdom. We cannot assert that cognition of small-scale space *must* precede cognition of large-scale space with any more confidence than we can assert the opposite. We do know, however, that the development of cognitive mapping abilities—the major building block and, in our view, the probable keystone of environmental cognition—advances quite rapidly through a child's early years. Cognitive mapping requires an understanding of environments the spatial scale of which are such that the child cannot directly perceive them at once. Figure 6.4 suggests some of the basic steps in this developmental process, and tries to tie them to major types of spatial experience.

To understand the basis for the statements in Figure 6.4, we must go back a bit in personal history to a bus travelling through the Brazilian countryside near Rio de Janeiro, during the Brazilian winter of 1968. One of the authors was a passenger on this bus, and leaning over the back of the seat in front of him was a four-year-old girl, babbling away

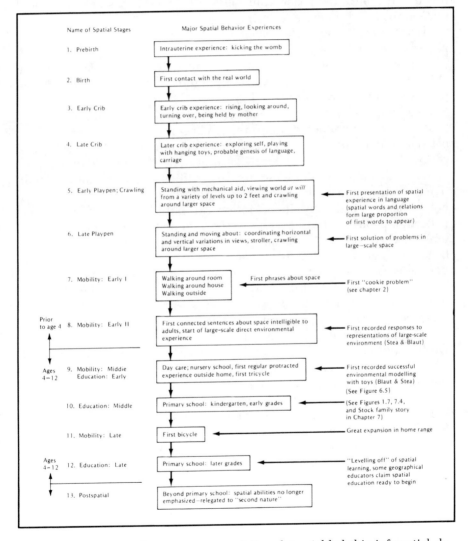

Figure 6.4. Filling in the gaps among existing data yielded this inferential developmental sequence of cognitive mapping skills.

as four-year-olds inevitably do. When, after an hour or so, he became tired of a running narrative on his bearded ugliness, he searched for something to distract the little girl. The only item at hand was a tourist guidebook to the region through which the bus was travelling, so he thumbed through the book until he came to an exceedingly poor-quality aerial photograph of the coastline. Small and grainy as it was, he thought that the photograph might provide a few moments of respite. He showed it to the girl, anticipating a story about "doggies and kitties." She took the book in her hands and said, "Well, there's the ocean and there's the beach, and there are some houses and trees, and that's a road and there's a train track . . ."

"*What* train track?" interjected the author, a train enthusiast who had seen no such thing.

"*There,*" she pointed disdainfully. And there it was. The eye of a child who had never seen the world from the air had caught what the sophisticated adult eye had missed.

What happened with that four-year-old radically changed the approach to an on-going research project concerned with the relationship between environmental learning in young children and the teaching of geography. To get at either the first "appearance" of cognitive mapping or its subsequent development are very difficult research tasks. Cognitive mapping is a classic example of an intervening process, which cannot be observed directly: Its operation can only be inferred from some pattern of behavior. But how can we be sure that the behavior is not an unwanted artifact of the techniques and methods used to generate the behavior? This is a difficult problem to resolve with adults, but its difficulty is compounded in the case of young children. We may unwittingly demand that the child make use of skills that have not yet been fully developed. Basic drawing skills, such as eye-hand coordination, are age-related. Command over language increases with age. It has been suggested that such generic spatial concepts as town, city, and world may not be accurately understood until the age of eight. Tasks may vary in the degree to which they motivate the children and maintain their attention. Tasks that are based on the lowest common denominator of skill may be considered babyish and uninteresting by the more advanced children. Variations in familiarity with the task may affect responses, especially in cross-cultural studies. Finding methods that avoid all of these problems is virtually impossible. Yet the responses to aerial photographs helped to suggest a whole range of related methods for studying the development of cognitive mapping in very young children.

Methods of research were not the only fruits of these casual insights into aerial photo interpretation. The unexpected nature of the original responses, together with those from a precocious two-and-a-half-year-old, provoked some questions about the process of interpretation.

Could it serve as an index to the development of cognitive mapping? An aerial photo is related to a cartographic map in both structure and function, and photo interpretation is a decoding process much like map reading. (Recall the discussion of mapping in Chapter 3.) If a child could interpret a *perspective* he or she had never seen before of some large-scale geographical environment, it was reasoned that no theory involving the lumping together of simple eye-level, land-based perceptions could possibly explain this achievement. Such a child would be using cognitive mapping to solve a problem of recognition and interpretation. Further, and even more startling, this photo-interpretation ability must involve several cognitive operations that the young child is supposedly incapable of performing: rotation of ninety degrees in perspective, reduction from three dimensions to two, drastic reduction in scale, and abstraction to semi-conic signs (i.e., comprehension of the meaning of the black-white tinted shapes on the photo). These are the key cognitive operations that underlie the use of a cognitive signature for map reading and mapmaking. The aerial photo is itself a perceptual stimulus, but aerial photos do not represent a view of the world that would be "perceivable" in the usual sense at ground level. Thus, the large-scale environment represented in the photo must somehow be cognized (i.e., recognized by the child in order to be identified and interpreted). It *can* be integrated by the child from a number of eye-level perceptions, or, more likely, generalized from a knowledge of what some terrestrial area *would look like if viewed from above*. One of the principal functions of cognitive mapping is to construct such hypothetical representations of places as yet unvisited or views as yet unseen.

Geographical educators have stated that children should not be fully capable of learning to interpret aerial photographs before the age of ten at the earliest. Two findings are remarkable in the face of this assertion. First, children display this interpretation ability nearly full-blown *before* school-entering age (Blaut and Stea, 1971). Development of the ability appears to be complete before the age of nine. Indeed, the skills attained go beyond simple recognition and interpretation. First-grade children can identify houses and roads, trace them, name the shapes drawn on the tracing (after the photo has been removed), color code the shapes, and finally, draw a pencil route over roads connecting two widely separated houses. Blaut and Stea (1971, p. 389) argue the following:

> If [the child] proved capable of drawing the outlines of houses and roads, and remembering the meaning of these shapes after the photograph had been removed, the child would demonstrate his ability to generate a simple form of map sign, a shape abstraction, and to understand its meaning. By color coding the signs, he would show that he could deal with at least one non-iconic meaning. . . . And finally, by solving the nav-

igation problem, the child would demonstrate that he can deal with the sign system as a whole: as a map.

All of these performances depend upon cognitive mapping for recognition, interpretation, manipulation, and spatial problem solving.

The second remarkable finding is that the photo-interpretation ability seems to be independent of a specific location, culture, or educational system. One study of aerial photo interpretation involved kindergarten children in four Puerto Rican communities (Stea and Blaut, 1973a). One hundred and eleven out of one hundred and fourteen children succeeded in identifying two or more features in *each* of the photographs of the four communities. The children did *not* perform significantly better with photographs of their own community than with photographs of the other three communities. Urban children did not perform poorly on rural images and vice versa.

The ability to cognize large-scale spaces, to *imagine* what a larger-than-perceivable world would look like, is further reflected in toy play. Children between the ages of three and five show a steadily increasing ability to use models of houses, trees, vehicles, and so on to make landscapes with organizational principles less based upon *similarities* of form, color, or function than upon basic physical principles of community organization (Blaut and Stea, 1971). Children not only know what a community *looks* like when viewed from above: They can construct one and supply *gestalt* landscape names for their constructions. Or perhaps they know what a community looks like because they have constructed not one, but many. We assume that this construction process is one surrogate for *direct* experience with large-scale geographical environments (see Figure 6.5). Together with such surrogates as television and photographs, toy play provides an "as-if" experience for the child who cannot move rapidly around a town, nor climb into an airplane and actually view the world from above (Stea and Blaut, 1973b). Physical models reflect and react upon cognitive models. Modelling is a creative means whereby children can explore and master cognitive signatures: They can actively manipulate and change perspectives, scales, and symbols. Different worlds can be built for use in a variety of games. Toy play is a source of enrichment for the child and an index of the developmental process for the researcher in cognitive mapping. Lest this interpretation should seem strained, field explorations into many parts of the Western Hemisphere (the U.S.A.; Puerto Rico, Haiti, and other islands of the Caribbean; Mexico; Venezuela; and Brazil) have failed to identify any area in which children do not play either with manufactured or with self-made environmental toys. It is almost as if a *drive* exists for experiences related to cognitive mapping, which, in children, is partly satisfied by toy manipulation.

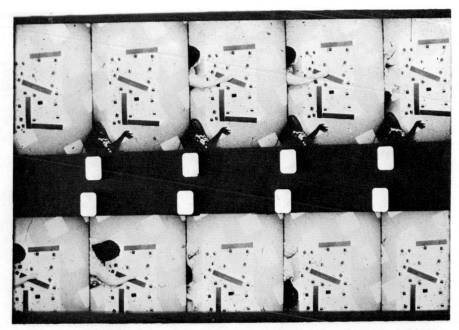

Figure 6.5. Time-lapse motion picture photographs of a preschool child constructing a "toy landscape." The child uses miniature buildings, trees, vehicles, and streets provided by the researchers, and is perfectly free to make whatever he or she wishes on a large sheet of "butcher paper."

DEVELOPMENT: SOME ALTERNATIVE VIEWS

Although these empirical studies of air photo interpretation and toy play point to the early emergence of cognitive mapping in young children, they must be viewed in the light of preexisting theories of development. The dominant theorist in today's world of developmental psychology is undoubtedly Jean Piaget. Piaget and his colleagues have traced the development of a range of concepts and abilities including physical causality, judgment, reasoning, mathematics, and space. A central concept in his overall theoretical position is the *qualitative* difference between child and adult cognition: Children are assumed to cognize differently from adults. (See Box 6.1 for a summary of Piaget's theoretical position.) This idea, while systematized by Piaget, is by no means unique to him; he was preceded by the literary record. In *A High Wind in Jamaica*, Richard Hughes (1929, p. 158) claimed

> ... babies have minds which work in terms and categories of their own which cannot be translated into the terms and categories of the human mind.

And fully ten years before the first English translation of Piaget's work appeared, Henry Kuttner, writing under the pseudonym Lewis Padgett, pointed to the cognitive gulf between adults and children:

> Youngsters are instinctive dramatists, for purposes of self-protection. They have not yet fitted themselves to the exigencies—to them partially inexplicable—of a mature world. Moreover, their lives are complicated by human variables . . . children are hopelessly dependent upon the caprice of those who give them birth and feed and clothe them . . . children lack subtlety. Children are different from the mature animal because they think in another way. We can more or less easily pierce the pretenses they set up—but they can do the same to us . . . A baby may be . . . so alien to an adult that only superficial standards of comparison apply. The thought processes of an infant are completely unimaginable. But babies think . . .
>
> Give a young child pencil and paper, and he will draw something which looks different to him than to an adult. The absurd scribbles have little resemblance to a fire engine, to a baby. Perhaps it is even three-dimensional. Babies think differently and see differently.

(Padgett, 1969 edition, pp. 54–56)

BOX 6.1

PIAGET I: THE DEVELOPMENTAL PSYCHOLOGY OF JEAN PIAGET

Of the two major theorists in cognitive growth (neither of whom deals explicitly with cognitive mapping), Jean Piaget is currently the more famous. He has what appears to be the best-integrated theory of cognitive development; indeed, some would argue that it is the best because it is, according to them, the *only* theory left in psychology. Piaget holds that a child's intelligence develops in distinct sequential stages, each marked by characteristic and identifiable ways of thinking that are qualitatively different. Through a wealth of ingenious experiments, he has—like a physician with a stethoscope—searched for evidence of the presence or absence of various cognitive structures. In his opinion, these structures, hierarchically arranged and integrated, underpin the step-by-step evolution of thought. According to Pinard and Sharp (1972, pp. 65–66):

Piaget divides this evolution into four major periods:

Sensorimotor (from birth to one and a half or two years), the time when a child acts directly upon reality, and before the appearance of language.

Preoperational (from one and a half or two to seven years). It now
becomes possible for the child to internalize actions into
thoughts through the use of symbols—a time of preparation for
the psychological operations.

Concrete Operational (from seven to 11 or 12 years). The child is
capable of internalized mental acts such as adding and
multiplying, arranging objects (seriation), and setting up
correspondence among objects. He cannot yet think about
abstractions, however.

Formal Operational (from 11 or 12 to 14 or 15 years). The child no
longer is tied to the concrete and can reason by hypothesis.
These periods are divided into stages and, where necessary,
into substages.

Several aspects of Piagetian theory must be considered central
to an understanding of his position. First, there is the idea that
children differ not only *quantitatively* in their cognition from adults,
but *qualitatively* as well. That is, they are not cognitive miniatures of
adults, but cognize in their own distinctive way. This idea is discussed
further in the body of Chapter 6.

Second, there is the notion of *stages* (or periods). The stages are an
ordered series; thus, while the *ages* associated with a specific stage are
somewhat variable, the *sequence* of stages is invariant and immutable
in Piaget's system. A child does not reach stage "X" without having
passed through stage "X-1" and all preceding stages. In a sense, this
resembles the idea of "critical periods," as the term is used in ethology
(the naturalistic study of animal behavior). Each animal, presumably including human beings, has a critical period for the acquisition of each
essential response to its social environment. If that response is not acquired during that critical period in the animal's life, it may not be acquired at all. If certain responses are not established during one critical
period, it becomes more difficult to establish new responses built upon
these during the succeeding period, and so forth.

Third, the stages are connected by a mechanism of development
and change. The mechanism is based upon two functional invariants,
two ever-present processes. The first process, *assimilation,* refers to the
attempt to incorporate new and different experience into existing cognitive structures. *Accommodation* involves the readjustment of these
cognitive structures to try to take in (or cope with) more of the external
world. Assimilation and accommodation work simultaneously, and development demands a progressive coordination of the two. The coordination stems from a constant interaction between environment and
representation. Cognitive representations are reconstructed so as to be
more stable and yet more flexible. It is this process of coordination,
called *equilibration,* that underlies cognitive development in the child.

If Pinard and Sharp (1972) convey the *essence* of Piaget, the *flavor* of Piaget is best exemplified in an article, which appeared in *The New York Times,* describing the visit of Piaget to Columbia University on October 17, 1972:

". . . I think that psychological research on emotion, especially psychoanalytical research, is quite provisional," (said) Mr. Piaget . . . "When the endocrinologists find certain answers, much psychoanalytical theory will be found entirely mythical."

"Studies of the brain will find the mechanisms (of learning) but will change nothing of the structure."

At (a later) session, Mr. Piaget alluded again to his revolutionary experiments in how children learn "conservation" — for example, that things can change their shape without changing their volume. He and his colleagues would take a ball of clay and, as children watched, roll it into a long, sausage shape. Small children would respond invariably that there was more clay in the sausage than in the ball.

Similarly, the Piagetians put down two rows of 10 checkers each, but with one row spaced out longer than the other. Up to age 5 or 6, children insist that there are more checkers in the longer row, even after they have counted them.

A questioner observed that recent tests among primitive tribes in Africa and in some slums in America showed an inability to grasp the concept of conservation, even among adults. He asked whether this did not call for a change in the Piagetian thesis.

"Absolutely not at all," Mr. Piaget retorted. "The development of children's intelligence implies a constant exchange with the social environment. Obviously, progress is slow or fast, according to the environment."

The Early Learners

In his institute in Geneva, he reported, the most precocious children were those of atomic physicists . . .

"Now I don't think these parents taught their children the notion of conservation," he said. "In fact, they don't understand it. The proof is that when I explained it to Einstein in Princeton, he was enchanted."

On the other hand, in tribal society, where tradition and the rule of elders impairs free inquiry, the attainment of complex ideas can be inhibited, he concluded.

Mr. Piaget shed a little light on the latest research in Geneva. A major area concerns the learning of abstract concepts. He illustrated, swinging a pocket watch from the end of a heavy gold chain. A child of 5, he said, soon learns how to let go of a swinging object so that it will land in a box. But not until about age 11, he said, could the child grasp the fact that he lets go at the top of the circle, not the point nearest the box, and thus master the concept of tangential trajectory.

Another colleague, Mr. Piaget revealed, had been giving similar tests to old patients suffering senile dementia and found that they unlearned concepts in reverse order to a child's learning growth. "It's very reassuring," he said with a smile . . .

Asked in an interview to sum up the Piaget talks, Professor Beilin acknowledged with a smile that it was not easy for the layman. He said he had met a girl on a train reading Piaget, and she told him it was for her poetry class at Sarah Lawrence. It must be fairly abstract poetry, he admitted.

(John Hess in *The New York Times,* October 19, 1972, p. 49 and 94)

Bearing in mind the hypothesized qualitative differences between adult and child thought processes, what does Piagetian theory have to contribute to our understanding of the development of cognitive mapping? Although Piaget has not dealt with cognitive mapping per se, Piaget and Barbel Inhelder (1956) have tackled the closely related problems involved in the development of concepts of space. However, in discussing this work, one important qualification must be kept in mind: The "space" that we are talking about in this book is not the perceptual-scale space that Piaget and his colleagues have dealt with in detail, but a much larger-scale, "transperceptual" space. Thus, because the two scales of space are quite distinct, the conclusions obtained from the study of one spatial scale neither necessarily contradict, nor support, those obtained from the study of another scale. Piaget's studies *do* provide an alternative viewpoint to the development of cognitive mapping.

One major question that concerns Piaget and Inhelder (1956) is the development of the child's ability to comprehend the geometric properties that link together objects in space. How does the child come to know (i.e., construct and comprehend) space as a geometric entity? Piaget and Inhelder see the developmental process as one culminating in the attainment of a Euclidean image of the world. The process commences with a world structured in terms of topological concepts (qualitative relations of proximity and separation, and descriptions of form as open or closed). This "primitive" topological world dominates from the age of two until about eight or nine years. Emerging alongside this world is an understanding of the environment based on a projective geometry. Projective concepts occupy the three or four to eleven year age range. Finally, a Euclidean world is erected around a series of axes or dimensions, beginning at the age of five or six. Piaget points out that these three frameworks for constructing a spatial representation emerge in the reverse of their original sequence of mathematical discovery and of the order in which they are taught in the school system.

However, we present this progression as part of the Piagetian *view*, rather than as established fact, simply because no *universal* progression towards a Euclidean conception of the world has ever been demonstrated. Despite Piaget and Inhelder's plausible arguments, the child's struggle to attain Euclidean functioning *is an assumption*. Even if a Euclidean model were observed everywhere in our own society, that would not make it less of an assumption on a global scale. Such a finding would show only that culture exercises an irresistible power over the course of cognitive development and learning, since our culture's geometry is fundamentally Euclidean. Other geometries *are* possible. Once again, Lewis Padgett (1969 edition, p. 61), speaking through the mouth of one of his characters, offers an alternative view:

> "Your mind has been conditioned to Euclid . . . But a child knows nothing of Euclid. A different sort of geometry from ours wouldn't impress him as being illogical. He believes what he sees.
>
> "Let's suppose there are two kinds of geometry—we'll limit it, for the sake of example. Our kind, Euclidean, and another, which we'll call X. X hasn't much relationship to Euclid. It's based on different theorems. Two and two needn't equal four in it; they could equal four in it; they could equal Y_2, or they might not even *equal*. A baby's mind is not yet conditioned, except by certain questionable factors of heredity and environment. Start the infant on Euclid . . . alphabet blocks. Math, geometry, algebra—they come much later. We're familiar with that development. On the other hand, start the baby with the basic principles of our X logic . . .
>
> "It wouldn't make much sense to us. But we've been conditioned to Euclid . . . I'm a psychologist. Unfortunately I'm conditioned to Euclid, too.

Despite these reservations about the degree to which a Euclidean image is imposed on a child's thinking, Piaget's ideas can be used to understand the emergence of cognitive mapping. Roger Hart and Gary Moore (1973) have made the greatest conceptual and empirical contributions to this understanding. By taking the four periods or stages of thinking and relating them to the three geometrical models, Hart and Moore show how the child develops frames of reference. These frames of reference allow the child to represent the spatial environment and, more importantly, to solve spatial problems within it. The first system, egocentric, is based entirely on the child's own actions and his own body, and it leads to representations in the form of disconnected spatial route maps (see Chapter 4). Landmarks and places are fixed only in terms of these routes and there is no sense of a *gestalt*, of space as an interrelated whole. The egocentric system is gradually superceded by a *fixed* frame of reference in which the child relates his position and his movements to fixed places in the spatial environment rather than egocentrically orienting the places to the child. Characteristically, it leads to a world made up of a series of disjointed "known" areas, the dominant one being centered around the home. These known areas emerge from the child's own explorations and movements, and are built around some "focal" point or points. The final frame of reference, termed *coordinated*, is equivalent to a spatial survey map (see Chapter 4). Representation of the world begins to approach an organized whole, with places connected by a variety of routes. The coordinates themselves need *not* be cardinal directions but can be proximate or ultimate systems (again, see Chapter 4). These coordinated frames of reference are the stable, flexible products of the equilibration process discussed in Box 6.1.

Once more we are provided with a plausible description of the ontogenetic development of cognitive mapping. Moreover, it is one that blends our own concepts with those of the Piagetian school. But how can we investigate the underlying developmental process? Piaget has marshalled an impressive amount of empirical evidence derived from his own imaginative experiments. One study, on the coordination of perspectives, is considered to be central to his account of the development of space as a geometric entity. In reviewing this we can get an added sense of the meaning of ontogenetic development *and* we can also appreciate the numbing difficulty of doing research with very young children. Just how do we pin down cognitive mapping, an elusive intervening process?

> In its broadest sense, coordination of perspectives refers to the *knowledge* that the appearance of objects is a function of the spatial position from which they are viewed, and to the *ability* to determine what that appearance will be for any specific viewing position.
>
> (Fishbein, Lewis, and Keiffer, 1972, p. 21)

To test this ability, Piaget and Inhelder (1956) constructed a three-dimensional model of some mountains, which they set on a square table top. A child was seated at one side of the table and a doll was then placed alternatively at each of the other three sides. After each placement, the child was shown a series of pictures, each representing the mountains as seen from a different viewpoint. The child was asked to pick the picture that corresponded to the doll's viewpoint. Three major stages of performance were identified. Children between four and seven years of age attributed their own perspectives to the doll; children between seven and eight seemed aware of perspectives other than their own, but operated imperfectly on these; while children between nine and ten generally gave "correct" responses. The errors made by children in the first stage were said to be "egocentric," and these tended to decrease with increasing age.

In the previous section of this chapter, we argued that no matter when the full comprehension of small-scale perceptual space develops, knowledge of large-scale geographic space is present at quite an early age. In fact, if we accept the Piaget and Inhelder findings, we would have to conclude that cognition of large-scale space *precedes* the cognition of small-scale space. Moreover, despite the apparent similarities between the underlying processes of spatial cognition and spatial perception, we might have to invoke two distinct sequences of development in order to explain these two abilities. But very recent results by Fishbein and his associates, building upon earlier studies (e.g., Dodwell, 1963; Houssidas, 1965; Laurendau and Pinard, 1970), indicate that some aspects of the comprehension of proximate space—and the coordination of perspectives in particular—may be advanced earlier in life than previously believed. Fishbein, Lewis, and Keiffer feel that one reason for the failure to detect such early cognition lies in the research techniques typically employed by developmental psychologists working on this type of problem. Their experience indicates

> . . . that one should be extremely cautious in applying age designations to any stage of thinking . . . (methodologically) we have always asked the child to identify the viewpoint of another human being, whereas the other researchers have asked the child to identify the viewpoint of a doll. The latter is in the realm of the hypothetical: "If a doll could see" or "if a doll could take a photograph." Dolls cannot see or take photographs, yet the child is asked to assume that they can. If young children have difficulty in dealing with the abstract or hypothetical, but can readily deal with the concrete . . . then methods which employ dolls instead of people should prove to be more difficult for these children.
>
> (Fishbein, Lewis, and Keiffer, 1972, p. 32)

Fishbein and his associates choose to discuss the ideas generated by their study in terms of *rules* rather than stages. These rules are (1) egocentric: "You see what I see"; (2) nonegocentric: "If you aren't in my place, you don't see what I see"; and (3) empathic: "If I were in your place, I would see what you see." Their results support the conclusion that as the use of Rule 3 increases with age, the use of Rule 2 decreases more rapidly than the use of Rule 1. Most significant for our argument is the experimenters' statement:

> . . . white middle-class children have clearly acquired Rule 3 by age 3–5, and probably much earlier than that.
>
> (Fishbein, Lewis, and Keiffer, 1972, p. 31)

This conclusion was somewhat differently phrased in an earlier and even stronger statement:

> . . . that children as young as 3½ years of age *are completely successful at coordinating perspectives under certain experimental conditions.*
>
> (Fishbein, Lewis, and Keiffer, 1972, p. 27, italics added)

These findings are entirely in accord with those of Blaut and Stea (1971), which were reported in the previous section. Air photo interpretation is related to the "coordination of perspectives" task. There appears to be a cognitive ability, which emerges in sophisticated form very early in life, and which permits the coordination and manipulation of perspectives in both large-scale and small-scale space. Thus, we can begin to understand the early stages of the development of cognitive mapping.

Our discussion of alternative views of development has been dominated by the enormous effect of Piaget's views. His nearest competitor is Jerome Bruner. (See Box 6.2 for a brief summary of Bruner's theoretical position.) Although Bruner's ideas emphasize the adaptive necessity of generating cognitive representations, they have had little impact as yet upon thinking in the area of cognitive mapping. However, as we will see in the final section of this chapter, they do allow us to get some valuable perspectives on Piaget's views, in particular, and on the development of spatial cognition in general.

BOX 6.2

THE DEVELOPMENTAL PSYCHOLOGY OF JEROME BRUNER

In contrast with Piaget, Bruner's views of cognitive development are not strictly tied to developmental stages. Some believe that his theoretical position, less "tight" than that of Piaget, has suffered somewhat from the passage of time, but his thoughts on early childhood education are still a source of fruitful and often controversial exchanges. In *The Process of Education*, Bruner (1960) summarized his view: "Any subject can be taught effectively in some intellectually honest way to any child at any stage of development." The contrast with Piaget's views cannot be drawn more forcefully.

Bruner's most relevant contribution to our concerns was entitled, "The Course of Cognitive Growth," and appeared in 1964. His comments on the infant's "drive for mastery of the environment" tie development to evolutionary necessity. Bruner draws explicitly upon the work of Washburn and Howell (1960) and Weston La Barre (1954), basing his argument firmly on the evolutionary record:

> As for integration, it is a truism that there are very few single or simple adult acts that cannot be performed by a young child. In short, any more highly skilled activity can be decomposed into simpler components, each of which can be carried out by a less skilled operator. What higher skills require is that the component operations be combined. Maturation consists of an orchestration of these components into an integrated sequence. The "distractability," so-called, of much early behavior may reflect each act's

lack of imbeddedness in what Miller, Galanter, and Pribram (1960), speak of as "plans." These integrated plans, in turn, reflect the routines and subroutines that one learns in the course of mastering the patterned nature of a social environment. So that integration, too, depends upon patterns that come from outside in an internalization of what Roger Barker (1963) has called environmental "behavior settings."

If we are to benefit from contact with recurrent regularities in the environment, we must represent them in some manner. To dismiss this problem as "mere memory" is to misunderstand it. For the most important thing about memory is not storage of past experience, but rather the retrieval of what is relevant in some usable form. This depends upon how past experience is coded and processed so that it may indeed be relevant and usable in the present when needed. The end product of such a system of coding and processing is what we may speak of as a representation (the three modes of which are) ... *enactive representation, iconic representation,* and *symbolic representation.* Their appearance in the life of the child is in that order, each depending upon the previous one for its development, yet all of them remaining more or less intact throughout life ... By enactive representation, I mean a mode of representing past events through appropriate motor response ... Iconic representation summarizes events by the selective organization of percepts and of images, by the spatial, temporal, and qualitative structures of the perceptual field and their transformed images. Images "stand for" perceptual events in the close but conventionally selective way that a picture stands for the object pictured. Finally, (symbolic representation) represents things by design features that include remoteness and arbitrariness. A word neither points directly to its referent here and now, nor does it resemble it as a picture.

(Bruner, 1964, p. 2; italics added)

AN ATTEMPT AT INTEGRATION

We have seen that cognitive mapping is likely to be manifested both phylogenetically and ontogenetically. We can point to patterns of spatial behavior in bees, wasps, rats, and chimpanzees that suggest the operation of some spatial problem-solving ability. Our observations on the evolutionary record, although speculative, reinforce the belief that cognitive mapping emerged as an adaptive necessity during the course of human evolution. Despite many controversies and uncertainties, researchers generally agree that the child develops a needed understanding of his spatial environment. The ability to engage in cognitive mapping is thus adaptive in both an evolutionary and an individual developmental sense. However, while there may be some rudimentary code in an individual's DNA directing a predisposition to map cognitively, we must assume that most of the specifics of cognitive mapping are acquired (i.e., are not genetically "given"), *and* that they develop with age. Although we see evidence of cognitive mapping appearing as soon as an individual learns to speak, we also have reason to believe that much cognitive development and environmental learning (which interact) occur at even earlier ages in *all* cultures (Box 6.3). The capacity or ability to map increases with age—to a point. There *may* be a levelling off—or even a decrease! (Stea and Blaut, 1973a)—occuring earlier than most people have assumed (between the second and fourth grades of elementary school). This levelling off occurs earlier than most geographical educators have assumed that a child is ready even to *begin* formal education in mapping. Finally, we are witnessing the emergence of the first neuropsychological evidence for the existence of cognitive mapping. New ideas concerning the functional specialization of the two hemispheres of the brain suggest a possible physiological "locus" for spatial problem-solving ability. Supporting this argument is the widespread belief that there is more than one kind of learning, and just possibly, more than one kind of development.

Our understanding, summarized above, has been generated in spite of a dearth of contributions from the major developmental theorists within psychology. Even the two most influential theorists of the past decade have not had much to say, directly, on this issue. Both Bruner and Piaget, who are intimately concerned with all other aspects of cognitive growth in the infant, have barely touched on our concerns. The basic differences between their two general positions have centered about the structure of the developmental process. Is it a stepwise process best described by stages (Piaget) or a more fluid developmental sequence (Bruner)? (See Box 6.4.) As far as the development of cognitive mapping is concerned, the available data do not yet allow us to choose between these two views.

BOX 6.3

PIAGET II: THE RELATIONSHIP BETWEEN DEVELOPMENT AND LEARNING

The relationship between development and learning is like that between "innate" and "acquired." Both involve "achievement"; but, in development, whatever one achieves depends upon *innate* structures, which develop over time—the changing capacity of the organism. In learning, the achievement is dependent upon the prior *acquisition* of information, reinforcement contingencies, and so on. In a sense, development must precede learning. An organism that has not developed the mechanisms for learning (sensory-motor coordination, for example) cannot learn.

Put somewhat differently, what might be the characteristics of an organism that exhibited learning but no development—or, alternatively, of an organism that exhibited development but no learning? An organism that fits the first category is the amoeba, sprung full-blown from the "forehead" of its "parent." The amoeba is capable of some very simple forms of learning, but displays no development whatsoever, save for the process of binary fission (which could hardly be called development). An organism that displays development but no learning is harder to find. Plants *may* fit this category, although not all scientists are entirely convinced that plants are incapable of learning.

Certainly, development depends upon time and learning depends upon behavior, employing the usual psychological definition that learning is a change in behavior due to practice. But while so simple an answer is obviously an inadequate response to a complicated question, more complex answers do not resolve the complexity of the development-learning relationship. For example, in Piaget's work, a child is said to *attain* a certain concept, almost as if he or she had been striving for it, although not consciously. This implies that there exists something like a blueprint for human development, which will be followed regardless of other influences. Evidence to the contrary is scant, although much of whatever criticism has been made of Piaget is centered about this idea, considered by some people to be a "lockstep" notion. Piaget's early results were based upon observations of very few children in one cultural context, although they were supported by the later and quite careful experimentation of Laurendau and Pinard (1970).

At least one observation—albeit a single instance—indicates that development and learning may interact in interesting ways. A seven-year-old girl had been "teaching" map reading to a researcher in cognitive mapping. She went to the closet to obtain a familiar USGS topographical sheet to use in her lesson. But she could not find it, and located another instead, a quite unfamiliar sheet. She brought it to the researcher, who perceived an unanticipated opportunity. "Find Twin Lakes," he said, and she pointed to a pair of lakes on the upper half of the sheet. "How far is it from the far shore of one lake to the far shore of the other?" Illustrating the behavior typical of her Piagetian "stage" of development, she discovered the scale of miles at the bottom of the sheet, and then placed her two hands at the opposite ends of the lake. Trying to keep them parallel, she moved them down to the scale. At this point the critical event occurred. "Do you believe that your hands remain the same distance apart when you move them from the lakes to the scale?" he asked. "No," she said, "But I don't know any other way." "Think," he said, "what else do you have available to you?" She found a Tinkertoy rod and attempted to use it as an instrument for transferring the measurement from the lakes to the scale. It was too short. Another rod was too long. The researcher then made his only obtrusive comment. "Get a pencil," he said, whereafter the researcher observed the nearest he has ever seen to a true "aha" experience. The child went to a nearby desk and returned with a pencil. She ran to the Tinkertoy rod, marked off the length of the lake, and brought the marked rod down to the scale in order to read off the mileage. She was very pleased with herself. The researcher was even more pleased. By giving the child a few tidbits of information in a spatial task (encouraging learning), he had carried her through several Piagetian substages (or several years of normal development) in a few minutes.

Investigations by Blaut and Stea (1971) suggest that map reading has considerable inherent attraction for children. The intrinsically appealing nature of the task indicated in the preceding paragraph thus may have facilitated the process described, but the result remains. This in no way necessarily impugns Piaget's ideas. It *does* call into question some educators' *interpretations* of Piaget, which attempt to force *all* of cognitive development into ages as well as stages—and into the same sequence. The above results, taken in conjunction with those of Bower (1966), Gibson (1970), and Blaut and Stea (1971) suggest that there *may be more than one* sequence of stages and substages, and that there may be a degree of flexibility in the temporal relation between sequences. What determines the exact nature of this relation may be environmental learning, which contributes to the establishment of a pattern of interaction between hypothesized cognitive structure and actual environment.

BOX 6.4
PIAGET AND BRUNER: SOME COMPARISONS

Both Bruner and Piaget view development as the acquisition or emergence of two forms of competence, one concerned with representing recurrent regularities in the environment and the other with integrating past, present, and future representations. But Bruner likens development to the growing emergence of "new technologies," proceeding in "spurts as innovations are adopted." While these spurts resemble Piaget's stages, it seems doubtful that Piaget would agree that innovations are adopted. He would be likely to disagree even more strongly with Bruner's statement concerning the *way* in which children acquire these innovations:

Most of the innovations are transmitted to the child in some prototypic form by agents of the culture: ways of responding, ways of looking and imaging, and most important, ways of translating what one has encountered into language.

(Bruner, 1964, p. 13)

Much of Bruner's recent work has been concerned with (1) the development and learning of language, (2) the relationship between nonlinguistic and linguistic learning, and (3) the development and use of prelinguistical symbol systems, where gesture, sensory events, and perceptual occurrences function as signs at all environmental scales (Bruner, 1968). Bruner calls this development of the linguistic from the nonlinguistic "the achievement of codes." The relationship of Bruner's "achievement" to Piaget's "attainment" is not yet clear, although the former might imply the developing organism's coming to grips with the external environment, the latter the organism's realization of a preordained and internally structured line of development.

Some of Bruner's comments on achievement indicate the extremely important role played by environmental experience—even microenvironmental experience—in language learning:

> ... the differentiation of *holding* and *operating upon what is held* may be the same rule as diffuse and focal attention and ... both may presage the development of *topic* and *comment* in human languages ... there may be rules or systems which, when learned, might predispose a human infant to language. The *channel* of language is doubtless dependent on the growth of interaction codes. The origin of the uniquely human *form* of language remains very much a mystery. I have proposed that it is a refinement or extension of human skill as exhibited in the attentional system and the motor system as represented by man's clever hands. It seems to be a not unreasonable hypothesis that human skill, human information processing, and human language might conceivably be a set of related responses that differentiated man as he evolved from his hominid ancestors.

(Bruner, 1968, pp. 63–64)

Elsewhere in this chapter, and in the next, we suggest that early environmental learning *may* constitute a prototype experience for the later learning of nondimensional language. It provides a necessary template, so to speak, for the acquisition, achievement, or attainment of the ability to understand written language. We view Bruner's comments on language as basically supportive of this view.

Some readers may by now have detected a slight Brunerian bias in our views. To our knowledge, no rigorous comparisons between the theoretical positions of Bruner and Piaget exist, perhaps because it is not always possible to determine precisely the points of agreement and disagreement in the two positions. For a valiant attempt at such a comparison, we refer the reader to a recent review of spatial cognition (Hart and Moore, 1973). Hart and Moore compare Bruner with Piaget and relate their respective positions to a variety of empirical findings, organizing these comparisons in terms of Bruner's categories of representation: *enactive, iconic,* and *symbolic* (see Box 6.2). In certain senses, the Hart and Moore bias is the opposite of ours, since their point of view is predominantly Piagetian.

Some of the necessary groundwork for a rigorous comparison between the Brunerian and Piagetian views of cognitive development is now being laid. For example, Patrice Horn (1975, p. 84) reports on the work of Bruner and Scaife:

> The infant's world may be less egocentric that Jean Piaget's child-development theories suggest. Jerome Bruner and M. Scaife, working at Oxford, have found that children as young as two months will follow the gaze of their mother or other adults. This action—not just looking at another person, but using her as a guide to something else—indicates that even very young babies can interact with their environment in a rather complex way.

Despite this one very provocative idea, the major obstacle to a comparison of Bruner and Piaget remains. Neither man has seriously tried to evaluate the other man's position! One possible reason for this situation is contained in a statement purported to have been made by Piaget during his 1972 visit to Columbia University:

> Provoked by a question about "cognitive style," a concept associated with Prof. Jerome Bruner, now at Oxford, Mr. Piaget struck another blow in a debate that has titillated the profession for some time. "I never understood Jerome Bruner," he said, "and I don't think he ever understood me."
>
> (John Hess in *The New York Times,* October 19, 1972, p. 49)

What changes, then, undeniably occur? Primarily, underlying all other processes, the individual undergoes physiological change, experiencing growth and physiological maturation. He also experiences psychological maturation, altering his cognitive frameworks and representations. In the views of certain researchers, this alteration in cognition is an immutable process, proceeding in accord with some pre-established templates. In other views, it can vary, particularly in accordance with the ambient culture and environmental context. Both views are in agreement, however, about the constraints on cognitive development. The *external* structuring of development regulates the *privileges* or *access* to the tools of society and its subenvironments, and determines at each developmental level what are to be called "suitable" goals, objectives, and so on, for the individual.

As the person develops, the role of instinct (innate characteristics) decreases, and the roles of learning and culture increase. Culture is viewed here as a system that determines the *ways* in which learning (including environmental learning) is to take place; *what*, specifically, is to be learned; and *where* and *when* it is to be acquired.

Phrasing all of this another way, as a person goes from age zero to age X he is both maturationally and developmentally capable of new things — we call this an increase in ability. In addition, we find it necessary to coin two new terms to describe what occurs. Societal press determines what is to be *required*. Societal license determines when, how, and under what circumstances an individual is *permitted* to experience the things of which he is now capable. Thus, while a person cannot be required to do that which he is not yet able, he *can* be prevented from experiencing that of which he *is* capable. The developing person is in the process of *learning how to learn* and developing the ability to *apply* what he has learned to new and novel situations. Society and culture determine the extent to which he is allowed to do so.

How can we relate these rather abstract views of the developmental process to the practical context of everyday life and spatial problem solving? Chapter 7 shows how the developing capacity for cognitive mapping is reflected in learning about new spatial environments. Learning about the world around us is a way of generating a personal sense of space, and of belonging. It forms the basis for nostalgia and for fantasy. Learning provides the raw material for spatial problem solving.

Chapter 7

LEARNING: HOW ENVIRONMENTS GET MAPPED

INTRODUCTION

To get to the center of Los Angeles, you go where it's all twinkley.

(Brenda Iredale, a recent migrant to L.A.)

WRONG DIRECTIONS: Man in Bellefonte the other day said "I'm going down to State College," thereby branding himself as a man who hasn't been around here too long.

Because, you see, you never go "down" to State College — you go "up." The same kind of local directions prevail in many a community and you have to be around a good while until you become familiar with them.

From Bellefonte, for example, you go "up" to Tyrone or Altoona; you go "out" to Pleasant Gap or Karthaus; "down" to Milesburg, Howard, Lock Haven, and "over" to Snow Shoe, Pine Glen, Centre Hall, Millheim. Why this is so is anyone's guess.

The term we like best around here is in the Woodward area. People there go "down through" to Harleton or Lewisburg. Even more, if you inquire for someone over there, you might get the explanation "He went down through."

(Paul Dubbs in *The Pennsylvania Mirror*, July 19, 1975).

No one knew exactly when (Ursula) had begun to lose her sight. . . . She did not tell anyone about it because it would have been a public recognition of her uselessness. She concentrated on a silent schooling in the distances of things and people's voices, so that she would still be able to see

"THE ROAD TO RIO DOESN'T LEAD TO ROME! THE ROAD TO MOROCCO DOESN'T LEAD TO ROME! THE ROAD TO..."

Figure 7.1. All roads do not lead to Rome.

with her memory what the shadows of her cataracts no longer allowed her to. Later on she was to discover the unforseen help of odors, which were defined in the shadows with a strength that was much more convincing than that of bulk and color, and which saved her finally from the shame of admitting defeat. In the darkness of the room she was able to thread a needle and sew a buttonhole and she knew when the milk was about to boil. She knew with so much certainty the location of everything

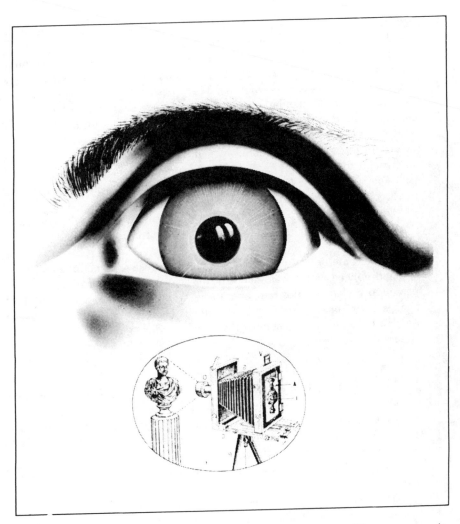

Figure 7.2. In primary school, we are taught that the eye is like a camera; in college, we are taught that it is not. Whatever our resolution of this conflicting information, we retain the idea that the camera offers a *metaphor* for seeing. "What to see" is built into the camera's structure, but it is something that the eye must *learn*.

that she herself forgot that she was blind at times. On one occasion Fernanda had the whole house upset because she had lost her wedding ring, and Ursula found it on a shelf in the children's bedroom. Quite simply, while the others were going carelessly all about, she watched them with her four senses so that they never took her by surprise, and after some time she discovered that every member of the family, without realizing it, repeated the same path every day, the same actions, and almost repeated the same words at the same hour. Only when they deviated from the meticulous routine did they run the risk of losing something. So when she heard Fernanda all upset because she had lost her ring, Ursula remembered that the only thing different that she had done that day was to put the mattresses out in the sun because Meme had found a bedbug the night before. Since the children had been present at the fumigation, Ursula figured that Fernanda had put the ring in the only place where they could not reach it: the shelf. Fernanda, on the other hand, looked for it in vain along the paths of her everyday itinerary without knowing that the search for lost things is hindered by routine habits and that is why it is so difficult to find them. . . . Sometimes unforseen accidents would happen. One afternoon when Amaranta was embroidering on the porch with the begonias Ursula bumped into her.

"For heaven's sake," Amaranta protested, "watch where you're going."

"It's your fault," Ursula said, "you're not sitting where you're supposed to."

She was sure of it. But that day she began to realize something that no one had noticed and it was that with the passage of the year the sun imperceptibly changed position and those who sat on the porch had to change their position little by little without being aware of it. From then on Ursula had only to remember that date in order to know exactly where Amaranta was sitting.

(Márquez, 1970, pp. 251–253)

In peace-time fogs, as she well knew, any [Thames] lighterman could tell which reach of the river he was in by the smell. "Cinnamon and cloves told you you were by the spice warehouses at Wapping Wall, malt was Deptford Creek and, when the river stank like a polecat, you were at Greenwich. War changed all that."

One yellow-blanketed day a barge was long overdue. The phone rang eventually.

"Took me seven hours to get 'ere, Missus. I got lorst!" said an outraged voice. "I dunno what the 'ell they're doing wiv this bleedin' war, now you can't even smell your way down your own bleedin' river!"

(Taken from an interview with Dorothea Fisher,
in a 1974 issue of the magazine, Woman.)

These assorted illustrations and stories reveal the ever-present need for spatial information, a need that is fulfilled by a continual process of environmental learning. Despite its essential role in spatial problem solving, learning does have its comic moments. All roads do not lead to Rome and the sooner that Dennis the Menace appreciates that fact, the sooner his admission to polite society. Yet, in a more serious vein, we do need to know which roads lead where so that we can find the way.

In the face of spatial uncertainty, we are often forced to ask someone for directions. To unravel the resulting instructions, we must be privy to the linguistic nuances and niceties of local orientation systems. We must learn the cognitive ups and downs, the ins and outs of an area. Not only must we learn at least something about each spatial environment that we encounter, we must also learn *how* to learn. Although seeing is said to be believing, even seeing does not come naturally to us. We learn to see just as we learn to map cognitively the world around us. The success of learning to learn varies dramatically. Some people always seem to know where they are while others get lost as soon as they step outside of their houses. Whether this propensity to get lost is the result of a "terrain intelligence deficiency," as Hewes calls it, or an inefficient strategy for spatial problem solving, no one knows. Nevertheless, everyone must generate cognitive maps and must synthesize innumerable bits and pieces of spatial information that are derived from *all* of our senses. We tend to emphasize the role of vision to such an extent that the roles of the other senses are often ignored. The loss of her sight forced Ursula to relearn the world in which she had lived for many years, to "see" it in a very different "light" by using her other senses. We make use of and often rely on these senses without realizing their importance. The Thames lighterman was literally at a loss in the absence of both visual cues *and* distinctive smells; the river that he knew, that he could *sense* his way along, did not exist.

The need to understand the world transcends the constraints of age and physical ability, the barriers of culture and language, and the requirements of particular spatial problems in particular environments. What is the underlying process that satisfies this need? When we speak of getting to know a place, what do we mean? What do we "get" and how do we get "it"? How does learning happen? The obvious place to seek answers to these questions is in the psychological literature, since, to many people, psychology and the study of learning are as inextricably intertwined as are geography and the study of maps. Unfortunately, environmental learning has suffered the same fate as cognitive mapping itself: It has been consigned to the obscurity of the backwaters somewhere between the mainstreams of psychology and geography.

Environmental learning, as a special class of learning, has not been entirely neglected by researchers, but the *environmental* aspects of the learning studied were rarely explicitly recognized. Psychologists concerned with human and animal *behavior* have regarded the surrounding physical environment as an inert background, and have neglected *spatial* behavior per se. Ironically, the experiments that such psychologists have performed, which constitute the basis for learning theory, have often involved distinctly spatial apparatus and evoked distinctly spatial behavior. Moreover, explanatory concepts (e.g., the ideas of field theory and topological psychology developed by Kurt Lewin) often employ spatial analogies and metaphors. Our book is based on the most obvious of these spatial metaphors: the cognitive map. Edward Tolman

(1948) popularized this concept, although he used it in a less patently spatial manner than we do.

Tolman was concerned with the classic twin questions, *What* is learned? and *How* is "it" learned? He proposed that all mobile organisms are capable of forming, and in fact do form, cognitive maps, which enable them to learn *places* and thus to move around in their spatial environment. This argument was in marked contrast at that time (the 1940s and 1950s) to the views of other learning theorists, especially those of Clark Hull. Hull claimed that what organisms learned were *not* places, but rather, chains of responses, which eventually got them to places where rewards were located. Thus, the terms *place learning* and *response learning* are derived from the description of one major area of conflict between Tolman and Hull concerning *what is learned* (Hilgard, 1956). Clearly, Tolman claimed that places were learned, while the Hullians stressed responses. These two antithetical views form a part of learning theory that is directly relevant to an understanding of environmental learning. We will suggest that the antithesis is more apparent than real, and that *both* forms of learning play a sequential and complementary role in cognitive mapping.

Sadly, however, with the exception of the above distinction, learning theorists have been even less concerned with spaces and places than have developmental theorists. Our attempt to explain the process of environmental learning must therefore build on even more meager resources than were available for the preceding chapter on the development of cognitive mapping. We will structure our argument around the ongoing experiences of a typical family who are confronted with the problems of learning a new city. In describing the reactions of the different family members, we can distinguish *what* is learned from *how* it is learned. We will discuss the relationships between learning and a series of influential factors, including age, length of experience, type of experience, and structure of the spatial environment.

LEARNING A NEW CITY

Let us consider a hypothetical but typical example of the process of environmental learning. Mr. Stock, an individual who has spent most of his life in Bull City, is moved by his company to its branch office in Beartown, to take up residence there for an unspecified period of time. He has a family who must also uproot themselves and move to Beartown. Initially, the Stock family is faced with a number of familiar problems. Starting out with temporary accommodations in a fairly expensive motel, they must find a place to live, rent some furniture (their own is in temporary storage in Bull City), buy staples for the kitchen, find the schools and parks, and so on. The source of each of these necessities has a whereness to it. And because Beartown is typical of most

American cities in that it has only the barest residue of a public transportation system, the Stock family cannot rely upon instructions of the "take the No. 21 trolley to Market Square" variety. Instead, they are dependent on their car and their own ability to find the "wheres" at which the "whats" they need are located. In short, they need to cognitively map Beartown as rapidly, accurately, and reliably as possible. This mapping must occupy so short a period of time that no development can be expected to take place in any of the family members; thus, their comfortable survival is dependent upon *learning*.

The goals and stimuli that will aid environmental learning are many. The Stocks' motivational state is high since the motel is expensive and quite unsatisfactory for family living. There are a number of resources that the Stocks can call upon to assist in the learning process. For example, Mr. Stock has visited Beartown on many occasions and already has a rough feel for the place. Moreover, as a consequence of his job he has visited a number of other cities and has developed a pattern useful in learning to map them cognitively; he has learned how to learn. Unfortunately, the rest of the family does not share this *spatial* learning advantage. The only model that they have is Bull City. All of the family, however, can draw upon the resources provided by Beartown itself. Cartographic maps of Beartown do exist, although they are neither particularly accurate nor designed with the newcomer in mind. There are innumerable aids to navigation, orientation, and direction finding built into the physical structure of Beartown. Some of these learning cues are called "signs," and many are literally just that—road signs giving street names, permitted directions of travel, and guides to neighborhoods within the city. Other cues take the form of gasoline station heralds, drug store shingles, and so on—these are especially useful if they are illuminated at night. Traffic signals are among the most useful signs. Not only are they visible both day and night, but they are eminently countable. Thus a person giving directions can state that an intersection is one, two, three, or more lights away from the place where he is standing. Some parts of the city are arranged in a grid pattern, producing city blocks that also provide excellent navigational aids. The utility of any of these cues is greatest at choice points, those locations at which an individual must make a change in direction (see Figure 7.3).

But initially, Beartown does appear to be a vast, blooming, buzzing confusion. Fortunately, Mr. Stock does not have to search for a job; hence, he need not learn the entire city in the process of finding a suitable place to work. His company, however, has given him only a little time in which to get settled and so, on the advice of a colleague, he route maps his way to work. He learns a system of paths by learning a connected series of signs and landmarks, the connections referring to the specific behavioral response that he must make at each point in a series in order to reach the next point. Learning involves a string of re-

Figure 7.3. Two aids to spatial navigation and one to societal navigation.

sponses to selected parts of the surrounding physical environment. Only later, when time allows and necessity demands that he learn where other places are located, does Mr. Stock begin to develop a comfortable feel for the layout of Beartown.

Mrs. Stock faces a set of spatial problems somewhat different from those encountered by her spouse. Not yet having been liberated either socially or spatially, her sphere of activity is differentiated from that of the other members of the Stock family. She is trapped in a narrow and restricted social world by the demands that are placed on her in the role of the wife of a business executive. These demands channel and constrain her spatial patterns of movement within Beartown. Not only is she restricted in her spatial experience of Beartown, but she is also restricted in the *way* in which she can familiarize herself with the city. This latter restriction reflects the impact of *past* spatial experiences on the present. For a long period during their early residence in Bull City, the Stocks were a one-car family, and Mr. Stock was forced to use the car for commuting to his job. Mrs. Stock was thus confined to their home in the suburbs, and her knowledge of the city was limited to areas within walking distance of home. Although she was able to use the car in the evenings and on weekends, her experience of Bull City was limited in time and space, and these limits influenced her strategies for learning the city and for solving spatial problems within it. For example, she has difficulty reading printed maps because she has not learned how to relate the cartographic map to the world beyond her immediate visual range. She cannot see how to use the map to solve spatial problems because her experience with Bull City neither demanded such a problem-solving strategy nor did it encourage it or even make it possible. As a consequence, she relies almost entirely on verbal route descriptions that are provided by her new friends in Beartown. These second-hand descriptions form the basis for her understanding of the spatial layout of the city. As time passes, Mrs. Stock increases her knowledge of Beartown through the tedious, piecemeal accretion of such route maps.

Mr. and Mrs. Stock started the learning process with virtually the same knowledge baseline. Both rely on a method of accretion to expand the spatial coverage and detailed linkage of their knowledge of Beartown. The specific form of the accretion process and, more importantly, its effectiveness differ between the two Stocks. In Mr. Stock's case, the result of the accretion process is a two-dimensional "layout" map—a spatial survey map (see Chapter 4)—in which the relation of one route to another route is clear. The original pieces of knowledge have been integrated and the learning process has generated a new type of cognitive structure.

On the other hand, Mrs. Stock does not know how one route map relates to another, except in situations where they share a common starting point (e.g., her home or the nearby shopping center). Over familiar paths, to which she now pays considerable attention, she navigates remarkably well in the family car. In a sense, her navigation over these routes is so automated that it has become habitual. She does not really pay attention because she could do it blindfolded. (Recall the discussion of habitual and conscious problem solving in Chapter 3.) But her sense of mastery of the spatial environment is fragile. As soon as she is forced to travel off the beaten track, her sense of direction deserts her; she has difficulty in constructing a new route connecting two places. Similarly, on those occasions when she is deprived of the use of the family car and must resort to the public transport system, she becomes lost quite easily. Her method of learning, effective for the solution of certain problems, has prevented her from comprehending the relationship between the pattern of the streets that she has driven over, and the fixed routes of the transit system. Mrs. Stock's accretional learning process, in other words, has left her with an *inflexible* understanding of the city.

The four Stock children present many contrasts to their parents, both in their patterns of spatial behavior and in their learning. The children experience a rather different Beartown from that of their parents — at different scales and velocities. None of them has a driver's licence. Hence, when they move under their own power, the world unfolds more slowly than it does for their parents. Further, they see it from different vantage points: The smaller they are, the further the distances appear and the larger loom the surroundings. As it is, the elementary school, which the two youngest attend, is within walking distance. (Interestingly, most of the children read maps more easily than does their mother.)

For amusement one evening, Mr. Stock asked each child to draw a map of the route that he or she took to school. Since the youngest two followed virtually the same route, it was easy to make a comparison (see Figure 7.4). The youngest children drew a jagged line indicating symbolic changes in direction, these changes having little relation to actual turns. The map displayed no sense of scale and relative distance. Another child, who attended junior high school, was beginning to be capable of drawing a sketch map, which approximated her spatial experience, and which could be used by another person in solving the wayfinding problem. (Refer back to Box 6.2 for Bruner's description of the stages of cognitive development and the types of representation that a child can produce at each stage.) The fourth, and oldest, of the Stock children was in the room at the time. He was attending the city high school and travelled each day by school bus. His father decided to try the same game with him, and was astonished to find that his representation of the route was much less close to his actual experience than that of his younger brother in primary school.

THE PROCESS OF ENVIRONMENTAL LEARNING

WHAT IS THE NATURE OF THE LEARNING PROCESS?

Throughout this book, we have drawn a chain of connections between spatial problems, cognitive mapping, and spatial behavior. But this

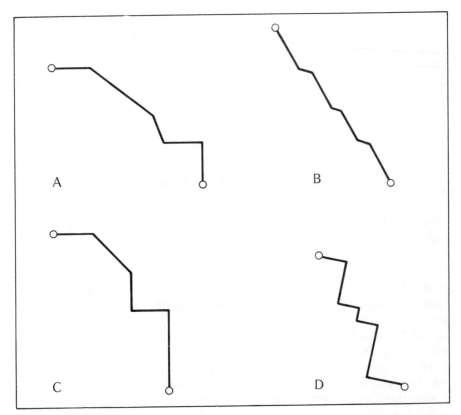

Figure 7.4. The actual route to school (A) and probable trip-to-school sketches (B, C, and D) provided by three of the Stock children. "B" is drawn by the youngest, "C" by the second oldest, and "D" by the oldest, who takes a bus to school (see text).

chain is missing one essential link: environmental learning. Environmental learning provides the raw material for the problem-solving process; it even provides the successful problem-solving strategies.

Despite its preeminent role, environmental learning is an even more obscured topic than cognitive mapping itself. Perhaps this obscurity may be attributed to its *incidental* nature. With very few exceptions, much of the learning process takes place while the person is ostensibly doing something else. It operates largely outside of the realm of conscious awareness, as does spatial problem solving (see Chapter 3).

Environmental learning is not something that we are taught to do, either informally or systematically. It is something that we just pick up on our own, and thus is even less associated with the teaching process than are other forms of learning. On infrequent occasions, we deliberately engage in environmental learning. We make a point of exploring an unknown neighborhood; we take an interesting side turn to see where it leads us; we get a different perspective on places from a tall building or hill; an air photo or map may catch our attention and we try to work out where various well-known places are located. Yet these conscious efforts are the exceptions. The rule is a continuous process hidden from consciousness. The process *is* continuous despite the popular assumption that learning necessarily involves the sporadic acquisition of discrete units of *new* information. Repeated confirmation of our existing spatial knowledge is just as central to the environmental learning process as is getting to know new things about a familiar place. Even the new information may be old information seen in a different light: for example, the realization that two streets join or that the pieces of the Boston Common form a five-sided figure, not a rectangle (see Figure 5.6).

All of the Stock family are engaged in environmental learning, a process that largely occurred "beyond their conscious awareness." However, although we have labelled the environmental learning process as incidental and unconscious, we should not overlook its goal-directed nature. The Stock's initial experiences of Beartown and, indeed, their subsequent experiences are largely dictated by their *plans.* Rarely are these plans for utilizing the spatial environment per se: Rather, they are plans for doing something in which the spatial environment is inevitably involved. It forms the stage and setting *within* which spatial behavior occurs. The formation, development, and execution of a plan taken together represent the basic building blocks for the environmental learning process. These building blocks determine the nature of environmental learning, and it is these blocks that we must strive to understand.

WHAT DO WE LEARN?

Traditional theories of learning, stressing contiguous associations *alone,* shed little light upon the relationship between environmental learning and cognitive mapping. Here, we adopt the view expressed earlier by several learning theorists, but most recently by Stea and Blaut (1973a) and Stea (1974): There are *several* distinctive *forms* of learning, each governed by its own set of laws. In the Stea-Blaut view, one general form of learning can be called *nondimensional.* An obvious example of this form is that area of experimental psychology traditionally called human verbal learning. The material to be learned is often a sequence of nonsense syllables, a sequence whose elements have no inherent meaning by themselves and whose only structure is one of serial order. The serial order offers only the most trivial sense of meaning in that one syllable precedes the next. Hence, the sequence has no sense of dimensional order to it, and the way in which it is learned can perhaps be explained within the contiguity framework of traditional stimulus-response psychology, *without* the need to invoke any other learning process.

The second general form of learning is *dimensional*. It involves the gradual acquisition of information that is explicitly or implicitly, literally or figuratively, distributed in space. The information derives at least part of its meaning and hence its utility from the inherent dimensions of spatial relationship—the qualities of separation into far and near, and of direction to and from. Dimensional information contains built-in properties of order and meaning that must be recognized in the learning process.

In getting to know their way around Beartown, the Stock family is engaged in dimensional learning. The Stocks must acquire knowledge of the whereness of people and things. The process by which their literal and figurative distribution in geographical space is learned is a particular class of dimensional learning that considers spaces ranging in scale from the architectural through the global. The Stocks are concerned with understanding spaces at the house, neighborhood, and city-wide scales.

Environmental learning (and hence cognitive mapping) is an interactive process (see Chapter 3). It cannot occur without some direct experience in the manipulation of environmental objects or their surrogates in space (see Box 7.1), or of oneself in the environment (Held and Rekosh, 1963).

BOX 7.1
AIDS TO ENVIRONMENTAL LEARNING

Struck by the fact that children display evidence of environmental learning from the age at which they begin to speak (Blaut and Stea, 1971), a few researchers have become concerned with the question, *how* does this learning come to be? Thus far, little attention has been focussed, in studies of early development, upon the *environmental* experience of the small child. Hence, *aids* to environmental learning are still being identified. These aids—which include pictorial magazines, television, and toys—are also *surrogates* for *direct* environmental experience at those ages at which the child is too small to have much direct experience. Thus, aerial and oblique views of a variety of landscapes are frequent features of pictorial magazines and television news broadcasts. However, it is noteworthy that even in areas of the world where television and pictorial magazines are rarities, children show the same advanced spatial cognition of the environment. The one feature of interest, which appears common to the lives of children in Massachusetts, Venezuela, Brazil, Puerto Rico, Haiti, and elsewhere in the Caribbean, is the possession and use of that group of objects that we call *environmental modelling toys*. If they cannot purchase toys, they make them. These toys, which include miniature houses, cars, trees, streets, and so on, go beyond magazines and television as aids to learning, for they can be *manipulated* to model any existing environment in the child's world or fantasized environment in the child's mind. A child can easily take a vicarious trip through his table-top village, and can *perceive* the relationship among objects in the environment that he can only *cognize* in the full-scale world.

Some psychologists in the 1930s were concerned with children's toy play in much the above sense. Their writings on this subject, however, were given a sound verbal thrashing by more psychoanalytically oriented psychologists, who claimed that the manifest content of such toy play was quite unimportant—what *was* important, they said, was the latent evidence of castration anxiety, penis envy, oedipal feelings, and so on. Consequently, most of the study of toy play by psychologists during the forties and fifties involved dolls, with which the child was assumed to be acting out interpersonal and intrafamilial conflicts. The *social* content was heavily studied while the environmental content was ignored.

Toy play is thus one route by which a *child* learns about spatial environments; recently, it has been shown that adults, as well, can effectively use toys to indicate the extent of their own environmental knowledge (Stea and Taphanel, 1974). Problems with the "freely drawn map technique," as used by Lynch (1960), led to the development of a variety of other techniques to assess environmental cognition. Among the criticisms of Lynch's technique, three are quite basic: (1) freely drawn maps produce less information than simple place listing; (2) they are heavily dependent upon graphic or spatial literacy and previous experience with maps; and (3) some people, particularly rural inhabitants of developing nations, find the task of drawing a map on a blank sheet of paper a threatening situation. Toys, representing important buildings, areas, nodes, and so on, can be used by the adult to reflect his knowledge of places and of their locations on an outline map of an urban area.

The toy play that enables the child to learn enables the adult to describe the extent of his own learning—but what aids to environmental learning does the adult have at his or her disposal? Clearly, he learns something about a variety of environments via his own set of "surrogates": television, movies, the travel section of his local newspaper, stamp collecting, reading, and so on. But he directly experiences more environments than ever before in this globe-trotting era. He or she travels through them, and the *mode of travel* is thus an aid to further environmental learning. The mode of travel may be local or long distance; it may be below, at, or above the surface of the earth; it may involve the rider passively, or the walker or driver actively, as described elsewhere in this chapter. Riding Boston's underground rail system gives a very different image of the city than driving its much-less-comprehendible maze of streets above. Some claim that the reverse is true for Manhattan. Among the "passive" transportation modes, trains now carry us *above* and *beneath* cities, and a few even operate *between* cities, while both long- and short-distance buses operate at ground level. But what about air travel?

We have mentioned the cognitive issues inherent in long-distance air travel (see the discussion of cognitive distance in Chapter 4). While attention has been focussed elsewhere upon disruption of the *time* sense, and its associated discomforts—disturbances in diurnal cycle because of rapid time-zone changes, and so on—much less attention has been directed to disruptions of one's *spatial* sense. The "eleven capitals" tour of Europe ("we offer a better tour because we give you *one more* city") is a point-to-point, genuinely *punctate* experience, because the connections *between* points are usually unknown and apparently regarded as irrelevant. The only information may be a sequence of time, as given by the itinerary ("if this is Tuesday, it must be Belgium"), and, to the traveller shuttled from city to city, the path connecting London, Paris, Brussels, Amsterdam, Frankfurt, Munich, Vienna, Milan, Rome, Athens, and Madrid might be a straight line, or a circle, or take any other form. He or she may learn something about the details of the *Tour Eiffel,* but learns nothing about the spatial relationship among areas and places, which has affected European geopolitics and contributed so much to the history of the Continent. Environmental experience is more than a temporal sequence of points, and travel may *not* be an aid to environmental learning.

But such interactive experience—such response to the spatial environment—is of a very different order than that considered in traditional stimulus-response (i.e., nondimensional) learning. How, for example, could one describe the acquisition of the knowledge of "home range" in either the younger Stock children or even animals as exclusive consequences of a simple series of stimulus-response connections? If we *always* assume the existence of a restricted system of pathways and if we further assume that the learning of *each* path occurs as the solution to a single, isolated spatial problem, only then can we explain what we consider dimensional learning in this nondimensional form. Indeed, some environmental learning in western cities, especially among people whose spatial patterns of movement are restricted (e.g., the oldest Stock child), may occur in this nondimensional manner. But one cannot thus explain how Mrs. Stock manages to find her way among rooms she has never visited, in the order in which she now traverses them, any more than one can explain how Mr. Stock knows the geographical configuration of the towns surrounding Beartown, towns that he has never visited. Even less can we explain the behavior of animals defending the invisible boundaries of their territories or avoiding places of danger in their home ranges as the *result* of the nondimensional learning of a series of stimulus-response connections. An animal that had to learn the spatial distribution of attractive and dangerous things in its physical environment in so atomistic a way would have scant chance of survival.

Can we use the example of an animal, "environmentally learning" a natural setting, to understand the process of dimensional learning? A natural setting is to be differentiated from the highly controlled, and hence also highly constrained setting of the psychological laboratory. It is inherent in the nature of environmental learning situations that the subject, the animal in this case, must at some point be left free to wander at will, to choose one path among many. It is equally as inherent in the nature of the laboratory situation that the subject cannot wander at will, lest control be lost. The laboratory situation gains precision at the expense of realism, while the natural setting represents the reverse; thus, we are often faced with a choice between results that are precisely meaningless or fuzzily meaningful.

Suppose we free an ordinary domestic cat from the confines of the laboratory and allow him to wander at will within a new house in Beartown. Wandering at will involves environmental familiarization, territorialization, and the establishment of home range, in roughly that order. It is undeniable that his sensory experience is different from ours. He sniffs, for instance, more than we do, and what he sees at eye level is generally but a few inches above the floor. Most of us have shared the Stock's experience of moving to a new house, of sealing up all of the available exits during the first day of residence, only to find the pet cat has disappeared a few minutes after completion of the sealing job. Our *umwelt* (von Uexkull, 1957) of possible exits is different from that of the cat, as is our way of integrating the exits with the layout of the house as a whole. Our goals, too, are different. To accomplish the goals enumerated at the beginning of this paragraph, the cat rapidly samples his new environment, establishing a series of *means-ends relationships* (Tolman, 1948, 1958) in a perfectly shameless display of what some would term teleology.

The cat's spatial behavior and learning are guided by anticipated goals and well-formed plans. It is hard to imagine that the cat would survive if it had to stroll about until it encountered goal objects or places by accident. Survival depends upon the emergence (through dimensional learning) of cognitive maps that suggest *where* certain things are likely to be found. Undoubtedly, nondimensional associative learning enables animals *and* people to build up initial cognitive maps of an area; to establish the early or "primitive" stages of each succeeding map; and thereafter, to extract segments of these maps. Thus, as Stephen Kaplan (1973) argues, the perception of environmental circumstances leads by association to possible next alternatives, and from these to possibilities still further down the road. (This argument underlies his neurophysiological model that was reviewed in Chapter 6.) But it *also* appears that such associative learning is only a small part of cognitive mapping and environmental learning.

We can complete this picture of environmental learning if we recall the spatial experiences of Mr. Stock. Over time, he began to feel at home in Beartown and graduated to an understanding of the overall spatial layout of the city. This "graduation" reflects a shift from nondimensional to dimensional learning, from associative or stimulus-response learning to place learning or cognitive mapping. His *initial* reactions to wayfinding problems necessarily involved stimulus response, or, more simply, *response* learning. The later acquisition of a comfortable "feel" for the place depended upon an integrated knowledge of the spatial relationships between many starting points and many goals (or many means and ends). This is *place* learning. The distinction between response and place learning lies in the nature of the learning process, the way in which spatial information is integrated, and what finally emerges as the way of coping with spatial problems.

Response learners such as Mrs. Stock engage in what Kevin Lynch (1960) calls *route mapping*, a process that produces a chain-like series of connections of choice points with their associated cues. (See Figure 7.5 for an example of a route map.) Place learners, on the other hand, engage in *survey mapping*, which leads to an array of places with a rich "mesh" of associated connections among them. These survey maps may *begin* as a collection of simple route maps, as a set of specific behavioral responses to specific problems and plans. Since Mrs. Stock, in her homemaker role, typically follows only a few well-established paths in her routine trips through Beartown, her mapping never gets beyond this stage. However, as Mr. Stock makes more varied trips around Beartown, he ceases to view his trips as following individual and quite separate routes. He recognizes a *spatial relationship* among the routes, which transcends the sequential elements of a specific trip. The comfortable "feel" he acquires comes from a qualitatively different form of knowledge of the city than that possessed by his wife. The response-learned "pieces" have been fitted into a new and more coherent whole. This new, dimensional whole permits a more flexible and "superior" approach to spatial problem solving. Thus, if a route to some goal is blocked, Mr. Stock knows how to detour onto other routes in order to get to his destination.

Place learning does *not* supercede response learning in all environmental contexts; rather, most people are (at least in principle) capable of doing both. People who employ survey mapping can shift to a route mapping when the occasion demands. Such "downshifting" often occurs when one first arrives in an area or when one is confronted with a

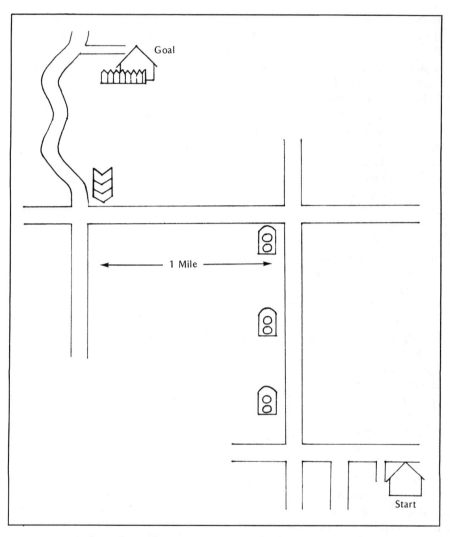

Figure 7.5. A hypothetical route *map* in which compass directions, street
    names, and some other cues are considered irrelevant. The corre-
    sponding *list* of instructions (a verbal route map) might read as fol-
    lows: (1) Leave your driveway and turn left; (2) go down two
    blocks; (3) turn right; (4) go past two traffic signals; (5) turn left at
    the third; (6) continue for about a mile until you come to a "Stan-
    dard" gasoline station; (7) turn right; (8) follow the road as it curves
    uphill; (9) look to your right just past the crest of the hill where
    you'll see a red house with a white picket fence; and (10) turn into
    the driveway.

physical environment that literally defies successful survey mapping.
In the sense that one kind of learning typically precedes the other, this
downshifting from the more advanced to the more primitive seems the
reversal of development. Other psychological evidence (e.g., White,

1965) suggests that a learner shifts from cognitive mapping to stimulus-response learning in states of stress or disturbance, or in the face of other difficulties and impediments.

The graduation from response to place learning is influenced by four major factors: the form of the physical environment, the type of spatial experience, the duration of that experience, and the age of the person involved. It is difficult to say that any one of these factors is more important than the others; however, it is possible to say that the nature of the physical environment always constrains the process (as well as the product) of environmental learning. These constraints apply equally to response and place learning.

ENVIRONMENTAL LEARNING AND THE
FORM OF THE PHYSICAL ENVIRONMENT

Plans are the building blocks for *all* environmental learning. A plan must be "energized," or motivated, in order to be put into action. But its execution depends upon feedback from the spatial environment. We seek cues that tell us how far we are along a path to the successful realization of our plan. In the spatial setting of *all* plans, these cues are the "signs we learn to read" (Brower, 1965). Thus Worcester, Massachusetts, is said to be a "city of drug stores and gas stations," since, in the outlying areas, these generally illuminated places are likely to be the only cues (or landmarks) visible at night. It is always possible to generate a route mapping by selecting cues and linking them to a sequence of behavioral actions. But for an area to be place mapped, it must lend itself to the formation of a set of *rules*, and the learner must have opportunities for a variety of travel experiences within it so as to test out these rules. Worcester is so irregular that almost no set of place-mapping rules seems to work. ("When you reach a drug store, change direction" is about the best advice that anyone has yet been able to offer!)

Some of the possible ways of place mapping an area will take precedence over others. We try to learn a set of rules that can cover as wide a range of spatial problems as possible. This search for generality and flexibility leads to the development of an heuristic—a general set of rules for coping with route choice, directional change, direction giving, and so on. The best-known heuristic, that for wayfinding in a grid-form city, is based on the following: "A set of streets runs east-west and a set of avenues runs north-south. The two sets lie at right angles to each other. One street serves as the origin axis for street numbering and one avenue as the origin for avenue numbering. Street and avenue numbers increase going in any direction from the point formed by the intersection of these two axes. A distinction is made between east and west numbers, and north and south numbers." To this basic spatial structure can be added problem-solving strategies: "If I turn in the same direction at four successive corners, I will be back at my starting point (since the blocks are always rectangular)."

Both survey maps and heuristics have many advantages for a person attempting to cope with the spatial environment. The simple grid-form heuristic will serve *almost* as well for such diverse areas as Manhattan Island (New York north of City Hall) and Puebla, Mexico. All that we have to do is to tailor the general rules to fit the specific identity of a particular city. If we add to our general rule system for Manhattan the fact that streets are numbered sequentially from north to south and avenues from east to west, and for Puebla the fact that street numbers are odd on one side of the Plaza Mayor and even on the other, we have completed most of the "picture" for both cities. And it *is* pictorial, in the sense that a good heuristic provides the basis for a *mental picture*. It can be visualized; it can be "read." It is perhaps the simplest way of coming to grips with the world around us. To use Lynch's (1960) terminology, the spatial environment must be both *imageable* and *legible* for a useful heuristic to be formed.

And once formed, heuristics can be *transferred* from one city to another sharing some common structural characteristics. We form a frame of reference via environmental learning, a template that acts very much like a psychological "set," predisposing us to attack new environmental learning situations in certain ways. Fortunately, the morphologies of Bull City and Beartown are similar so that Mr. Stock faces no great problem in adapting his earlier heuristic to his new location. There is no question that his earlier environmental experience is affecting the way in which he now engages in environmental learning. How does past mapping affect future mapping? Two sets of factors act upon future problem solving: (1) *what* has been learned before, and (2) *how* it has been learned. Both the what and how relate to the application of learning acquired in one situation to a new situation, that is, to the *transfer* of learning. They also relate to the acquisition of principles or heuristics of learning, a process known as "learning to learn."

The latter deserves some additional clarification. Suppose that a group of tasks are to be learned, all of which have certain principles in common. One can either learn each task as an individual enterprise independent of all others (response learning) *or* learn the underlying principles (developing heuristics via place learning in the spatial case). The first is fairly typical of the way that things are taught in public schools; the second involves learning to learn. Paradoxically, the best-known studies of learning to learn have been done with monkeys (Harlow, 1949).

The environmental learning process is *so* unconscious and seems *so* incidental in comparison to apparently more demanding aspects of everyday life that we have little realization of just *what* we have learned and *how* demanding the learning process is. Getting to know the physical structure of a new city is an arduous, time-consuming, and, above all, worrisome process. Robert Coles (1971) has provided some insights into the stresses associated with environmental learning through his interviews with migrants from rural areas who have moved to a city. These people are confronted with a *novel* physical and social environment, one that is beyond their normal experience and yet one that must be learned rapidly. A man from Tunica County, Mississippi, sheds revealing light on those things that we normally take for granted in a city:

> But now he is in a city, up North in one. Now he lives there. Now, every single day, there are those streets. And now he is "used to things." What things, though? What up North has he day by day come to accept as the ordinary, the expected? "It started with the sidewalks and the sewers," he will say. He is trying to convey what took him by surprise when he "hit" Chicago, when he entered the city and saw one street and then another. They were beautifully paved. And black people lived all around. He had never before seen so many people, so many black people, and so many sidewalks and paved streets and sewers "that belong to them, the colored man."
>
> (Coles, 1971, p. 4)

A Black who moved from Georgia to Harlem contributed this vivid picture of *what* is learned and what this learning *costs*:

> He describes all the "trouble" he met up with and came to understand — and not to fear so much. He describes the things he gradually took for granted: those junkies, the soot in the air, the roar of the buses and garbage trucks and freight trucks and the elevated railroad and the machines being used to build or tear down or repair buildings. He describes gutters and hydrants and lampposts and automobile meters; they are all part of the city, part of the streets of Harlem — and it was only when his family at last did come up, and when he saw *them* noticing all those things, and complaining about any number of these things, it was only then that he realized what *he* had gone through; . . .
>
> And almost invariably he finds that when he lets his mind go back, when he dwells upon the past, he ends up remembering not the South but himself as new to the North, new to New York City and Harlem and those streets he now drives over, all over — to the extent that sometimes his wife will wake up in the middle of the night and hear him reciting them, their numbers, their names, their origins, their endings.
>
> (Coles, 1971, pp. 22–23)

Coming to terms with the physical structure of New York City is a difficult and demanding task. Some parts do lend themselves to survey mapping and place learning — other parts are only partially known as a disconnected maze of routes. Despite these problems, the "whereness" of the people and things must be learned — whereness is intimately associated with directions. We may dispute a recent advertisement's contention that "in New York the last person you should ask for directions is a New Yorker," *if* we take it as implying that the person most ignorant of an area is the one who lives there. A second possibility is that people are *too* familiar with their home areas, so familiar in fact that they cannot understand the navigational problems of strangers. A third implication, so commonplace now as to be part of popular "wisdom," is that New Yorkers know *less* about New York than other people do about their own home towns.

Although this plausible and, to many people, appealing third contention has *not* been substantiated, it is true that major cities are difficult places with which to come to grips. Perhaps the group of people who could be expected to have the most coherent, flexible knowledge system for coping with any city are taxicab drivers. Yet New York cab drivers are achieving a dubious reputation as wayfinders. The cab driver interviewed by Robert Coles must be an exception because his colleagues do not seem to know the city (The Empire What Building?). Whatever the truth, they certainly pale in comparison with London cab drivers. In large part, the New York-London difference can be attributed to the *nature* of the environmental learning process. Would-be cab drivers in London are required to spend over a year bicycling around the city in order to practice following 450 routes that connect major points of interest; they learn the city by *actively* interacting with it. They must also pass several stringent examinations before they are granted a taxicab license. The examinations, called "the knowledge" by the drivers themselves, assess detailed awareness of the spatial layout of London. No such elaborate learning is required by New York law. But cab drivers in other cities also face wayfinding problems, although the problem lies not in the learning process itself, but in the nature of what is to be learned. One would expect, for example, that since cab drivers have the greatest opportunity to experience the physical form of the city *and* the greatest need to know how the parts of the city relate together, cab drivers will form survey maps. Unfortunately, Worcester, Massachusetts, does not lend itself to such a place-learning process, and Rand (1969) found that Worcester taxi drivers were route mappers. Michon (1972, p. 100) reports that Parisian taxi drivers come close to achieving an overall survey map of the city:

> Some studies by Pailhous (1968) on the internal representations of Paris taxi drivers show the existence of a basic grid and several secondary grids, which are confined to small parts of the town and are related only to the basic grid.

This knowledge structure is part way between a route map and a survey map. In developmental terms, it falls between the egocentric and coordinated spaces that children construct (see Chapter 6). The volume of research involving taxi drivers is surprising. Along the same lines, Psathas and Henslin (1967) have analyzed the ways in which taxicab dispatchers communicate the location of potential customers using a fairly simple but effective "spatial language" in their radio messages.

How does the ordinary New Yorker cope with his city? He can turn to learning aids, which help to simplify the city, to make it legible and imageable. Thus, *Flash Maps* (Lasker, 1972) is supposed to be an aid to learning New York. In the opinion of the editors of *Flash Maps*, however, accomplishment of this task requires the sacrifice of cartographic accuracy and veracity. With the exception of the first map, which presents an overall view of the city (Figure 7.6), the shape of Manhattan is seriously distorted (e.g., Figure 7.7).

If *Flash Maps* reduces Manhattan to a squat shadow of its former self, another learning aid, "New Subway Routes," published by the New York City Transit Authority (Figure 7.8), makes Manhattan almost unrecognizable. This schematically simple structure is generated in order to depict subway routes in what the Transit Authority perceives to be the clearest way possible. In spite of a complex and conceptually difficult city layout, the learning process *can* be made easier; thus, distortion in the service of clearer plans is no vice.

The discerning reader will have noticed in comparing Figures 7.7 and 7.8 that the direction of "north" is indicated in neither map *and* that the two Manhattans have different orientations as well as shapes. The alteration is small but easily recognizable. However, it causes no difficulty in itself to those accustomed to "conventional" map orientation (i.e., to those who have "learned" that maps have "tops" and "bottoms"). New Yorkers seem to be remarkably cavalier in their approach to map orientation. A writer for *The New York Times* (Burks, 1971) noted that the official working maps for the Borough of the Bronx were "sideways"; i.e., west was at the top of the map instead of north:

> Yankee Stadium is in the upper Bronx, right? And the New York Giants are moving up to Jersey, right? Also, as any Bronx official could tell you, the Hudson River on his official borough map seems to flow from west to east.
>
> If all this sounds like things aren't on the up and up, it's because of that strange official map. Things are officially atilt.
>
> Nobody seems to know for sure how and why it started, but for some years the official borough map shows the borough in a sideways position. ... The effect is somewhat like trying to tell time when the "12" on the clock face is where the "3" should be.
>
> That means that the Hudson River runs across the top of the map like some Northwest Passage. And City Hall in Manhattan would be far out in left field for the Bronxite studying his official map.

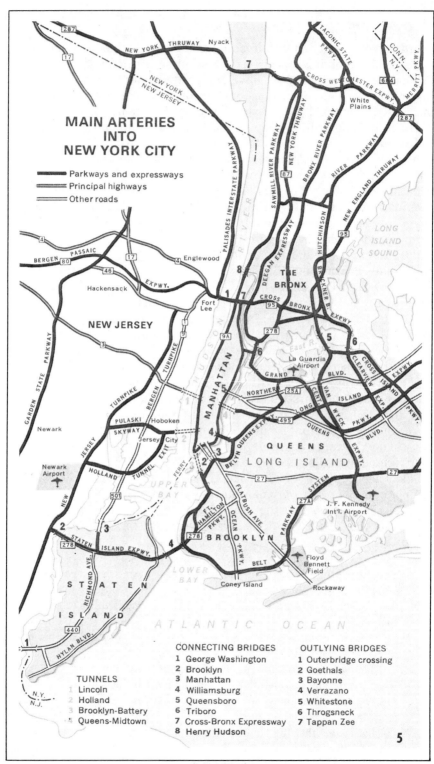

Figure 7.6. The *actual* form of New York City (from *Flash Maps*).

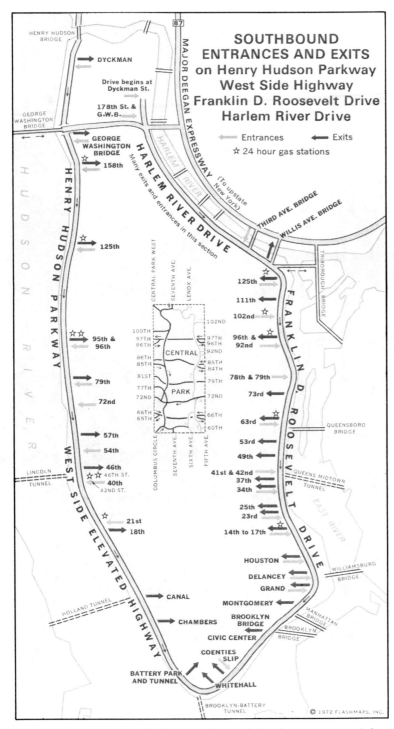

Figure 7.7. A "squat" Manhattan, distorted for the purposes of depicting highway entrances and exits.

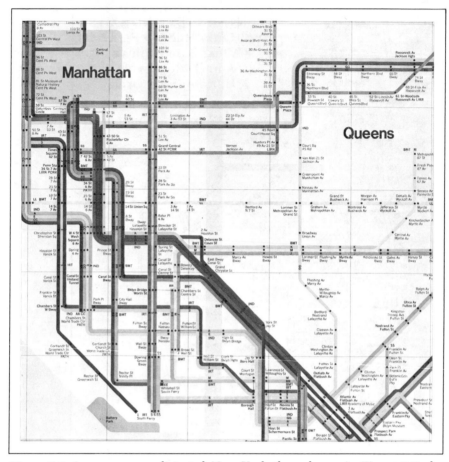

Figure 7.8. An even more distorted New York than shown in Figure 7.7, designed to help New Yorkers (and others) find (and even learn) subway routes.

While the Bronx Public Information Officer

> ... claims to have no difficulty in reading the askew map, it is not uncommon to observe others canting their heads sharply to the right to get their bearings ... "Up here (he should have said, "out here") everyone orients himself by the Grand Concourse and the Concourse on these maps runs directly across them."

However, the consulting engineer to the Borough President pointed to the problems of a tilted Bronx and said:

> ... at least as far back as 1895 the official map was sideways. He surmised that turning the map sideways made it easier to read the name of

the major streets like the Concourse, but he added: "People look at it and say, 'Gee, where's Riverdale?'"

(He) also confessed that in his own office he had turned the sideways map around so that the north was at the top, as on other maps. "I got confused so I turned it around to match the rest of the city," he said.

(Burks, 1971, p. 77)

THE ROLES OF EXPERIENCE AND AGE IN LEARNING

Although we have focussed on the relationship between environmental learning and the form of the physical environment, the outcome of the learning process is also influenced by a host of other factors. Preeminent among these influences are the tangled effects of the type of environmental experience, the length of this experience, and the age at which it occurs. Unravelling this tangle is virtually impossible because, as we have argued in Chapter 6, learning and development are but two facets of the same ongoing process.

We can use the Stock family's experience as a means of breaking into this age and experience relationship. Mrs. Stock solves spatial problems in a different way than does Mr. Stock: She is a route mapper while he is a survey mapper. But, just as significantly, Mrs. Stock's approach to the world differs from that of her children. She is less adept at map reading and thus avoids these learning aids whenever possible. She finds that maps are confusing and time consuming, and she makes mistakes when forced to use them. The opposite is true of her children.

One explanation for this apparently paradoxical situation is contained in our argument that environmental learning begins to occur at a very early point in the child's development (prior to school-entering age). But what *may* occur then as the result of a continually *decreasing* exposure in school to representations of things in geographical space (e.g., via maps, aerial photos, models, etc.) is a *diminution* in geographical knowledge as the child grows older. By diminution, we do not mean a loss of information, but a fundamental change in how this information is known (i.e., stored and processed). The child understands environments less well in a *spatial* sense because of the reinforcement in school of another specifically *verbal* mode of information processing. In the Brunerian sense (see Box 6.2), the symbolic mode of representation comes to supercede the iconic (or image-based) mode: The educational system strongly reinforces this shift. Bruner emphasizes that having shifted to the symbolic does *not* mean that the child has left earlier modes of representation behind; supposedly, a return to the iconic and the enactive is always possible. But we are suggesting that the ability to return to and make use of earlier forms of representation may decrease with time. Evidence cited in Chapter 6 argues that environmental learning is developmentally "primitive"; that is, we now suspect that it begins early in life and that it may even be a prototype for other forms of learning. However, the adults who create educational systems often regard the child's mind as essentially a *tabula rasa*, blank and waiting to be written upon. It is often said that large-scale environments (i.e., at the geographical scale) are difficult for children to comprehend. Thus, it is assumed that environmental learning must be *introduced* quite formally, fairly late in the child's schooling. But Stea and Blaut (1973a and b) suggest that children may have reached the *asymptote* of environmental learning, under the present system of teaching, at about the age where "orthodox" educational theories propose that a child is ready to *begin* such learning (grades 4–6 or ages 10–12). Children can deal with, and enjoy dealing with, maps — the graphic representations of the world around them. Unfortunately, the same is not true of all adults; many share Mrs. Stock's reaction to a map. "Sorry but I can't read maps" is *not* a phrase out of the mouths of babes.

The processes by which children learn and *mentally* represent their environments are subjects of conjecture; their representational outputs or cognitive maps are not. Between the ages of about three and six, the normal child "graduates" from grouping "environmental modelling toys" — houses, cars, trees, and so on — by common form or color, to arranging them so as to represent the spatial structure of a portion of his world — a town, for example. A similar change in the form of representation occurs in the child's drawing of the familiar route from home to school (see Figure 7.4). The data provided earlier in this chapter were distilled, with some liberties, from an unpublished study of Scottish school children by T. G. R. Bower. Bower found that children "graduate" from straight-line depiction to more realistic sketches of the home-school route during the first few years of schooling. That the motoric ability to depict *graphically* an environment lags behind the ability to *model* it, and that development of the latter parallels (or may even lag behind) the ability to identify abstracted environmental features in aerial photos, is quite understandable. A high level of development of motor ability is decreasingly involved in this sequence of mapping skills.

What seems essential for normal environmental learning to occur, however, is the interaction of sensory perception and motor experience. One has to *feel* that one is moving through a space to really perceive it as it is or to learn it in its full richness. (And even movement does not guarantee *full* understanding; recall the difference between the sighted and the blind person's description of the same work-to-home route that we discussed in Chapter 3.) The Stock's oldest child does not interact with the environment in the same way as do the younger children. They walk, whereas he rides a bus. T. G. R. Bower has reported that at least one group of adult tourists, after a bus ride through a town, drew route maps much like those of his six-year-old children! In another study done several years ago, however, a group of people who were strangers to an area of Rio de Janeiro were taken on a walk through the area and then asked to draw maps of the route. Some of the sketches showed considerable detail and quite sophisticated knowledge of spatial structure. Clearly, there is a major difference between walking through a place and being bussed through it, as anyone knows who has "done" a place both alone and on a guided bus tour.

We are emphasizing the distinction between *active* and *passive* spatial experience, previously discussed in Chapter 3. Active spatial experience involves walking, cycling, driving; passive experience involves riding or being driven around. There is an important difference, when approaching an intersection, between having to decide what direction to take *and* feeling the results of that decision, and to having both the decision and action taken for you. Thus, to learn how to learn spatial environments, one must experience a variety of environments and experience them actively.

Passive experience of a new environment can result in confusion and uncertainty; one never seems to get the layout of a place "straight" in one's mind. Alfred Binet (1894) presented a series of accounts of orientation problems and this one, by a French physiologist, shows how mistaken impressions are formed:

I arrived for the first time at Croisic one morning at the break of day. I had slept in the train on leaving St. Nazaire, and it was only a few moments before arriving at Croisic that I was wakened by the voice of one of my travelling-companions. He showed us the sea just coming into view in the distance. It was at this moment that from the general direction of the river (only a small part of which I saw) and from the general direction of the railroad I deduced the direction of the north and the sea. I left the train with this orientation. Croisic is situated on a peninsula, so that in going through the town and its surrounding country I often saw the sea in different directions. I then chose unconsciously that one of the directions which coincided with the orientation which had been established in my mind at the moment I left the train. I repeated this many times, visiting Croisic and its surroundings, and comparing everything with this orientation. I discovered that this was false by seeing a boat start out from the pier for a certain destination which I thought lay in quite the opposite direction.

By means of a compass I corrected the error. During the rest of my stay at Croisic I had two very distinct orientations: the first, the false one, which had imposed itself on my mind, persisted in spite of me; and the second, the true one, which I found only at certain moments thereafter by reflection with a marked effort of will. When I was in the streets of the town or in a house, I suffered no annoyance from this fact; but when I made an excursion into the surrounding country, or when someone mentioned to me the name of a distant place, Belle-Isle, England, New York, I suffered very great inconvenience in representing the place to myself in its true situation. This annoyance, this indefinable distress, slightly comparable to that which one suffers when dizzy, persisted during the whole time of my stay at Croisic (about a month and a half). This state left an impression in my mind so disagreeable that now, whenever I arrive in a place which I do not know, I take care to orientate myself properly.

(Binet, 1894, pp. 344–345)

Such impressions, though false and misleading, are curiously ineradicable. They literally stick in our minds, and both Trowbridge (1913) and Gatty (1958) have commented on this persistence, which runs counter even to later spatial experiences. Binet (1894, pp. 342–343) quotes one man who even learned to live with his mistaken view of the world:

> When I think of a place, a street, a monument in Lyons, I myself being at Paris, I picture to myself a map of Lyons turned around. A certain side of Lyons is nearest to Paris, that by which I enter Lyons in going *as the crow flies* from Paris to Lyons. I invariably picture Lyons in such a way that the wrong part of it is brought around in the direction of Paris ... This habit of orientation takes such hold upon me that I prefer to arrive in Lyons at the depot on the side which I picture toward Paris, although the other depot would be more convenient.

Could there be a more convincing demonstration of the power of cognitive maps?

In disentangling the roles of age and type of experience in channeling what we learn and how we learn it, we should not forget that children form impressions of more than just their neighborhoods or cities. They learn to cognize their nations as well. Their knowledge changes, both quantitatively *and* qualitatively, over time (and space):

> As a small part of a much larger study investigating residential perception surfaces in Sweden, the preferences of many children were sampled at Jonkoping, a town in south-central Sweden ... between the three main urban focuses of Stockholm, Goteborg, and Malmo. The children worked directly upon large maps showing the seventy ... functional regions, with major roads, towns, and water bodies shown as a light blue underprinting to give some general orientation.

(Gould, 1973, p. 236)

From age seven-and-a-half to thirteen-and-a-half, the Swedish children in Gould's study demonstrated a lawful sharpening of their spatial preferences. These preferences are obviously related to knowledge of the country as a whole. Thus, for example, when asked to write down the names of all the Swedish cities and towns that they could produce in five minutes, the children generated:

> ... information surfaces — surfaces that develop in such a regular manner that one can almost use the first series of maps as a crude model to predict the next in the sequence ... Younger children seem to store only the strongest signals of information from small places close to them, or the very large places far away. Older children ... store the cumulative impact of many weak signals that never appear to be received by the youngest group.
>
> (Gould, 1973, p. 244)

These signals are the result neither of active nor of passive spatial experience. Instead, they are the residual impacts of the mass media: television, radio, and the press. Much knowledge of the world, even of our local areas, is indirect, second- or even third-hand. Learning the world involves far more than the simple and rather obvious consequences of patterns of spatial behavior. Learning is a blending process in which we mix "spatial fact" with imaginative fiction and in which we progress from "real" to fantasy worlds.

CONCLUSIONS

Psychologists claim to know a great deal about the process of learning, and very much less about what is learned. Environmental psychologists and behavioral geographers know about the environments that are learned, but very little about the process. In this chapter, we have attempted to unite the two, to bring the processes and products of environmental learning together through a number of examples. We know that such learning plays an extremely pervasive role, beginning to appear in infancy, but continuing through various stages in life. But the "practical" importance of the learning process may not be fully evident until after adolesence (and may be hidden even then). In our mobile society, people are continually forced to occupy, and to adjust to, brand-new environments. Because of the paucity of public transportation and the great expense of moving within the U.S.A., these same people often must drive their own vehicles from one location to another and then around the new place after arrival. Learning must be rapid and veridical, for the costs of mistakes are high. Lynch's legible city may have been an aesthetic nicety in the nineteenth century; whether aided by signs or not, it is indispensable today.

Chapter 8

COGNITIVE MAPPING IN EVERYDAY LIFE

INTRODUCTION

We began this book by evoking a sense of place, that comfortable feeling of being at home in and belonging to some particular part of the world. At the base of this feeling is the uncharted world in the head, the mysteries of which we tried to penetrate by viewing a series of "snapshots" that "caught" some of the links between cognitive maps and everyday life. In going beyond these fragmentary glimpses, we were forced to explore the world in the head, an exploration that, to adapt some appropriate spatial metaphors, has taken us far afield to the four corners of the mind. Thus, cognitive maps and cognitive mapping are no longer shadowy peaks emerging from a distant *terra incognita;* we have probed into many of these previously unknown areas. We have, for example, talked about the learning of new places and the development of the capacity to learn. By focussing on two particular places (Puluwat and Boston), we have seen cognitive mapping at work. Mapping as a process and maps as products have been distinguished and explained. Throughout this exploration, we have tried to stay close to the central idea that there is an intimate link between cognitive mapping and everyday life. By drawing examples from a wide variety of everyday contexts, we have metaphorically "been all over the place." As a consequence, we are of necessity in danger of losing sight of the wood for the trees. To redress the balance and to regain our overall sense of perspective on the world in the head, this concluding chapter will emphasize four themes that are reflective of and central to everyday life. By appreciating the role of cognitive mapping in each theme, we can gain added understanding of the design of urban spaces, the use of wayfinding signs, the role of games, and the worlds of fantasy and imagination.

THE DESIGN OF URBAN SPACES

From all that we have presented in the previous chapters, the reader might reasonably assume that cognitive mapping and its associated baggage has already been well harnessed in the service of the many urban and environmental crises:

> The urban crisis — supplanted now by new ones (pollution has spun off into its own full-blown crisis) — seems to have diminishing urgency precisely as the situation becomes increasingly critical. Not that the urban crisis was ever quite defused; we each supply our own definition according to where we live, how quickly we accept ready answers, and how much we are inconvenienced, threatened or thwarted by our separate urban worlds. Thus, to some, the most important paperback on the urban crisis will be "Park-A-Plan: Garage Parking in Central Manhattan" (Wry Products, $1.25), 13 pages of maps for the frustrated driver.
>
> (*The New York Times Book Review,* February 21, 1971)

Perhaps we may be able to assist in the solution of crises in the near future, but, as yet, we workers in this field cannot even take credit for the *Park-A-Plan* book. And unfortunately, the field is now a bit too well established for us to fall back on the "it's in its infancy" excuse for our lack of practical impact. For the most part, we have willingly remained incarcerated in our laboratories, making occasional and tentative forays into the field in order to collect some data. We hastily return to the warm nurturance of academia to prepare reports such as this one.

In a recent interview, Kevin Lynch, one of the acknowledged founders of cognitive mapping research, bemoaned the fact that studies of urban cognition have had few demonstrated applications (and quite a few misapplications), and that his own pioneering studies have been adopted by social scientists rather than planners. A few urban designers have taken Lynch's argument one step further: Because cognitive mapping research has been little applied, they claim that it cannot be applied and that it is an amusing intellectual tool of no particular value to planning practitioners. We obviously disagree! It is true that the high hopes aroused by Lynch's beguiling work have foundered on the rocks of everyday planning practicalities. However, although we have not produced a new cognitive design paradigm, we do believe that we have developed a powerful method of design analysis and evaluation.

Cognitive mapping provides a vehicle for assessing the impact and effectiveness of designs at both the urban and architectural scales. In this vein, cognitive maps generated by seasoned inhabitants of existing cities have been examined and reexamined. These examinations have detected areas of confusion, areas of great civic or wayfinding importance, "unknown" areas, and the "edges" of such areas as neighborhoods or downtown. But strangely, there have been few cognitive assessments of new towns. Even fewer have been the attempts to make design recommendations based upon such assessments. Donald Appleyard's work on the Venezuelan new town of Cuidad Guayana is one of these rarities. The problem, as he saw it, was clear:

> ... the planners' view of the city was ... culture bound. Their work environment—the symbolic world of maps, models, and data—created unknowingly a conception of the city quite distinct from the reality of those who lived there. Not that the population's view was monolithic. They, too, saw the same city in different ways.
>
> (Appleyard, 1969b, pp. 422–423)

Appleyard's survey regarding urban cognition was based on a series of interviews, the purpose of which was

> ... to test the effectiveness of different environments and measure the role of various environmental factors—physical, social, and functional—in the inhabitants' urban perception; and to learn if there were significant group differences in environmental attitudes and knowledge. This was an effort to give the designer a clearer picture of life in the city and to allow him to develop a more meaningful vocabulary of forms, functions, and social groups to use in designing the future development.
>
> (Appleyard, 1969b, p. 423)

By 1964, only the plans for the new town, which some expected to reach a population of 600,000 by 1980, had yet been formed. Over 300 persons from each of six environmentally distinct districts were interviewed, under the assumption that the responses of future populations to Cuidad Guayana could be predicted by the current population's cognitions of existing environments. Appleyard attempted to assess these cognitions using refinements of the techniques developed by Kevin Lynch. Graphic descriptions (freely drawn maps) and responses to questions were elicited; these included journey descriptions, assessments of current and future states of the area, and descriptions of idealized cities, using Cuidad Guayana as a base of comparison.

Subjects local to the area recalled the elements mentioned in their maps because of imageability, exposure, use, or significance, while strangers' recall was primarily because of visibility. New arrivals noted elements of economic significance and those related to environmental quality first, and more frequently used places later. Differences, both in elements mentioned and total organization, were found between the townspeople and the planners, between the educated and the relatively uneducated. Appleyard discovered land use and site plans to be inadequate descriptions of urban experience, the form of these representations being more appropriate depictions of building location and road construction than of the actual behavior, perception, and cognition of its inhabitants. The distinction was particularly noteworthy in this rapidly changing complex of communities, perhaps because the planners felt no particular need to inform the inhabitants about the changes that were taking place. The ambiguous information gleaned by the area's inhabitants concerning the future course of urban growth was of the sort that generates anxiety, insecurity, and fear of unpleasant surprises, that destroys the existing sense of structure without indicating the elements and connections from which new structure will eventually emerge.

> Patterns of social and functional significance . . . played a structural role. Territory occupied by similar social groups was looked upon as an entity, and for some respondents the need to identify with areas occupied by higher social groups distorted actual distances and intervening groups to gain desired relationships. One social worker living in apartments adjacent to the squatter area of Castillite insisted that her home was really part of the Puerto Ordaz model community some distance away . . . structural redundancy will be necessary for those of the population who structure by . . . methods (other than the sequential method provided by the design group). The pattern of physical character should be designed around the settings and patterns of habitual journeys in different travel modes. Prominent and visible sites, skylines, hilltops, and spurs should be selected now to give future landmarks a high range of visibility. The pattern of social significance and the naming of related elements should be part of the design. . . . Environmental values polarize around two sets of opposite qualities: concepts like unity, order, simplicity, dominance, symmetry, articulation, boundary, and control; and notions like diversity, richness, interest, choice, meaning, ambiguity, flexibility, and independence. Historically, city design has been more under the influence of the former set of concepts than the latter, and during the design of Ciudad Guayana there was a perceptible shift in the design group's attitudes from the first to the second set as their understanding of the problem grew. We have seen that the inhabitants, too, visualized the city in a variety of ways. If the first set of qualities are to be the only criteria for success, then Ciudad Guayana will have difficulty in succeeding, for its design will be based on a narrow set of values and will require an unrealistic degree of control.

(Appleyard, 1969b, pp. 442–444)

Appleyard's discussion of his results focuses on the gap between the ideas and efforts of the new town planners, and the cognitions of the area's inhabitants. The nature and form of urban knowledge possessed by the two groups is clearly distinct, as are the modes of representation of this knowledge. The Appleyard interview procedure expanded upon the Lynch approach in both the breadth of the survey (number and variety of knowledge probes) and the level of analysis attempted. Not only were the "potencies" of individual elements measured, but the overall map form classified and the accuracy of representation measured as well. The six interview areas were socially and physically distinguishable, so that the aggregate representations derived were genuinely pluralistic, and it is from these aggregate representations that Appleyard drew his conclusions and his recommendations to planners.

Appleyard's study of new town imagery was, in some ways, a form of "projective" cognitive mapping (see Saarinen, 1973), asking the Ciudad Guayanans not only to map what exists but also to project into the future. What *will* exist was the explicit content of some questions and the implicit concern of others. It was also a study of urban (or to-be-urban) cognitive mapping. Relatively few applications of cognitive mapping to small-town or rural settings have been attempted. Two exceptions are a recent analysis of the Mammoth Lake community in Central California (Reiff, 1972), and a somewhat earlier survey of the U.S. Wilderness Areas.

Mammoth Lake is a ski resort located some 300 miles (or more than six grueling hours' drive, as it is often measured) from Los Angeles. Drawing its trade almost exclusively from Southern California, it has succumbed to many Southern California "ills." Unlike many European ski resorts, it is a very dispersed village; like Los Angeles, it is dependent entirely upon the automobile for transportation, and again like Los Angeles, its newer buildings are of questionable architectural quality. A University of California planning team was asked by an organization known as the Friends of Mammoth to plan some alternative futures for the area, and the team used community attitude surveys, interviews, mapping exercises, and observational techniques to get a sense of the place.

In the Mammoth Lake section of the Sierra Nevada Mountains, summer, when the ground is clear, is a beautiful season for fishing and hiking, while winter, when the area is buried under deep snow, beckons skiers. Thus, two major seasonal changes occur: (1) the user groups are different, and (2) the visual quality of the landscape undergoes profound alteration The plain and even ugly buildings, which are pleasantly cloaked by snow in the winter, emerge into stark visibility in the summer, to the dismay of many:

> The heavy winter snow not only has a large impact on the perception of
> buildings but also on the images people form of the layout and structure

of the town. A major finding after attempting two different mapping exercises was that Mammoth's image was defined by the roads and a first conception of the structure of the community is generally a series of roadside corridors. . . . There was little recognition of any spatial depth beyond the buildings and the trees. The snow piling along (Route) 203 and the location of cars in front of the stores decreases the legibility of the area and makes it difficult to identify certain businesses and to determine points of access.

(Reiff, 1972, p. 1.4)

Reiff's report differs from other attempts at application in that it specifies what are called "visual quality implementation tools," and projects the effects upon visual quality of the choice of each of several alternative urban futures.

Few people, with the possible exception of residents of Central Manhattan, would ever classify the Mammoth Lakes community as "wilderness." But much of the National Forest surrounding Mammoth *is* wilderness to most, an area that is largely devoid of paved roads and is open primarily to the backpacker. In between are "transition" areas, wilderness to some but not to others. What, then, is wilderness? Clearly, it has an *official* designation, since the Sierra Club and other conservation organizations will battle to have a precisely bounded space declared a Wilderness Area. It has had a *legal* definition, since enactment of the Wilderness Act by Congress in 1964. But what is *cognized* as wilderness is another question (see Roderick Nash's (1967) attempt to trace the varying answers to this question throughout American history). Robert Lucas argues:

Much needs to be learned about the perception of individuals or of small, integrated, operating groups, such as a hiking party . . . Different types of visitors and resource managers may differ widely in their perception of the wilderness . . . in the Boundary Waters Canoe Area . . . a National Forest wilderness-type area, it was learned that there were two main types of visitors with two very different areal perceptions of wilderness. Neither "perceived wilderness" agreed closely with the officially designated area. . . . For one type of visitor, the wilderness was larger than the established area; for the other it was smaller. . . . The basic question posed by these differences is: What components of a landscape seem essential for its perception as wilderness, or critical in preventing such perception?

(Lucas, 1966, pp. 120–121)

Lucas (1966, p. 125) also comments trenchantly upon the relation between urban and wilderness landscape cognition:

Wilderness research may also contribute to the more general study of landscape (cognition). Although the complexity of wilderness research has been stressed, yet the problems are relatively simple compared to those of most environments. In the wilderness the visual environment seems far simpler than in Boston. . . . Furthermore, the motivation of the wilderness visitor with regard to the environment is probably simpler. Presumably, he seeks the wilderness environment to experience it. Boston, in contrast, is the backdrop to making a living for many observers, and this may complicate and confound the reaction to the environment. The urban environment likely is loaded with more involved, more varied, and more obscure symbolism.

Without doubt, the urban environment *is* loaded with and colored by symbolism. The symbols are value-laden, evoking positive and negative responses. A striking illustration of this valuational process is exemplified in the ambiguous feelings towards high-rise buildings. As skyscrapers, as part of the existing skyline, they evoke a mixture of awe and self-congratulatory pride. They stand for *the city* and provide a measure of our positive mastery over the physical world. But as proposed interlopers, as potential high-rise buildings that will violate the existing skyline, they evoke anger and outrage. Different reactions may be present in one person, but are more likely to represent the positions of conflicting interest groups. San Francisco provides a classic example of the course of such conflict.

The architect Frank Lloyd Wright once claimed, "San Francisco is the only city I can think of that could survive all the things people are doing to it and still look beautiful." But a significant and vocal portion of the city's inhabitants did not share this optimistic assessment. They saw proposed high-rise buildings as a destructive threat to the city's beauty. They campaigned against the "bigger is better" approach to urban design; they rallied around such slogans as "Skyscrapers are economically necessary, but only if you own one" (*Newsweek*, December 28, 1970, p. 47). Alcira Kreimer (1971) focused on the effect of these high-rise buildings upon cognitive maps of San Francisco. She ingeniously analyzed the myths surrounding the construction of high-rise buildings in San Francisco, and pointed to the central role played by the metaphors that were used to portray the effects of such construction upon the image of "The City."

Parenthetically, we may note that only two cities in the United States are regularly referred to as The City by the inhabitants of surrounding areas: San Francisco and Manhattan. The City does not apply to locations immediately north, south, or east of San Francisco nor to the other boroughs of New York City. Thus, a resident of Brooklyn, about to embark on the subway for Manhattan, will usually say: "I'm going to The City."

Some of the ideas behind Kreimer's work understandably resemble those of her teacher, Donald Appleyard. She has pitted the "real" against the "ideal" city, conceiving the fundamental controversy as one between San Francisco's romantic image and the problem images of such cities as New York (an image that is especially powerful among those who have never been to New York). In a larger sense, she is investigating mythologies concerning cities, how these mythologies are generated and the cognitive maps they generate in turn, and the specific effects of this generating process upon San Francisco. Her concern is the role of mass media in shaping cognitive maps; one significant conclusion is that designers base their designs upon patterns considered acceptable to the public, and that the nature of such acceptance is strongly influenced by the communications media.

Another conclusion is that the media tend to focus upon a single aspect of environmental change, while ignoring other aspects. In the high-rise building controversy in San Francisco, the focus has been on *height,* to the exclusion of form or color. Height, the vertical dimension of The City, is cognitively tied in with the overall humanity, or livability, of The City. The traditional image of San Francisco, of "civilized scale," of "reasonableness," of "humanized nature" is set against The Other City, Manhattan, which is seen as "out of scale," "unreasonable," "inhuman," and "superurbanized." Objectively, Manhattan is as visually accessible to a large body of water as is San Francisco, perhaps even more so since it has fewer dense fogs; despite this, it is rarely thought of as a maritime city (the same appears true of Boston). Some San Franciscans attribute this landlocked image to the plethora of tall buildings in New York. The evil image of New York is indeed so strong that the adjective "Manhattanization" has been coined by San Franciscans to describe the consequences of building construction that they envision. One respondent referred to " ... all those dark buildings thrown up by newcomers with cold New York hearts who think this town is Chicago. It's hard to measure how much damage they've done to San Francisco, but it's considerable."

The "vertical evil" (unrestricted height) was certainly seen as paramount, but consequences of *horizontal* spread of this building type were recognized as well. In this case, the metaphor chosen was the "Chinese Wall," imparting to an imposing building row the solidity (and impenetrability) of the Great Wall of China. The Chinese Wall was imaged as a barrier to the waterfront view from The City's vantage points, destroying San Francisco's maritime image. The points of reference were not only Manhattan, but Honolulu's Waikiki Beach, as well; Hong Kong and Rio de Janeiro's Copacabana went unmentioned.

Individual buildings did not escape from the deluge of metaphors. The pyramidal Transamerica Building was compared with a dunce cap; the United States Steel slab with a giraffe; the Ferry Building with a whale. As Kreimer recognizes, these metaphors are partly a function of the adaptation level, or reference levels of San Franciscans. Six stories were once considered tall enough. What they see as tall, she observes, might well be termed normal in New York or Chicago. San Franciscans have a positive flair for constructing graphic images: In a later controversy over the location and design of a collosal television antenna, the offender was memorably described as "a giant thumb in the eye of San Francisco" (*Time*, January 3, 1972, p. 54).

In the formulation of such images of San Francisco, learning plays a key role. Short-term learners (tourists) acquire one kind of cognitive map, long-term residents another. Those who have never visited San Francisco have still a third. Most often, the tourist who visits a place tries to regenerate or revivify the images previously generated by postcards or travel photographs. He or she looks, in short, for the picturesque—to *view* something—and the something he or she comes to view was previously seen in pictorial images and described in a tantalizing way. Most of us have had the experience of viewing airline billboards that present visual images of the cities served, and on which a clever choice of perspective and symbolization can make Gary, Indiana, or Bridgeport, Connecticut, as attractive as Monterey, California, or Williamsburg, Virginia. Other advertisements portray Boston as an arctic waste, or Los Angeles as a Bosch-like hell. They are both places to be escaped *from*.

But the tourist who arrives in the picturesque location he or she has chosen for a vacation requires something more. He or she wants to feel that it's possible to discover something and, perhaps more important, to be able to report this discovery to friends back home. His or her destination must offer at least a hint of exploration possibilities, of chances for a bit of discovery, of some *choice*. The drive to seek the picturesque, however, remains unaltered. The tourist still looks for that peculiar kind of beauty in the landscape that would "go well" in a photograph (recall the statements by Huxtable in Chapter 3). And in this sense, few cities offer more possibilities for panoramic picturesqueness than San Francisco—possibilities clearly disturbed and frequently diminished by high-rise towers on the city's horizons. Natural panoramas are many, while panoramas of human-made environments are few. In Manhattan, one must ascend a human-made tower for a panoramic view of the human-made city; in San Francisco—that sculptural city of steep slopes and sharp profiles (*Time*, January 3, 1972, p. 54)—the natural topography provides the vantage points. It's no small wonder, then, at the concern for these fragile and exquisitely picturesque views that contribute more than perhaps any other factor to the image of San Francisco. As Curt Gentry (1968) eloquently states, it has *fewer* attractions in terms of exciting tourist places than its sprawling but much less well-liked sister city to the south. San Francisco relies on its visual charm.

Perhaps nowhere in North America is a cognitive map so strongly linked to the *vertical* dimension of a city. As the architect Charles Moore (1965, pages 44 and 46) puts it,

> . . . some of the big new buildings are on the city's edges, blocking the view; some are on the hilltops, enhancing the view, and some are at the bases of the hills, efficiently erasing the hills as the essential features of a skyline that used to be unique . . . The spot where this picture was made used to be one of the most exciting urban spaces in the world, a city square on top of a city, with air all around. Now it isn't. There are buildings (especially the Hartford Building) instead of air. There is no dollar loss, and no protest; even preservationists don't protest the removal of air. But something very special, and presumed capable of lasting for a very long time, is gone.

Images of the results of certain environmental transformations are projected both verbally and graphically. As the verbal portrayal can mislead the reader by the selection of metaphors, so can the graphic portrayal mislead the observer by the selection of viewpoints, of perspectives, and by the selective exclusion of certain portions of buildings or building complexes. In a rendering of a limited area, the effect of a building on the remainder of a city can be easily obscured from view. The distortions may be very much greater, showing an idealized group of buildings on an idealized day with idealized small numbers of idealized stick figures idyllically promenading. Such a picture excludes some building masses, emphasizes others, and represents the structures in such a way that they appear to block no one's view, and so forth. In the case of San Francisco, the antihigh-rise forces employed similar techniques, choosing perspectives and points of view in such a way that the new and proposed buildings appeared maximally dissonant in the urban fabric, obscuring cherished landmarks and looming taller than elements (such as the Bay Bridge piers) already deemed tall by San Franciscans.

While virtually everyone would agree that San Francisco *is* beautiful, that it is worth fighting to protect, and that its symbols are worth reading, who could possibly make the same claims for Las Vegas and its world-famous Strip? When Robert Venturi, Denise Scott Brown, and Steven Izenour released *Learning from Las Vegas* in 1972, the book caused an immediate furor. What *positive* environmental learning could emerge from the study of what *everybody* knew to be the crassest caricature of architecture, urban planning, and culture to be found on the North American continent?

We view this book from a somewhat different perspective. Leaving aside the question of whether Las Vegas is or is not an appropriate subject for study by serious students of architecture, and as well, with some reluctance, the question of Venturi's overall philosophy (see

Goodman, 1971), we would like to consider the effort as a provocative attempt to apply the cognitive mapping process to city planning. That Las Vegas itself did not use the ideas generated by the Yale group is immaterial. What is important is that these ideas argued *against* the creation of a "coherent image" for the Strip as a whole, contrary to the arguments of many researchers in urban imagery. After their study had been completed, Venturi, Brown, and Izenour learned that the Las Vegas Beautification Committee

> ... would continue to recommend turning the Strip into a western Champs-Elysees, obscuring the signs with trees and raising the humidity level with giant fountains, and that the local planning and zoning agencies would continue to try to persuade the gasoline stations to imitate the architecture of the casinos, in the interest of architectural unity.
>
> (Venturi, Brown, and Izenour, 1972, p. x)

The students who attempted to learn from Las Vegas (and to try, however unsuccessfully, to influence its physical future) were interested in many facets of the urban scene. They produced maps illustrating such interesting things as illumination levels on the Strip, the distribution of churches, food stores, wedding chapels, auto rental agencies, and "heraldic symbolism." They analyzed the spatial experiences of Las Vegas, as these related to varying velocities of movement, in a manner somewhat reminiscent of — if much less rigorous than — the work of Appleyard, Lynch, and Myer (1964) on travel experiences within Boston. The Las Vegas study was of course done in private autos. Even the Yale team failed to recognize the existence of Las Vegas' bus system, probably the best urban public transportation system in the southwestern U.S.A.

Their implicit objective was The Sign. Las Vegas is without question the illuminated sign capital of the world, boasting the highest and the largest illuminated signs to be found anywhere on earth. The basic elements of the typical (and typically huge) casino signs were so consistent from one establishment to another that the students found it possible to specify the physiognomy of a typical sign as consisting of "Heraldry" above, visible from a considerable distance and at high speeds, and "Information" below, visible from a moderate distance and at moderate speeds of travel. But they could not show this, nor other aspects of the atmosphere of Las Vegas, on a typical architectural plan. For such *atmosphere* is a cognitive representation difficult to externalize either verbally or graphically. Why so?

> The representation techniques learned from architecture and planning impede our understanding of Las Vegas. They are static where it is dynamic, contained where it is open, two-dimensional where it , is three-

dimensional—how do you show the Aladdin sign meaningfully in plan, section, and elevation, or show the Golden Slipper on a land-use plan? Architectural techniques are suitable for large, broad objects in space, like buildings, but not for thin, intense objects, like signs; planning techniques are able to depict activity (land use), but in excessively general categories, for the ground floor only, and without intensity.

We need techniques for abstracting, for example, to represent "twin phenomena" or to demonstrate concepts and generalized schema – an archetypal casino or a piece of the urban fabric – rather than specific buildings. The pretty photographs that we and other tourists made in Las Vegas are not enough.

How do you *distort* these to draw out a meaning for a designer? How do you differentiate on a plan between form that is to be specifically built as shown and that which is, within constraints, allowed to happen? How do you represent the Strip as perceived by Mr. A. rather than as a piece of geometry? How do you show quality of light – or qualities of form – in plan at one inch to 100 feet? How do you show fluxes and flows or seasonal variation, or change with time?

(Venturi, Brown, and Izenour, 1972, p. 15)

In the light of this plea, one might expect, or at least hope that some answers could be found in the existing literature on cognitive mapping. But the students examined at least some of that literature, and found it sadly wanting:

. . . combinations between signs and buildings, between architecture and symbolism, between form and meaning, between driver and the roadside are deeply relevant to architecture today and have been discussed at length by several writers. But they have not been studied in detail or as an overall system. The students of urban perception and imageability have ignored them, and there is some evidence that the Strip would confound their theories. How is it that in spite of "noise" from competing signs we do in fact find what we want on the Strip?

(Venturi, Brown, and Izenour, 1972, p. 4)

The last question, in a city characterized as an Ocean of Signs, is the heart of the matter. Researchers in cognitive mapping have simply not addressed themselves very effectively to this issue. But another, and equally perplexing question might be raised: How do we find "what we want" or "where we want to go" in the *absence* of distinctive signing? If the typical nocturnal cognitive map of Las Vegas could be titled the City of Augmented Signs, then the typical nocturnal map of State College, Pennsylvania (home of one of the authors of the present volume), might have to be titled the City of Subdued Signs. In a country probably more dependent upon illuminated signs for its casual commercial activity than almost any other nation in the world, signlessness is more distinctive than an overabundance of signs. In fact, it was the extreme signedness that characterized Las Vegas, Los Angeles, and some New Jersey towns that prompted State College to enact an ordinance explicitly forbidding signs greater than a certain size (a very small size by American standards). A sprinkling of other small- and moderate-sized communities have taken a similar course toward sign control. Such actions may gratify those architects who object to signs in or on buildings, an objection based on the claim that "if the plan is clear, you *know* where to go."

YOU CAN'T GET THERE FROM HERE

How can designers and architects cope with the seemingly irreconcilable conflict between, on the one hand, the need for a legible and comprehensible spatial environment and, on the other hand, the ugliness inherent in a profusion of eye-catching advertising and directional signs? Often we seem to be faced with the worst of all worlds: The plan is *not* clear, you *can't* seem to get there from here, *and,* to make matters worse, you are assaulted by a massed phalanx of gaudy, flashing, rotating signs. Yet, despite this conflict, designers continue to strive for a humane environment, to search, as did the American Institute of Planners, for the "Optimum Environment with Man as the Measure" (Ewald, 1967). For *any* spatial environment to be humane and livable, it must be legible. It may well be impossible for designers to cope with the overwhelming problems of noise pollution, of traffic congestion, and of street crime, but surely they can contribute to the creation of a legible environment. As urban residents, we must try to come to terms with the scale and complexity of the built environment by reducing it to a human level of comprehensibility. We must be able to read the world in which we live in order to extract the necessary information for wayfinding and spatial problem solving. With legibility outside and comprehension inside comes that all-important bond of a sense of meaning and a sense of place.

Unfortunately, designers and planners have not been noticeably successful in converting this apparently simple need into a set of design principles and guidelines. The obvious answers do not work. For example, the alternative to the bewildering complexity of a neon jungle is not the spartan regularity of a rigidly simple plan. The simple but monotonous structure of a grid-form layout is not the panacea to all wayfinding ills. As Charles Dickens lamented after a visit to Philadelphia,

> It is a handsome city, but distractingly regular. After walking for an hour or two, I felt that I would have given the world for a crooked street.
>
> (Dickens, 1897–1899, p. 116, quoted in Warner, 1968, p. 5)

And even the carefully shaped intertwined curves and crescents of the instant suburb are not the answer to the design dilemma. Whenever we speak of the city as a jungle, a rabbit warren, or a maze, we are reflecting in part our inability to cope with its scale and complexity; it is *illegible* and thus *incomprehensible*. Since neither simplistic regularity nor illuminated cacophony will work, can an understanding of cognitive mapping help to generate strategies and tactics for building a legible world?

An answer to this central question depends upon answers to three further questions. What sort of signs do we need? Where should they be placed? How can we learn to make effective use of them? Since wayfinding touches so many aspects of our daily routines, it is not surprising that answers to these three questions are to be found in a wide variety of sources and contexts. It is distressing, however, to discover that, with two notable exceptions, these answers are not assembled into coherent bodies of knowledge that can guide designers and planners. Instead, the answers reside in the realm of personal expertise, painfully accumulated on a trial-and-error basis while others are to be found within highly specialized technical reports in obscure libraries or equally generalized popular articles in magazines and newspapers.

The most thorough investigation of the relation between sign systems and wayfinding comes from the literature on the design of highway systems. That the investigation is not yet complete comes as no surprise to any driver in any part of the country. We can all recount horror stories in which we were unable to get "there" from "here" and, even more frustrating, in which we did not know where "here" was in relation to anywhere else. Perhaps Chuck Davis speaks for us all:

Permit me to fanaticize for a moment.

The scene is Lewiston, Idaho. We (my family and I) are driving east along Highway 12 from the Oregon coast to Spokane to attend the opening day of Expo 74. The road map tells us we must leave Highway 12 at Lewiston and turn north onto Highway 95. We are therefore very attentive as we drive through Lewiston for signs directing us to Highway 95.

There are no such signs.

There are lots and lots of signs indicating where Highway 12 is: little white signs by the side of the road, signs of assorted other colors on the sides of buildings—all indicating the location of Highway 12. There is none telling us where Highway 95 is.

Finally someone points out the right route, but not until we get a mile north of town do we finally come across its marker: Highway 95.

The message is clear: Lewiston's leaders are firmly convinced no one ever enters or leaves their city via Highway 95. It's as prominent on the road map as number 12, the road itself is just as wide, and there is lots of traffic on it. But, in downtown Lewiston, its existence remains a secret.

We ran into sign trouble at Expo itself. By the time we got there we were all eager to find the washrooms, but there were no signs on the grounds indicating their location. We bought an official guide to the fair. The official guide has no map in it.

We bought an official map. The official map did not show the location of washrooms. About 75,000 people wander around, gritting their teeth, searching, searching.

This sort of thing has been going on for millenia and it drives me crazy. You're affected too.

(Davis, 1974, p. 6)

How do we fight our way through the cloak of secrecy that often hides the spatial relationship between a road network and the surrounding geographical environment? The problem is frequently exacerbated by highway signs themselves. In an eye-opening discussion entitled "Danger: Signs Ahead," James Conniff (1975) lists the pitfalls of current highway sign practices. Foremost among the problems encountered by travellers are signs placed too close to the decision point; signs that list distant, small places while overlooking nearby, major points; junctions that are festooned with a blizzard of signs; roadside signs that can be obscured by truck traffic; and signs that use unfamiliar official route designations while failing to mention commonly used route names. Not surprisingly, there have been sincere attempts to solve these problems. Consider, for example, the following problem. Once you are fortunate to get on a freeway system, how do you know where to get off? Sad to say, the answer to this question is neither simple nor obvious, as was discovered in Los Angeles. A few years ago, a 47-mile stretch of the Santa Monica and San Bernardino freeway system was provided with new, numbered exit signs. Underlying the signs was an elaborate spatial rationale, which was intended to provide a better means for identifying appropriate off-ramps. Thus the exit numbers, based upon the existing freeway milepost system, increased from west to east and decreased from east to west on a major freeway. Crossing freeways, naturally, had numbers that ascended from south to north and descended from north to south. As an added (and hopefully helpful) refinement, letters (A, B, C, etc.) were used in conjunction with the numbered signs *if* there was more than one exit within one freeway mile. This $75,000, federally sponsored pilot scheme (an ironic label in itself!) was well meant and designed especially to help those who do not make frequent use of the freeway system. Its result? Confusion, frustration, and accidents: You cannot teach an old motorist new tricks might be an apt assessment. The old-timers were scornful of the expense involved: Who needed the new signs? They were confused because they had to learn a new spatial language and reference system, and they were forced to relate this system to their preexisting cognitive map of the freeway system.

One obvious conclusion from this pilot scheme is that driver education must go beyond simply teaching the rules of the road and the mechanics of driving skills. We must be taught to comprehend the meaning of highway signs. Conniff (1975, p. 33) cites the specific problems associated with interpreting one sign that resembles a milk bottle outlined in black and filled with vertical lines of dashes. Although intended to convey a lane drop or narrowed highway ahead, it is known by highway safety experts as the "rain ahead" sign and is responsible for both confusion and accidents. In a similar vein, we need assistance in forming cognitive maps relating highway systems to the surrounding environment. We need to understand the spatial rationale or logic that the sign systems employ. Many American drivers, for example, do not know the rationale underlying the numbering of the interstate highway system: even numbers are east-west routes, odd numbers north-south, and the prefixes "3," "5," and so on designate the route's relation to an urban area (i.e., whether it passes through or around a city).

Not all highway design is concerned with making the highway system legible and thus *easier* to read and to use. Occasionally, strategies are designed to produce the opposite effect; there is a deliberate, rather than unintentional, effort to make some areas of the city *illegible*. The reasons for such a seemingly paradoxical move are to improve the area made illegible. By turning the area into an obstacle course, drivers will be forced to abandon long-favored short cuts through the area and will have to stick to the designated main routes; better still, they will abandon their cars and use public transport. If the strategy is successful, it will reduce congestion, cut down the number of accidents, lessen air pollution, and return the local streets to the people. Parts of London were made illegible by widening the sidewalks, by narrowing the streets, and (the key to the design strategy) by creating a system of mazes, one-way routes, and dead ends. The following two comments illustrate the game being played between the determined motorist and the equally determined designer. A taxi driver reacted, "It's crazy, . . . How do they expect anyone to find their way around here?" A planner answered, "You can't make it just difficult, . . . You have to make it nearly impossible or you won't win" (*Newsweek*, June 15, 1970). Winning involves the destruction of well-developed cognitive maps of the city. The area must be changed from a place known like the back of one's hand to the land of the lost: "You can't miss it" becomes "you can't get there from here." A planner embracing such a design strategy would do well to find out how people have come to know the city and how they solve spatial problems within it.

Assuming, however, that we wish to *assist* people in solving spatial problems, what techniques can we use? Some are obvious. For example, in response to the problems encountered in connecting *whats* and *wheres*, New York has a Cityphone in the Times Square Information Center. This connects the caller with a staff member who, according to *The New York Times* (August 8, 1972, p. 37), can help the New Yorker to find such things as a suit of armor or a rickshaw. Similarly, some bus stops in New York have "bus-stop information kiosks," which display bus-route maps *and* directional information concerning nearby public facilities and subway stations. These kiosks help the New Yorker to integrate information about surface and rail public transport systems, leading in turn to an appreciation of the spatial layout of the city and to a better sense of the interconnections among the pieces of everyday spatial experience. That such interconnections are currently difficult to form was evident from a recent comment made by the Chairman of the New York Metropolitan Transportation Authority. He emphasized the need for new route designations on buses, designations that would include origin, route, and destination in such a manner that "you won't have to have a master's degree to figure it out."

Cartographic maps are supposed to be one of the more useful devices for helping people to figure things out. They form a versatile communications bridge between the world in the head and the world outside. They are portable or they can be placed in appropriate locations; they are eye-catching and visually appealing; maps employ well-known conventions and yet they can be tailor-made to assist specific people in the solution of specific spatial problems. However, despite the versatility of the map form and the good intentions of the cartographer, many maps do not work. The Chairman of the Metropolitan Transportation Authority also listed as a high priority the need for yet *another* attempt to produce an easily readable map of the New York subway system. Some maps are literally incomprehensible; we cannot make sense out of them. Although the symbols are carefully chosen, the colors appealing, and the drafting immaculate, the map does not help us to solve our spatial problem. Despite the "you are here" arrow, we can neither see how the map relates to the surrounding environment nor can we use it to work out an appropriate route. Some people have great difficulty in mentally rotating a fixed wall map so that it is correctly oriented with the surrounding street system. Often, the map does not contain the information that we need; it does not indicate one-way streets and the public restrooms, nor does it use the commonly accepted names for different parts of the city. And, all *too* often, there is no map available. Airports, bus stations, and large supermarkets never seem to offer us the sense of security that comes from knowing where we are going. However, there are some imaginative attempts to provide useful and readable maps. For example, most maps are designed to show the *stranger* the way around an area. But, as the New Thing Art and Architecture Center in Washington (D.C.) demonstrated, maps can be designed to serve a different audience in a different way (*The Washington Post*, August 13, 1972). The Center produced a neighborhood map for the Adams-Morgan community that helped to give the *residents* a sense of neighborhood and also an appreciation of *what* services were available and *where* they were located. Since the community is linguistically mixed, the map captions were in English and Spanish. Moreover, the task of producing the map forced the cartographer to walk around the neighborhood and to talk to the local people. During this process of getting to know the community, he realized that there was a need for a public information system, a system designed to tell the people *how* to make use of the full potential of the city in which they were living. The solution to this need came in the form of a street graphics system in which appropriately located signs could make the streets *explain* the community to itself.

As the Adams-Morgan community example suggests, no matter how carefully a cartographic map is designed, its ultimate effectiveness depends on the physical form of the spatial environment. Both map *and* environment must be readable, and thus a legible physical environment is a necessary precondition for spatial problem solving. Designers have a range of tools available to them in their quest for legibility. Color coding is a widely used design technique. At Tampa airport, color codes are used in conjunction with conventional signs to guide the traveller through the building complex. European cities use colors to designate specific subway lines. Large arenas are color coded so that patrons can get to and from the appropriate seating area; for example, Long Island's Nassau Colliseum has a geographical color-coding system in which compass directions (north, east, etc.) are paired with distinctive colors. Such color-direction links are common in the mythology of many traditional cultures throughout the world; unfortunately, we have not developed a widely understood geographical color-coding system. As a consequence, we are forced to learn each specific system and cannot take full advantage of a universally known system in which, for example, red would always refer to north, yellow to east, and so on. There are many aids to the wayfinding process that are not obvious and that must be learned (and hence taught) before they can be effective. How many New Yorkers realize that each borough in the city uses distinctive pairings of letter color and background color for its street signs? Despite the need to learn the intricacies of some wayfinding systems, there are a few systems that are so simple and obvious that they seem to be overlooked by designers. One example is a system that requires the wayfinder to look down, not up. In observance of the European Architectural Heritage Year, the city of London has designed two Heritage walks, the routes of which are marked by studs set within the pavement.

A wealth of ingenious techniques exists for making environments at architectural and urban scales legible and humane places within which to live. These techniques can offer more than just wayfinding assistance: They can help to educate us to an understanding of the history and meaning of the area in which we live, and to an appreciation of a sense of place. Yet our overall success in using these techniques is sadly limited. For some unaccountable reason, legibility has been taken for granted, or, if considered at all, often treated as a problem of "icing the design cake." The "wayfinding need" is *not* superficial; it is a problem integral to the design process, but only in the last few years has the seriousness of this need for legibility been acknowledged. Two impressive books show just what can be done to render the spatial environment comprehensible. Henry Dreyfuss' *Symbol Sourcebook* (1972), a massive compendium of over 8000 graphic symbols taken from all aspects of everyday life, is more than just a symbol dictionary. Dreyfuss defines graphic symbols as nonlingual conveyers of instant information, and he explores the scope and limitations of symbols as a communication system. It is the untapped potential of the system that is more apparent than its limitations. More directly relevant to our interests is Stephen Carr's (1973) *City Signs and Lights,* a report prepared for the Boston Redevelopment Authority and the U.S. Department of Housing and Urban Development. It is the most comprehensive study yet produced linking environmental design and human wayfinding, and it generates a series of provocative policy guidelines. But it is provocative only because it points clearly to the many problems that we must confront before we can achieve a legible and humane spatial environment.

GAMES

The links between urban design and cognitive mapping are immediate and rather obvious. The need to understand the visual impact of proposed high-rise buildings and to develop an effective highway sign system is easily appreciated. These needs reflect problems that are worth solving, that we *must* solve. But what on earth is the connection between cognitive mapping and games? We would argue that when the seriousness and magnitude of "real world" problems threaten to overpower us, one response is to seek sources of diversion. Yet, even as we escape from the contraints of the world around us, the games to which we turn often utilize the same cognitive mapping ability that is essential for everyday life.

Where Are You?, advertised as a guessing game for the whole family, is a book of map puzzles that challenges one's knowledge of the spatial layout of the U.S.A. The task for the reader is to identify the state that is shown in a circular cut out from a cartographic map. Clues are provided, and, as the advertisement says, "Some are geared for relative newcomers to geography, some are difficult enough to challenge the map buff; all are fun and informative." Jigsaw puzzles of such areas as the U.S.A., its states, or the London Underground system offer constructional variations on the same theme: Sometimes "the only game in town" is town itself. In an article prompted by the recent surge in the popularity of jigsaw puzzles, Norah Smaridge (1975, p. 45) points to the early links between puzzles and maps:

> Most of the early puzzles were educational, with maps a favorite subject. They were aimed at well-to-do families, such as those in Jane Austen's novels. In "Mansfield Park," Fanny Price is ridiculed by her cousins because she can't put together the map of Europe.
>
> The "surround," or outer frame of those first puzzles was left in one piece; it showed the sea or neighboring countries. John Spillsbury, the first puzzle-maker, advertised his wares at lower prices when they were "without the sea." This was to save the expensive cedar and mahogany from which puzzles were carved in those days.

But we can go beyond simple identification and reconstruction tasks to games that involve the creative development of spatial problem-solving strategies. Although Monopoly has only a tenuous connection with spatial problem solving, it has imprinted certain places in the popular imagination. (Recall the furor over the suggested renaming of streets in Atlantic City, discussed in Chapter 2.) However, Battleship is a game combining chance and spatial skill. With a carefully plotted spatial strategy, one can work out where the enemy is located. Success in Tic-tac-toe depends upon the consistent application of some very simple spatial rules. Games such as Risk, Diplomacy, and the various battle "replay" packages represent a qualitative leap in the demands that are placed on the players. The rapid assessment of alternative tactical moves and the creative development of long-term spatial strategies are mandatory for success in Diplomacy. Perhaps the most severe test of spatial strategy and problem solving is provided by chess. D. Keith Mano (1974, p. 6), in a review of books analyzing the Fischer-Spassky chess tournament, wrote: "Chess is heightened experience like being lost in space, perhaps like being lost spatially."

Although few people enjoy being lost in the city or in the wilderness, there is one device that allows us to experience the challenge of wayfinding without suffering excessive physical or emotional penalties if we fail to solve the task. A maze is a cunningly designed structure that presents us with an intricate and confusing network of paths. Until recently, mazes were relegated to the status of such amusing landscape curiosities as gazebos and follies, or were the incidental means by which learning theorists probed the subtleties of rat behavior. For some unknown reason, mazes are now in vogue, and their popularity is continuing to increase. Martin Gardner (1975, p. 10) recently reviewed over 25 books of paper-and-pencil mazes. Greg Bright (1973), for example, has been at the forefront of this popular movement with *The Great Maze Book*, which, as its subtitle claims, produces extraordinary mazes for extraordinary people. Bright himself is no ordinary person, since he was reported as saying: "I've always very much dug the feeling of being lost. I've always been turned on by it" (*Time*, April 21, 1975, p. 86). In *The Great Maze Book* and a subsequent volume, Bright elaborates his two principles of maze design: the idea of "partial valves," which control the tides of movement, and the development of "mutually accessible centers," which help to keep the maze alive. Given structures based on these two principles, Bright convolutes the entire system to produce a finished maze. The resultant patterns are visually exciting and are attractive both as graphic designs and as puzzles. But wherein lies the appeal of a maze?

> The fun of a maze is the excitement of getting lost, of finding a way back, and ultimately a way out or to a goal. . . .
> But the labyrinth's most disturbing metaphor springs from the infernal possibility that there *is* no path to exit or goal. . . . To solve a paper maze is to escape, in a tiny symbolic way, from Nightmare. This is the dark secret hidden within every labyrinth. It is the secret that explains its eternal fascination.
>
> (Gardner, 1975, p. 10)

We have already hinted at the connection between games and cognitive mapping in our discussion of the development of spatial cognition (Chapter 6). For the developing child, *toy play* is a vital educational process that allows the child to comprehend the spatial organization of the surrounding environment. Toy play is the child's surrogate for direct spatial experience. As we grow older, games also play an important role as a diverting alternative to the routine of everyday spatial experience. But, more than providing a simple diversion, they offer us the vicarious pleasure of access to otherwise unobtainable spatial experiences. Games permit us to engage in spatial problem solving in a way that is amusing yet challenging, wherein the rewards of success and the costs of failure are not unacceptably high. Some games are educational and demand creative spatial thinking, which produces rewards that go well beyond their simple entertainment value. Not all games draw on cognitive mapping abilities, but there is a stronger link than we would acknowledge at first sight. To progress from urban design to games is not to go from the sublime to the ridiculous; rather, it is to go from the public to the private, from the communal to the personal. What underlies both of these progressions is the cognitive ability to solve spatial problems.

THE WORLDS OF FANTASY AND IMAGINATION

We have the power to escape *completely* from the confines of the world around us into the world in the head. Cognitive mapping can free us from the constraints of everyday routine and mundane existence. Many people, when confronted with Rorsach ink blots, "see" in these apparently meaningless shapes the outlines of countries and continents. We speak of flights of fancy, and Jerome Singer, a professor of psychology, has promoted the positive benefits of creative daydreaming (Dickinson, 1975). Singer argues that armchair travel, especially to exotic places, is a calming, tension-relieving process that helps us to cope with the stresses of everyday life. To some people, the travel pages of magazines and newspapers stimulate the vicarious pleasures of daydreaming. There are occasions when the gap between fantasy travel and real travel is unclear. Edward Zuckerman (1975, p. 799) was interviewed for a job as a bus driver for a European tour company:

> The applicant interviewed before me, when asked what countries he thought he would have to drive through to get from Belgium to Greece, thought for a moment and replied "Norway, Poland, Wales, Cuba . . ." By comparison, I was Marco Polo.

But, unlike this applicant, we all know that if this is Tuesday, it must be Belgium!

Although fantasy worlds can be humorous, they are not to be taken so lightly. Many novels depend upon a sense of place within which characters and plot and landscape are woven together. Alan Sillitoe (1975) explored the dimensions of the sense of place and revealed that some of his novels are literally crafted with the aid of cartographic maps, some real and the remainder products of his imagination. That such a writing technique is not unusual is a point made by Phillip and Juliana Muehrcke (1974) in their review of the use of maps in literature.

But for those who thrive on fantasy worlds, the richest mine is to be found in J. B. Post's (1973) An Atlas of Fantasy. From between these covers you can range forth to Treasure Island by way of Barsetshire and Middle-Earth, and you can stop off in the environs of Toad Hall and Pooh's Turf on the way home. Such wanderings, though prompted by the maps themselves, are the byproducts of the same cognitive mapping ability that solves the down-to-earth problem of getting to work in the morning.

CONCLUSION

Endings are difficult. To write one for any book is a problem, but even more so for this one. We have tried to take something that is hidden and expose it to scrutiny. On exposure, it becomes obvious. Everyone

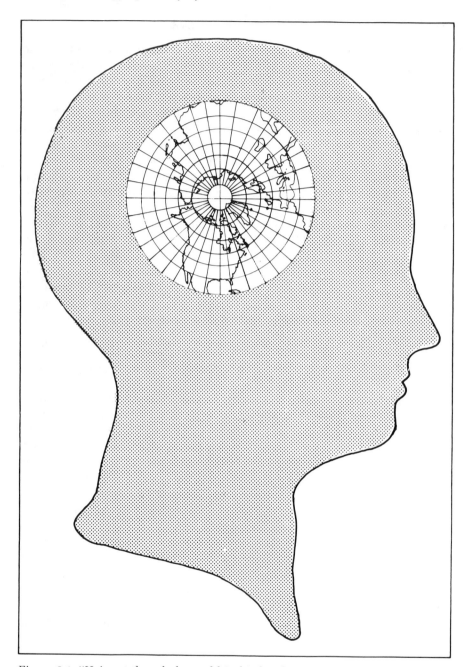

Figure 8.1. "He's got the whole world in his head."

does "know" about cognitive mapping precisely because it is so important and it touches so much of our everyday lives. It is difficult to conceive of a normal day in which one's cognitive mapping ability is not called upon. Perhaps one way to end is to think of a series of spatial metaphors and images. Atlas was reputed to carry the world on his shoulders; we, in our more exhilarated moments, occasionally feel in the same position as Charlie Chaplin in the famous poster advertising the movie, *The Great Dictator* — on top of the world. Some people are said to have the map of Ireland etched upon their face; others have stars in their eyes. Cyrano de Bergerac labeled his own nose "a rock, a crag, nay a promontory!" But the ultimate accolade thus far awarded to a cognitive mapper must be that given to David Brower, the environmentalist. The headline to an article about him claimed: "He's got the whole world in his head."

BIBLIOGRAPHY

Abbott, E. (1936) *The Tenements of Chicago, 1908–1935.* Chicago: University of Chicago Press.

Abbott, E. A. (1963) *Flatland: A Romance of Many Dimensions.* New York: Barnes & Noble.

Adams, R. L. (1973) "Uncertainty in nature, cognitive dissonance, and the perceptual distortion of environmental information: weather forecasts and New England beach trip decisions." *Economic Geography,* **49,** 287–297.

Alexander, C. (1965) "A city is not a tree." *Architectural Forum,* **122,** (1), 58–62 and (2), 58–61.

Appleyard, D. (1969a) "Why buildings are known." *Environment and Behavior,* **1,** 131–156.

Appleyard, D. (1969b) "City designers and the pluralistic city," in Rodwin, L. (ed.) *Planning Urban Growth and Regional Development: The Experience of the Guayana Program of Venezuela.* Cambridge, Mass.: M.I.T. Press.

Appleyard, D. (1970) "Styles and methods of structuring a city." *Environment and Behavior,* **2** 100–118.

Appleyard, D., Lynch, K., and Myer, J. (1964) *The View from the Road.* Cambridge, Mass.: M.I.T. Press.

Asimov, I. (1951) *Foundation.* New York: Doubleday & Company.

Banham, R. (1971) *Los Angeles: The Architecture of Four Ecologies.* London: Penguin Press.

Barker, R. G. (ed.) (1963) *The Stream of Behavior.* New York: Appleton-Century-Crofts.

Bergamini, D. (1971) *Japan's Imperial Conspiracy.* New York: William Morrow and Company.

Binet, M. A. (1894) "Reverse illusions of orientation." *Psychological Review,* **1,** 337–350.

Blaut, J. M., and Stea, D. (1971) "Studies of geographic learning." *Annals of the Association of American Geographers,* **61,** 387–393.

Bogen, J. E., De Zure, R., TenHouten, W. D., and Marsh, J. F. (1972) "The other side of the brain, IV." *Bulletin of the Los Angeles Neurological Societies,* **37,** 49–61.

Bogen, J. E., Marsh, J. F., and TenHouten, W. D. (1970) "A theorem of cognitive functioning and social stratification." Unpublished manuscript, University of California at Los Angeles.

Bowen, E. S. (1964) *Return to Laughter.* Garden City, N.Y.: Doubleday & Co.

Bower, T. G. R. (1966) "The visual world of infants." *Scientific American,* **215,** 80–92.

Briggs, R. (1973) "Urban cognitive distance," in Downs, R. M., and Stea, D. (eds.) *Image and Environment.* Chicago: Aldine, pp. 361–388.

Bright, G. (1973) *The Great Maze Book.* New York: Pantheon Books.

Bright, J. O., and Bright, W. (1965) "Semantic structures in Northwestern California and the Sapir-Whorf hypothesis." *American Anthropologist,* **67,** 249–258.

Brower, S. (1965) "The signs we learn to read." *Landscape,* **15,** 9–12.

Bruner, J. S. (1959) "Learning and thinking." *Harvard Educational Review,* **29,** 184–192.

Bruner, J. S. (1960) *The Process of Education.* Cambridge, Mass.: Harvard University Press.

Bruner, J. S. (1964) "The course of cognitive growth." *American Psychologist,* **19,** 1–15.

Bruner, J. S. (1968) *Processes of Cognitive Growth: Infancy.* Worcester, Mass.: Clark University Press.

Bruner, J. S., Goodnow, J. J., and Austin, G. A. (1956) *A Study of Thinking.* New York: John Wiley & Sons.

Burks, E. C. (1971) "City's Bronx map is drawn askew." *The New York Times,* October 3, p. 77.

Burton, R. (1973) "A Christmas Story." *The American Way,* **6,** 13–17.

Canby, V. (1974) "New York's woes are good box office." *The New York Times,* Sunday, November 10, Section 2, pp. 1 and 19.

Canter, D., and Tagg, S. (1975) "Distance estimation in cities." *Environment and Behavior,* **7,** 59–80.

Carr, S. (1973) *City Signs and Lights.* Cambridge, Mass.: M.I.T. Press.

Carr, S., and Kurilko, G. (1964) "Vision and memory in the view from the road." Unpublished manuscript.

Carr, S., and Schissler, D. (1969) "The city as a trip: perceptual selection and memory in the view from the road." *Environment and Behavior,* **1,** 7–36.

Cather, W. S. (1913) *O Pioneers!* Boston: Houghton Mifflin Company.

The Centre Daily Times; material in the issue dated July 7, 1972.

Claparède, E. (1903) "La faculte d'orientation lointaine (sens de direction, sens de retour)." *Archive de Psychologie, Genève,* **2,** 133–180.

Cleaver, E. (1969), "The Flashlight." *Playboy,* **16,** pp. 122 and 124.

Coles, R. (1971) *The South Goes North.* Boston: Little, Brown and Company.

Coles, R., and Erikson, J. (1971) *The Middle Americans.* Boston: Little, Brown and Company.

Conniff, J. C. G. (1975) "Danger: Signs ahead." *The New York Times Magazine,* March 30, 32–36.

Davidson, R. P. (1973) "A letter from the publisher." *Time,* November 5, p. 2.

Davis, C. (1974) "Can I get there from here?" *The Vancouver Sun,* June 13, p. 6.

De Jonge, D. (1962) "Images of urban areas, their structures and psychological foundations." *Journal of the American Institute of Planners,* **28,** 266–276.

Dickinson, E. (1975) "Armchair travel as therapy." *The New York Times,* April 27, Section 10, pp. 1 and 16.

Disley, J. (1967) *Orienteering.* Harrisburg, Pa.: Stackpole Books.

Dodgson, C. (1939) *The Complete Works of Lewis Carroll.* London: The None-such Press.

Dodwell, P. C. (1963) "Children's understanding of spatial concepts." *Canadian Journal of Psychology,* **17,** 141–161.

Dreyfuss, H. (1972) *Symbol Sourcebook.* New York: McGraw-Hill.

Ewald, W. R. (ed.) (1967) *Environment for Man.* Bloomington, Ind.: Indiana University Press.

Fellman, G., and Brandt, B. (1970) "A neighborhood a highway would destroy." *Environment and Behavior,* **2,** 281–301.

Fellman, G., and Brandt, B. (1971) "Working class protest against an urban highway: some meanings, limits, and problems." *Environment and Behavior,* **3,** 61–79.

Firey, W. (1945) " 'Sentiment' and 'symbolism' as ecological variables." *American Sociological Review,* **10,** 140–148.

Firey, W. (1947) *Land Use in Central Boston.* Cambridge, Mass.: Harvard University Press.

Fishbein, H. D., Lewis, S., and Keiffer, K. (1972) "Children's understanding of spatial relations: coordination of perspectives." *Developmental Psychology,* **7,** 21–33.

Forman, R. E. (1971) *Black Ghettos, White Ghettos, and Slums.* Englewood Cliffs, N.J.: Prentice-Hall.

Forster, E. M. (1972) "The machine stops," in Hoskins, R. (ed.) *Wondermakers.* Greenwich, Conn.: Fawcett Publications, pp. 112–149. Originally published in Forster, E. M. (1928) *The Eternal Moment and Other Stories.* New York: Harcourt Brace Jovanovich.

Franke, D., and Franke, H. (1972) *Safe Places.* New Rochelle, N.Y.: Arlington House.

Fried, M. (1963) "Grieving for a lost home," in Duhl, L. (ed.) *The Urban Condition.* New York: Basic Books, pp. 252–272.

Fried, M., and Gleicher, P. (1961) "Some sources of residential satisfaction in an urban slum." *Journal of the American Institute of Planners,* **27,** 305–315.

Frisch, K. von (1954) *The Dancing Bees: an Account of the Life and Senses of the Honey Bee.* London: Methuen.

Galton, Francis (1872) "On finding the way," in *The Art of Travel; or, Shifts and Contrivances Available in Wild Countries.* London: John Murray.

Gans, H. (1962) *The Urban Villagers.* New York: Free Press.

Gardner, H. (1975) *The Shattered Mind.* New York: Alfred A. Knopf.

Gardner, M. (1975) "Labyrinthian way." *The New York Times Book Review,* July 27, p. 10.

Gatty, H. (1958) *Nature Is Your Guide.* New York: E. P. Dutton & Co.

Gazzaniga, M. S. (1972) "One brain—two minds?" *American Scientist*, **60**, 311–317.

Geertz, C. (1972) "Deep play: notes on the Balinese cockfight." *Daedalus*, **101**, 1–38.

Gentry, C. (1968) *The Last Days of the Late, Great State of California*. New York: Ballantine Books.

Gibson, E. J. (1970) "The development of perception as an adaptive process." *American Scientist*, **58**, 98–107.

Gittins, J. S. (1969) *Forming Impressions of an Unfamiliar City: A Comparative Study of Aesthetic and Scientific Knowing*. Unpublished M.A. thesis, Clark University, Worcester, Mass.

Gladwin, T. (1970) *East Is a Big Bird*. Cambridge, Mass.: Harvard University Press.

Golledge, R., and Zannaras, G. (1973) "Cognitive approaches to the analysis of human spatial behavior," in Ittelson W. (ed.) *Environment and Cognition*. New York: Seminar Press, pp. 59–94.

Goodman, R. (1971) *After the Planners*. New York: Simon and Schuster.

Gould, P. (1966) "On mental maps." *Michigan Inter-University Community of Mathematical Geographers*, #9.

Gould, P. (1973) "The black boxes of Jönköping: spatial information and preference," in Downs, R. M., and Stea, D. *Image and Environment*. Chicago: Aldine, pp. 235–245.

Gulliver, F. P. (1908) "Orientation of maps." *Journal of Geography*, **7**, 55–58.

Haggett, P. (1966) *Locational Analysis in Human Geography*. New York: St. Martin's Press.

Hallowell, A. I. (1967) *Culture and Experience*. New York: Schocken Books.

Harlow, H. F. (1949) "The formation of learning sets." *Psychological Review*, **56**, 51–65.

Hart, R. A. and Moore, G. T. (1973) "The development of spatial cognition: a review," in Downs, R. M. and Stea, D. (eds.) *Image and Environment*. Chicago: Aldine, pp. 246–288.

Harvey, D. W. (1972) *Society, the City, and the Space-Economy of Urbanism*. Washington, D. C.: Association of American Geographers, Commission on College Geography, Resource Paper Number 18.

Haugen, E. (1957) "The semantics of Icelandic orientation." *Word*, **13**, 447–459.

Heathcote, R. L. (1965) *Back of Bourke*. Melbourne: Melbourne University Press.

Hebb, D. O. (1949) *The Organization of Behavior*. New York: John Wiley & Sons.

Heinlein, R. A. (1966) *The Moon is a Harsh Mistress*. Berkeley: Medallion Books.

Held, R., and Rekosh, J. (1963) "Motor-sensory feedback and the geometry of visual space." *Science*, **141**, 722–723.

Hilgard, E. R. (1956) *Theories of Learning*. New York: Appleton-Century-Crofts.

Honan, W. (1973) "They don't sell flight insurance at the Grand Canyon heliport." *Saturday Review of the Society*, **1**, March 17, pp. 24 and 26.

Horn, P. (1975) "Child Development: Babies see more than you think ("Newsline"). *Psychology Today*, **9**, (2), 84–85.

Houssidas, L. (1965) "Co-ordination of perspectives in children." *Archiv Fuer Die Gesamte Psychologie*, **117**, 319–326.

Howard, I. P., and Templeton, W. B. (1966) *Human Spatial Orientation.* New York: John Wiley & Sons.

Howell, R. W. (1969) *A Study of Informal Learning.* Office of Education: Final Report, Project #8–B–125, Grant #OEC–2–9–420125–1009.

Hughes, R. (1929) *A High Wind in Jamaica.* London: Chatto & Windus.

Huxley, Julian (1973) *Memories II.* New York: Harper & Row.

Jackson, J. B. (1957) "The stranger's path." *Landscape*, **7**, 29–35.

Jackson, R. H. (1972) "Myth and reality: environmental perception of the Mormon pioneers." *Rocky Mountain Social Science Journal*, **9**, 33–38.

Jackson, S. (1959) *The Haunting of Hill House.* New York: Viking Press.

Jacobs, J. (1961) *The Death and Life of Great American Cities.* New York: Random House.

Kaplan, S. (1973) "Cognitive maps in perception and thought," in Downs, R. M., and Stea, D. (eds.) *Image and Environment.* Chicago: Aldine, pp. 63–78.

Keeton, W. (1974) "The mystery of pigeon homing." *Scientific American*, **231**, 96–107.

Khopreninova, N. G. (1956) "Orientation of locality by sightless persons." *Uchenyye Zapiski Chkalovskogo Gos. Pedagogicheskikh In-ta* (Chkalov State Pedagogical Institute), #8. Cited in Shemyakin, F. N. "Orientation in space," in Ananyev, B. G., et al. (eds.) *Psychological Science in the U.S.S.R.*, Vol. 1, Washington, D.C.: Office of Technical Services, 1962, pp. 186–225.

Kreimer, A. (1971) *The Building of the Imaginary of San Francisco: An Analysis of the High-Rise Controversy.* Unpublished M.A. thesis, University of California at Berkeley.

La Barre, W. (1954) *The Human Animal.* Chicago: University of Chicago Press.

Ladd, F. C. (1970) "Black youths view their environment: neighborhood maps." *Environment and Behavior*, **2**, 64–79.

Lasker, T. (1972) *New York in Maps.* New York: *New York Magazine* and Flashmaps, Inc. (1972–1973 edition)

Laughlin, W. S. (1968) "Hunting: an integrating biobehavior system and its evolutionary importance," in Lee, R. B., and DeVore, I. (eds.) *Man the Hunter.* Chicago: Aldine-Atherton, pp. 304–320.

Laurendau, M., and Pinard, A. (1970) *The Development of the Concept of Space in the Child.* New York: International Universities Press.

Lawrence, D. H. (1959) *Lady Chatterley's Lover.* New York: New American Library.

Lee, T. R. (1963–1964) "Psychology and living space." *Transactions of the Bartlett Society*, **2**, 9–36.

Lee, T. R. (1970) "Perceived distance as a function of direction in the city." *Environment and Behavior*, **2**, 40–51.

Lewis, C. S. (1957) "The Shoddy Lands," in *The Best from Fantasy and Science Fiction.* New York: Doubleday & Company.

Lewis, D. (1971a) " 'Expanding' the target in indigenous navigation." *Journal of Pacific History*, **6**, 83–95.

Lewis, D. (1971b) "A return voyage between Puluwat and Saipan using Micronesian navigational techniques." *Journal of the Polynesian Society*, **80**, 437–448.

Lewis, D. (1972) *We, the Navigators*. Hawaii: University Press of Hawaii.

Lewis, S. (1920) *Main Street*. New York: Harcourt Brace Jovanovich.

Ley, D. (1972) *The Black Inner City as Frontier Outpost: Images and Behavior of a Philadelphia Neighborhood*. Unpublished Ph.D. dissertation, The Pennsylvania State University.

The Los Angeles Times; material in the issues dated March 19, 1972; April 16, 1972; August 13, 1972.

Lucas, R. C. (1963) "Wilderness perception and use: the example of the Boundary Waters Canoe Area." *Natural Resources Journal*, **3**, 394–411.

Lucas, R. C. (1966) "The contribution of environmental research to wilderness policy decisions." *Journal of Social Issues*, **22**, 116–126.

Lundberg, U. (1973) "Emotional and geographical phenomena in psychophysical research," in Downs, R. M., and Stea, D. (eds.) *Image and Environment*. Chicago: Aldine, pp. 322–337.

Lupo, A., Colcord, F., and Fowler, E. P. (1971) *Rites of Way: the Politics of Transportation in Boston and the U.S. City*. Boston: Little, Brown and Company.

Luria, A. R. (1968) *The Mind of a Mnemonist*. New York: Basic Books.

Lynch, K. (1960) *The Image of the City*. Cambridge, Mass.: M.I.T. Press.

Mann, T. (1970) *Tonio Kroger and Other Stories*. New York: Bantam Books.

Mano, D. K. (1974) "Reviews of B. Darrach *Bobby Fischer vs. the Rest of the World* and G. Steiner *Fields of Force*." *The New York Times Book Review*, October 13, p. 6.

Marchand, M. (1975) "Encounter: beware of Greeks bearing the best of intentions." *The New York Times*, July 20, 1975, Section 20, p. 9.

Márquez, G. G. (1970) *One Hundred Years of Solitude*. New York: Harper & Row.

Marx, L. (1964) *The Machine in the Garden*. New York: Oxford University Press.

McCarthy, M. (1973) "The Watergate notes." *The New York Review of Books*, July 19, 1973, p. 5.

Menzel, E. W. (1973) "Chimpanzee spatial memory organization." *Science*, **182**, 943–945.

Michon, J. A. (1972) "Multidimensional and hierarchical analysis of progress in learning," in Gregg, L. W. (ed.) *Cognition in Learning and Memory*. New York: John Wiley & Sons, pp. 89–115.

Millar, R. (1972) *The Piltdown Men*. New York: St. Martin's Press.

Miller, G. A., Galanter, E., and Pribram, K. H. (1960) *Plans and the Structure of Behavior*. New York: Holt, Rinehart and Winston.

Millet, K. "On Angela Davis." *Ms.* **1**, 54–60 and 105–116.

Moore, C. (1965) "The San Francisco skyline: hard to spoil, but they're working on it." *Architectural Forum*, **123**, November, pp. 40–47.

Muehrcke, P. C., and Muehrcke, J. O. (1974) "Maps in literature." *The Geographical Review*, **64**, 317–338.

Nash, R. (1967) *Wilderness and the American Mind*. New Haven, Conn.: Yale University Press.

Neruda, P. (1974) *Toward the Splendid City* (Nobel Lecture). New York: Farrar, Straus, & Giroux.

New York; material in issue dated July, 1972, p. 84.

The New York Times; material in the issues dated for the year 1972, July 23, August 8, September 24, October 4, October 13, October 19, November 24; for the year 1973, January 9, February 10, February 21, March 8, April 16, April 22, June 9, July 8, July 16, July 22, October 14, November 25; for the year 1974, November 15.

The New York Times Book Review; material in the issue dated February 21, 1971.

The New York Times Magazine; material in the issue dated November 18, 1973.

Newsweek; material in the issues dated June 15, 1970; December 28, 1970; January 18, 1971; January 22, 1973; March 19, 1973.

Oatley, K. (1974) "Mental maps for navigation." *New Scientist*, **19**, December, 863–866.

Orleans, P. (1973) "Differential cognition of urban residents: effects of social scale on mapping," in Downs, R. M., and Stea, D. (eds.) *Image and Environment*. Chicago: Aldine, pp. 115–130.

Padgett, L. (1969) "Mimsy were the Borogroves," in Elwood R., and Chidalia, V. (eds.) *The Little Monsters*. New York: MacFadden Bartell Corporation.

Pailhous, J. (1968) "Algorithme de deplacements chez le chauffeur de taxi." Paris: Laboratoire de Psychologie du Travail.

The Pennsylvania Mirror; material in the issue dated July 19, 1975.

Pfeiffer, J. E. (1969) *The Emergence of Man*. New York: Harper & Row.

Piaget, J., and Inhelder, B. (1956) *The Child's Conception of Space*. London: Routledge and Kegan Paul.

Pinard, A., and Sharp, E. (1972) "I.Q. and point of view." *Psychology Today*, June, pp. 65–68 and 90.

Post, J. B. (1973) *An Atlas of Fantasy*. Baltimore: The Mirage Press.

Pribram, K. H. (1971) "The brain." *Psychology Today*, September, pp. 44–48 and 89–90.

Psathas, G., and Henslin, J. (1967) "Dispatched orders and the cab driver: a study of locating activities." *Social Problems*, **14**, 424–443.

Rand, G. (1969) "Some Copernican views of the city." *Architectural Forum*, **132** (9), 77–81.

Reiff, I. (1972) "Visual quality," in *Facing the Future: Five Alternatives for Mammoth Lakes*. Los Angeles: University of California.

Rivers, C. (1972) "The specialness of growing up in Washington, D.C." *The New York Times Magazine*, May 7, 1972, pp. 34 and 100.

Ryan, C. (1974) "Man of Montreal." *Saturday Review/World*, November 2, pp. 14–20.

Saarinen, T. F. (1973) "The use of projective techniques in geographic research," in Ittelson, W. H. (ed.) *Environment and Cognition*. New York: Seminar Press, pp. 29–52.

The San Francisco Chronicle; material in the issue dated August 24, 1967.

Shemyakin, F. N. (1962) "Orientation in space," in Ananyev, B. G., et al. (eds.) *Psychological Science in the U.S.S.R.*, Vol. 1, Washington, D.C.: Office of Technical Services, Report # 62- 11083, pp. 186–255.

Sillitoe, A. (1975) "A sense of place: one man's maps." *Geographical Magazine*, **XLVII**, 685–689.

Smaridge, N. (1975) "Jigsaw puzzle makers can be merciless." *The New York Times*, December 7, Section 2, pp. 45 and 53.

Southworth, M. (1969) "The sonic environment of cities." *Environment and Behavior*, **1**, 49–70.

Spreiregen, P. D. (1965) *Urban Design: The Architecture of Cities and Towns* New York: McGraw-Hill.

Stea, D. (1974) "Architecture in the head: cognitive mapping," in Lang, J., Burnette, C., Moleski, W., and Vachon, D. (eds.) *Designing for Human Behavior*. Stroudsberg, Pa.: Dowden, Hutchinson, and Ross.

Stea, D., and Blaut, J. M. (1973a) "Some preliminary observations on spatial learning in school children," in Downs, R. M., and Stea, D. (eds.) *Image and Environment*. Chicago: Aldine, pp. 226–234.

Stea, D., and Blaut, J. M. (1973b) "Notes towards a developmental theory of spatial learning," in Downs, R. M., and Stea, D. (eds.) *Image and Environment*. Chicago: Aldine, pp. 51–62.

Stea, D., and Taphanel, S. (1974) "Theory and experiment on the relation between environmental modelling (toy-play) and environmental cognition," in Canter, D., and Lee, T. (eds.) *Psychology and the Built Environment*. London: Architectural Press, pp. 170–178.

Steinbeck, J. (1962) *Travels with Charley*. New York: The Viking Press.

Steinitz, C. (1968) "Meaning and the congruence of urban form and activity." *Journal of the American Institute of Planners*, **34**, 233–248.

Strauss, A. L. (1961) *Images of the American City*. Glencoe, Ill.: The Free Press.

Symanski, R., Harman, J., and Swift, M. (1973) "No Arby's in Appalachia." *Clifton*, **1** (2), 12–21.

Time; material in the issues dated January 3, 1972; April 13, 1972; July 17, 1972; April 21, 1975.

Tinbergen, N. (1951) *The Study of Instinct*. New York: Oxford University Press.

Tolman, E. C. (1948) "Cognitive maps in rats and men." *Psychological Review*, **55**, 189–208.

Tolman, E. C. (1958) *Behavior and Psychological Man: Essays in Motivation and Learning*. Berkeley: University of California Press.

Trowbridge, C. C. (1913) "On fundamental methods of orientation and imaginary maps." *Science*, **38**, 888–897.

Tuan, Y. F. (1974) *Topophilia*. Englewood Cliffs, N.J.: Prentice-Hall.

Twain, M. (1929) *Tom Sawyer Abroad* (Stormfield Edition). New York: Harper and Brothers.

Uexkull, J. von (1957) "A stroll through the world of animals and men," in Schiller, C., and Lashley, K. (eds.) *Instinctive Behavior*. New York: International Universities Press.

Venturi, R., Brown, D. S., and Izenour, S. (1972) *Learning from Las Vegas*. Cambridge, Mass.: M.I.T. Press.

Walter, G. (1972) "The national birthday mess." *Saturday Review*, **55**, June 17, 81–82.

Warner, S. B. (1968) *The Private City*. Philadelphia: University of Pennsylvania Press.

Washburn, S. L., and Howell, F. C. (1960) "Human evolution and culture," in

Tax, S. (ed.) *The Evolution of Man*, Vol. 2. Chicago: University of Chicago Press.

Washburn, S. L., and Lancaster, C. S. (1968) "The evolution of hunting," in Lee, R. B., and DeVore, I. (eds.) *Man the Hunter*. Chicago: Aldine-Atherton, pp. 293–303.

Wells, E. F. (1971) "Imagineering." *TWA Magazine*, 24–29.

White, M., and White, L. (1962) *The Intellectual Versus the City*. Cambridge, Mass.: Harvard University Press and M.I.T. Press.

White, S. D. (1965) "Evidence for a hierarchical arrangement of learning processes," in Lipsett, L., and Spiker, C. (eds.) *Advances in Child Development and Behavior*, Volume II. New York: Academic Press.

Whittaker, J. O., and Whittaker, S. J. (1972) "A cross-cultural study of geocentrism." *Journal of Cross-Cultural Psychology*, **3**, 417–421.

Wolfe, T. (1966) *You Can't Go Home Again*. New York: The New American Library Edition.

Wooten, J. (1973) in *The Philadelphia Inquirer*, August 26, p. 1-B.

Wright, H. M. (1972) "Radburn revisited." *Ekistics*, **33**, 196–201.

Wright, J. K. (1925) *The Geographical Lore of the Time of the Crusades*. New York: American Geographical Society Research Series # 15.

Wright, R. (1970) *The Weekend Man*. New York: New American Library.

Young, J. Z. (1962) "Why do we have two brains?" in Mountcastle, V. B. (ed.) *Interhemispheric Relations and Cerebral Dominance*. Baltimore: The Johns Hopkins Press, pp. 7–24.

Zuckerman, E. B. (1975) "Fun touring." *New Statesman*, June 20, pp. 799 and 802.

NAME INDEX

Abbott, E., 3, 79
Abbott, E. A., 100
Adams, R. L., 122
Alexander, C., 164
Annenberg, W. H., 38
Appleyard, D., 79, 81, 157–158, 159, 242–244, 246, 250
Asimov, L., 130–131
Austin, G. A., 84
Banham, R., 121
Barker, R. G., 202
Bergamini, D., 79–80
Binet, M. A., 156, 237–238
Blaut, J. M., 77, 183, 186, 191–192, 201, 203, 205, 220–222, 236
Bogen, J. E., 177–181
Bowen, E. S., 48, 49, 140, 142
Bower, T. G. R., 188, 205, 236
Brandt, B., 159
Briggs, R., 140
Bright, G., 260
Bright, J. O., 127
Bright, W., 127
Brower, D., 263
Brower, S., 227
Brown, D. S., 249–251
Bruner, J. S., 81–82, 84, 173, 201–203, 205–207, 235
Buckland, W., 134
Burks, E. C., 231–235

Burton, I., 122
Burton, R., 138
Canby, V., 93–95
Cannon, J., 37
Canter, D., 143
Carr, S., 79, 90, 158–159, 258
Carroll, L., 4, 45, 46, 52–53, 65–66
Cather, W. S., 109
Chaplin, C., 263
Churchill, W., 109
Claparède, E., 156
Cleaver, E., 78
Colcord, F., 159
Coles, R., 45, 71, 86, 229–230
Columbus, C., 29
Conniff, J. C. G., 254–255
Cook, J., 146
Darwin, C., 125
Davidson, R. P., 64
Davis, C., 253–254
De Jonge, D., 79
De Zure, R., 180–181
Dickens, C., 252
Dickinson, E., 261
Disley, J., 72
Disney, W., 4
Dodgson, C. See Carroll, L.
Dodwell, P. C., 200
Drapeau, J., 80–81
Dreyfuss, H., 134, 258

Dubbs, P., 209
Einstein, A., 196
Erikson, J., 86
Ewald, W. R., 252
Faulkner, W., 25
Fellman, G., 159
Fields, W. C., 37–38
Firey, W., 78, 160
Fishbein, H. D., 199–201
Fisher, D., 212
Fisher, E., 104
Folsom, V., 72
Forman, R., 78–79
Forster, E. M., 49
Fowler, E. P., 159
Franke, D., 18
Franke, H., 18
Fried, M., 160
Frisch, K. von, 30–31
Galanter, E., 202
Galton, F., 144
Gans, H., 159–160
Gardner, H., 173–174, 178–180
Gardner, M., 260
Gatty, H., 76, 133, 141, 154, 238
Gazzaniga, M., 177
Geertz, C., 130
Gentry, C., 248
Gibson, E. J., 205
Gittins, J. S., 102
Gladwin, T., 146, 148–149, 153
Gleicher, P., 160
Golledge, R., 143
Goodman, R., 80, 159, 249–250
Goodnow, J. J., 84
Gould, P., 17, 238–239
Gulliver, F. P., 156
Haggett, P., 26
Hallowell, A. I., 133, 141
Hardy, T., 25
Harlow, H. F., 228
Harman, J., 116
Hart, R., 173–174, 198–199, 206–207
Harvey, D., 18
Haugen, E., 126–127
Heathcote, R., 43
Hebb, D. O., 175
Heinlein, R. A., 132–133
Held, R., 73, 221
Henslin, J., 231
Hess, J., 197, 207
Hewes, G., 182–183, 185–187, 213
Hilgard, E. R., 214
Holmes, S., 96

Honan, W., 73–74
Horn, P., 207
Houssidas, L., 200
Howard, I. P., 176
Howell, F. C., 201
Howell, R., 128–130
Hughes, R., 193
Hull, C., 214
Huxley, J., 142
Huxtable, A. L., 75, 248
Inhelder, B., 197–200
Iredale, B., 209
Izenour, S., 249–251
Jackson, J. B., 81
Jackson, R. H., 116–117
Jackson, S., 131–132
Jacobs, J., 160, 169
James, H., 95–96
James, W., 174
Jucius, A., 64
Kaplan, S., 121, 175, 224–225
Kates, R., 122
Keeton, W., 124
Keiffer, K., 199–201
Khopreninova, N. G., 69–70
Klein, D., 142
Kreimer, A., 246–249
Kurilko, G., 158
Kuttner, H. See Padgett L.
La Barre, W., 201
Ladd, F., 105
Lancaster, C. S., 183
Lasker, T., 231
Laughlin, W. S., 183
Laurendau, M., 200, 204
Lawrence, D. H., 104
Lee, T. R., 105–107, 143, 156
Lenkiewicz, I., 64
Lewin, K., 213
Lewis, C. S., 100
Lewis, D., 146–147, 151, 153–155
Lewis, Sinclair, 118
Lewis, Susan, 199–201
Ley, D., 15
Lucas, R. C., 109, 245–246
Lundberg, U., 142
Lupo, A., 159
Luria, A. R., 97–98
Lynch, K., 5, 27, 71, 83, 127,
    137–138, 156–158, 222, 225, 228,
    241, 242, 250
McCarthy, M., 134–135
McLuhan, M., 101
Mann, T., 187–188

Mano, D. K., 259
Marchand, M., 133
Márquez, G., 47–48, 82, 209–212
Marsh, J. F., 177–181
Marx, L., 76–77
Menzel, E. W., 183–185
Michon, J. A., 230
Millar, R., 134
Miller, G. A., 202
Millett, K., 64
Moore, C., 249
Moore, G., 173–174, 198–199,
    206–207
Muehrcke, J., 261
Muehrcke, P., 261
Myer, J., 157–158, 250
Nash, R., 245
Neruda, P., 109
Oatley, K., 152
Orleans, P., 78
Padgett, L., 194, 198
Pailhous, J., 230
Parker, D., 37
Parker, E., 42
Passer, I., 94–95
Pfeiffer, J. E., 183
Piaget, J., 172–173, 193–201,
    203–207
Pinard, A., 194–195, 200, 204
Post, J. B., 261
Pratolini, V., 71
Pribram, K. H., 188, 202
Psathas, G., 231
Rand, G., 230
Reiff, I., 244–245
Rekosh, J., 73, 221
Rivers, C., 136
Ryan, C., 80–81
Saarinen, T. F., 128, 244
Scaife, M., 207
Schissler, D., 79, 158
Shakespeare, W., 66
Sharp, E., 194–195
Shemyakin, F. N., 69–70, 101, 125
Sillitoe, A., 261
Singer, J., 261
Smaridge, N., 259

Southworth, M., 76, 158
Spender, S., 27
Spreiregen, P. D., 80, 135–136
Stea, D., 77, 191–192, 201, 203, 205,
    220–222, 236
Stein, G., 135
Steinbeck, J., 113, 115, 117, 133–134
Steinitz, C., 158
Strauss, A., 92–93, 120–121
Swift, J., 4
Swift, M., 116
Symanski, R., 116
Tagg, S., 143
Taphanel, S., 222
Templeton, W. B., 176
TenHouten, W. D., 177–181
Thomas, L., 3
Tinbergen, N., 31–32
Tolkien, J. R., 4
Tolman, E., 32–34, 185,
    213–214, 224
Trowbridge, C. C., 157, 238
Tuan, Y. F., 138
Twain, M., 26, 75, 76–77
Uexkull, J. von, 20, 224
Venturi, R., 249–251
Vrangel, F., 125
Walter, G., 37–38
Warner, S. B., 252
Washburn, S. L., 183, 201
Weaver, D., 53
Wells, E. F., 72
White, L., 96
White, M., 96
White, S. D., 226–227
Wittaker, J. O., 103
Wittaker, S. J., 103
Wolfe, T., 2, 108
Wooten, J., 37
Wright, F. L., 246
Wright, H. M., 74
Wright, J. K., 79
Wright, R., 120
Young, B., 116–117
Young, J. Z., 179–180
Zannaras, G., 143
Zuckerman, E. B., 261

PLACE INDEX

Appalachia
  stereotypes of, 116
Athens, 114
Atlanta
  "boosting" of, 91
Atlantic City
  street renaming in, 42
Australia
  Aborigine's navigation in, 124, 138
  place names in, 43
Baltimore
  investment potential map, 18–19
  street patterns, 43–44
Belfast
  cognitive maps of, 83
Berlin Wall, 109
Bermuda
  advertisement for, 75
Berrens River
  Saulteaux navigation of, 133
Bogotá
  locations in, 44
Boston, 156–170
  Back Bay, 166–167
  Beacon Hill, 160, 163, 167
  The Common, 164–166, 220
  highway signs for, 51–52
  images of, 137, 156–158, 246
  neighborhood maps of, 159
  North End, 168

  Roxbury, 105, 168
  South End, 167–168
  territories in, 166–167
  underground rail system, 164, 222
  Union Park, 168
  West End, 159–160
Boundary Waters Canoe Area
  areal extent of, 109, 245
California, 4, 8. See also United
      States
  earthquake hazard, 123
  orientation systems in, 127
Cambridge (England)
  birthplace of cognitive
      mapping, 156
  neighborhood maps of, 105–106
Cambridge (Massachusetts)
  cognitive maps of, 168–169
  educational institutions, 161
  highway protest in, 159
Canada
  Maritimer's map of, 8–9, 11, 12, 17
Caroline Islands. See Puluwat
Chicago
  cognitive maps of, 84–86
  images of, 120–121
  directions in, 163
  location of, 81–82
  migrant's reactions to, 229
  neighborhoods in, 79

Chile
  cognitive distance from U.S., 142
China Sea
  shape of, 89
Ciudad Guyana
  cognitive maps of, 242–244
  inference in, 81
  knowledge of, 79
Cleveland
  recent migrants to, 71
Columbus (Ohio)
  cognitive distance in, 143
Croisic
  orientation problems in, 237–238
Delta Regional Primate Center,
  183–185
Dundee
  cognitive distance in, 143
Ealing
  knowledge of location of, 134
Europe
  air tours and cognitive maps, 223
  jigsaw puzzles, 257
  tour buses, 261
Fargo
  Steinbeck's stereotypes of, 117
Florence
  wayfinding in, 71
Florida, 4, 20
Galesville (Wisconsin), 111
Gilbert Islands
  swell systems in, 151
Gopher Prairie (Minnesota), 118
Grand Canyon
  scale of, 73–74
Great Britain
  driving in, 72
  Londoner's map of, 8, 10–12, 24
  regional differentiation in, 104
Greece
  wayfinding directions in, 133
Hartford
  brighter image for, 91
Iceland
  navigation systems in, 126–127
Indiana, 112
Jersey City
  images of, 137
Jerusalem
  Crusader maps of, 79
Las Vegas
  cognitive maps of, 249–251
Lewiston (Idaho)
  wayfinding problems in, 253–254

London. *See also* Great Britain,
  Londoner's map of
  cognitive peak, 128
  Henry James' view of, 95–96
  neighborhood re-design, 255
  representations of, 20
  taxi drivers, 76
  Underground system, 164
  walking tours, 257
Long Island
  expressway navigation, 70, 72
  Nassau Colliseum, 257
Los Angeles
  "beautiful people" places, 18
  compared to Mammoth Lake, 244
  freeways, 254–255
  images of, 95, 137
  model of historical growth, 121
  spatial behavior and cognitive
    maps in, 78
  street system, 209
  symbols for, 95
Luna City, 132–133
Lyons
  orientation problems in, 238
Maine, 53
Mammoth Lake Community
  cognitive maps of, 244–245
Metropolis (Illinois), 113
Mexico, 11
Mexico City
  city guide for, 47
  colonias, 166
  street system, 164
Mississippi River
  pilots, 76–77
Montreal
  Expo wayfinding problems, 254
  hiding the slums of, 80–81
  Westmount, as a symbol in, 91
Moscow
  mnemonics of, 97–98
  wayfinding in, 69–70, 134
Nebraska
  homestead location in, 109
New England, 4
  highway signs in, 161–163
  origins of name, 161
  place names, 51
  wayfinding in, 51–52
  weather forecasts and spatial
    behavior, 122
New Jersey
  symbols for, 115–116

New York City
  Bronx maps, 231–234
  city block system, 43–44
  Columbus Circle, 41
  East vs. West Side, 104
  Harlem bus tour, 90
  information systems, 256
  Manhattan, 15, 44, 46, 51,
    231–234, 241, 246
  migrant's reactions to, 229
  as a movie symbol, 92–95
  negative images of, 94–95, 247
  representations of, 76
  skyline, 92–94
  Staten Island, 109–110, 128–130
  subway system, 14–15
  and tourism, 110–111
  wayfinding directions, 14, 51–52,
    228, 230, 256
North Central U.S.
  children's knowledge of, 81–82
Oakland
  Gertrude Stein's comment on, 135
Osaka
  "unknown" park in, 79–80
Paris
  orientation systems in, 163
  street system, 164
  symbols for, 95
  taxi drivers in, 230
  tourist's view of, 102
Philadelphia, 15–16
  images of, 37–38
  street grid, 252
The Poconos, 114
Puebla
  street system in, 51, 228
Puerto Rico
  studies of air photo interpretation,
    192
Puluwat, 146–155
Radburn
  scale of, 74
Rio de Janeiro
  child's air photo interpretation,
    189–190
  cognitive maps of, 236–237
River Thames
  wayfinding on, 212
Rocky Mountains
  wayfinding problems in, 182
Rome, 210, 212
Sahara
  Tuareg navigation in, 124

Salt Lake City
  locations in, 44
Salt Lake Valley
  Mormon settlement of, 116–117
San Francisco
  cognitive maps of, 107–108
  high-rise controversy in, 246–249
  symbols for, 20
San Quentin
  geography of, 64
Siberia
  navigation in, 125
South Carolina
  addresses in, 45
  advertisement for, 110–112
South Vietnam
  airport signs in, 116
Southwest Metroplex. See Texas
Soviet Union. See also Moscow;
    Siberia
  cognitive maps of, 103
  maps and names, 41–42
State College
  sign ordinance in, 251–252
  street names in, 126
Sweden
  residential preferences in, 238–239
Tampa
  airport sign system, 257
Texas, 8, 11–12
  symbols for, 115
Toledo (Ohio), 113–114
"Truth or Consequences"
  origins of name, 113
Union Place (Toronto)
  suburban spread of, 120
United States
  changes in map of, 70
  model of settlement spread, 121
  regional differentiation in, 26, 89,
    104
  representations of, 100–101, 257
  safe places in, 18
  Texan's map of, 8, 10, 17, 24
  viewed from Alabama, 24
  viewed from California, 17, 24
  world viewed from, 142–143
Ussuri River. See Soviet Union
Virginia, 111
Wales, 138
Washington (D.C.), 20
  being lost in, 135–136
  bird's eye view of, 96
  maps of Adams–Morgan, 256–257

Washington (D.C.) *(cont.)*
  street systems, 164
  wayfinding in Watergate, 134–135
Wessex, 25
Worcester
  cognitive maps of, 166

taxi drivers in, 230
wayfinding systems, 164, 227
World
  cognitive maps of, 103
Yoknapatawpha County, 25

SUBJECT INDEX

Addresses. *See* Location, state
    description of
Aerial photograph interpretation
    as a cognitive mapping process,
      191–192
    as an index of development, 189–191
    as a universal process, 192
Anthropology, 5
Augmentation. *See* Inference
Cardinal directions. *See* Location,
    state description of
Cemeteries, 80, 160
Cognition
    age differences in, 193–194. *See*
      also Development of cognitive
      mapping
    cognitive structure, 40, 88. *See*
      also Cognitive maps; Frames of
      reference; Representations
    as knowing, 40–41
Cognitive distance, 139–140
    accuracy of estimates of, 143–144
    factors affecting, 48–49, 142–143
    generating mechanisms, 140–141
    means of expressing, 47–48, 49,
      141–142
Cognitive mapping
    and age, 24. *See also* Development
      of cognitive mapping
    as the basis for spatial behavior,

12–24. *See also* Spatial problem
    solving
in bees, 30–32
birthplace of, 156
in chimpanzees, 183–185
definition of, 6
and experience, 24. *See also*
    Environmental learning
flexibility of, 70, 96
as an interactive process, 73. *See*
    also Environmental learning,
    active vs. passive experience in
and mnemonics, 27, 97–98
neurophysiological basis of,
    174–175
neuropsychological basis of. *See*
    Neuropsychology
ontogenesis of, 182. *See also*
    Development of cognitive
    mapping
organizing nature of, 83–84, 88,
    123
and perspectives on the world,
    20–24. *See also* Cognitive maps,
    and regional viewpoints;
    Stereotypes
phylogenesis of, 182–186. *See also*
    Development of cognitive
    mapping
predictive role of, 81–82, 121–123.

Cognitive mapping *(cont.)*
See *also* Fantasy worlds
process of, 4, 66–68, 82–83, 96
purposes of, 68–69
in rats, 32–35, 184–185
and residential desirability, 16–18, 59–60, 238–239
role of distinctiveness in, 79. See *also* Imagery, spatial elements of
role of functional importance in, 76–77
and value systems, 79–81
in wasps, 31–32
Cognitive maps
accuracy of, 99–102
of the blind, 23, 69–70, 75–76, 101, 209–212
of the deaf, 23
definition of, 6
of the everyday spatial environment, 7
examples of, 7–12
and personal meaning, 27, 37–38, 83–84, 105–107, 138–139, 161
and regional viewpoints, 24, 104. See *also* Frames of reference, as stereotypes
as representations, 6–7. See *also* Frames of reference; Representations; Route maps; Symbols
of river boat pilots, 76–77, 212
of safe and dangerous places, 15, 18, 104
of scientists vs. writers, 102–103
similarities among, 102–107, 166, 168–169
of taxi drivers, 76, 230–231, 255
vertical dimension of, 128–130
of wilderness areas, 245–246
Cognitive representation. See Cognitive maps; Representation
Cognitive structures. See Cognition
Compass directions. See Location, state description of
Constructivist theory. See Cognitive mapping, process of
Copy theory. See Cognitive mapping, process of
Design,
and imageability, 26–27. See *also* Frames of reference
and legibility, 26–27, 252. See *also* Frames of reference

relation of cognitive mapping to, 241–242, 249–252
of small towns, 244–245
of urban areas, 241–244
of wayfinding systems, 134–135, 161–163, 250–258. See *also* Maps, cartographic
Development of cognitive mapping
Bruner's theory of the, 201–202
and the comprehension of space, 197–198. See *also* Frames of reference, development of
and the coordination of perspectives task, 199–201. See *also* Aerial photograph interpretation
comparison of Piaget's and Bruner's views on, 205–207
distinguished from learning, 174, 203–205
an integrated view of, 202–203, 207–208
nature of process, 172–174. See *also* Cognitive mapping, neurophysiological basis of; Environmental learning, in children; Toy play
as ontogeny, 172
as phylogeny, 172. See *also* Environmental learning; Neuropsychology
Piaget's theory of the, 193–197. See *also* Cognition, age differences in
of small- vs. large-scale spaces, 188–189
Direction. See *also* Orientation; Wayfinding
and coordinate systems, 49–51. See *also* Location, state descriptions of
problems of expressing, 51–53
Directions, See Location, process descriptions of
Directories
Baedeker, 14
Guia Roji, 47
Michelin Guide, 114
Triptiks, 47
Yellow Pages, 12, 67
Disorientation. See Wayfinding, being lost
Distance
cognitive. See Cognitive distance

Distance *(cont.)*
  perceived, 140
  relating "real" and cognitive, 141
Environmental learning,
  active vs. passive experience in,
    77, 221, 223–224, 236–238. *See
    also* Cognitive mapping, as an
    interactive process
  aids to, 215, 221–223. *See also*
    Design; Maps, cartographic
  in children, 218–219, 235–236.
    See also Toy play, role in
    environmental learning
  distinguished from development,
    174, 203–205
  effects of social roles on, 216–217
  human "costs" of, 228–229
  nature of, 40–41, 72–73, 135,
    212–214, 218–220, 239
  need for, 214–215
  as place learning, 214, 221. *See
    also* Plans; Route maps
  as response learning, 214–216,
    220. *See also* Plans; Route maps
Fantasy worlds, 4, 82, 96, 100,
  187–188, 261. *See also* Cognitive
  maps, and personal meaning
Frames of reference
  definition of, 68
  development of, 74–75, 198–199
  as models, 89–90
  spatial, 124. *See also* Route maps
  as stereotypes, 25, 89–91, 103–104,
    116–117, 146
  structure of, 88, 137–139. *See also*
    Time; Route maps
Games, 26, 44–45, 258–260. *See also*
  Mazes
Geography, 5, 25–26
Goal. *See* Wayfinding, the discovery
  of the objective
Heuristics. *See* Plans
Highway construction
  effects of, 159
Home
  feeling at, 3, 159–160
  nostalgia for, 2–3
  returning to, 1–2
Imageability. *See* Design, and
  imageability
Imagery
  spatial elements of, 83–84, 86,
    137. *See also* Frames of
    reference; Route maps; Symbols

Inference. *See* Cognitive mapping,
  predictive role of
Learning. *See* Environmental
  learning
Legibility. *See* Design, and legibility
Location. *See also* Orientation;
  Wayfinding
  process description of, 43–44,
    45–47, 49, 126
  state description of, 43–44, 45–47
Locational preference. *See* Cognitive
  mapping, and residential
  desirability
Lost. *See* Wayfinding, being lost
Mapping. *See also* Maps
  definition of, 61–62. *See also*
    Representations
  mapmaking, 62–63
  map reading, 62–63
  perspective in, 63–64
  purpose of, 63–64
  scale in, 63–64
  signature, 66, 85–86
  symbolization in, 63–64
Maps
  cartographic, 42, 64–66, 133–134,
    256–257, 258–259. *See also*
    Design, of wayfinding systems;
    Wayfinding, use of cartographic
    maps in
  sketch, 79, 100–101
Mazes, 33–34, 259–260. *See also*
  Games
Mnemonics. *See* Cognitive mapping,
  and mnemonics
Models. *See* Frames of reference, as
  models
Mystery tour. *See* Wayfinding,
  mystery tour
Names. *See* Place, and identity
Navigation. *See* Orientation;
  Wayfinding
Neuropsychology
  and brain function, 176–177
  and cognitive mapping, 179–180
  defintion of, 174–175
  influences on, 180–182
  and modes of thinking, 177–179
  nature of evidence on, 176
Nostalgia. *See* Home, nostalgia for
Object
  definition of, 54–55
  identification of, 54–55
Objective. *See* Wayfinding, the

Objective (*cont.*)
    discovery of the objective
Orientation. *See also* Wayfinding
    as a cognitive act, 53, 124–125
    local systems of, 51, 126, 161–164,
        209
    the myth of innate, 125
    proximate, 126–130
    ultimate, 126–130
Paths
    layout of, 46, 51, 164, 252–253.
        See also Design, of wayfinding
        systems; Route maps
Perception
    role of development in, 188. *See*
        also Spatial problem solving,
        role of perception in
    and spatial behavior, 73–74. *See*
        also Frames of reference,
        development of
Perspective. *See* Mapping
Photographs, 74–75, 248
Place
    as an equivalence category,
        117–119
    and identity, 41–43, 108–109,
        111–115, 246
    uniqueness of, 109–111, 165–170.
        See also Location;
        Representations, identity
        categories in
Plans
    as heuristics, 60, 72–73, 86,
        227–228
    for solving spatial problems, 58,
        224–225
Propaganda, 24–25
Psychology, 5
Real estate market, 18–19
Representations. *See also* Cognitive
    maps, as representations
    contents of, 84
    equivalence categories in, 84–85,
        108
    identity categories in, 84–85,
        107–108. *See also* Place, and
        identity
    modes of, 62
    storage of, 62. *See also* Mapping;
        Maps
Route maps. *See also* Frames of
    reference; Plans
    sequential, 69–70, 135, 217–218,
        225–227

spatial or survey, 136–137,
    217–218, 225–227
Scale. *See* Mapping
Science fiction, 50, 130–133
Sensory modes
    and cues, 57, 151
    differential roles of, 23–24,
        157–158
Signature. *See* Mapping, signature
Signs. *See* Design, of wayfinding
    systems
Sociology, 5
Spatial behavior, 35
Spatial problem solving. *See also*
    Wayfinding, role of cognitive
    mapping in
    conscious, 72. *See also* Plans, for
        solving spatial problems
    habitual, 70–72
    nature of spatial problems, 35–39
    role of perception in, 57. *See also*
        Perception
    strategies for, 36, 55–58
Stereotypes. *See* Frames of reference,
    as stereotypes
Streets. *See* Paths, layout of
Structure, cognitive. *See* Cognition
Symbolization. *See* Mapping
Symbols, 20, 91–96, 115–116,
    245–249. *See also* Frames of
    reference; Place
Taxi drivers. *See* Cognitive maps, of
    taxi drivers
Territoriality, 78–79, 138
Time. *See also* Frames of reference
    frameworks of absolute, 121
    frameworks of relative, 120–121
Topophilia. *See* Cognitive maps, and
    personal meaning
Tourism. *See* Travel
Toy play. *See also* Development of
    cognitive mapping;
    Environmental learning, aids to
    as a cognitive mapping process,
        77, 192–193
    role in environmental learning, 26,
        221–222, 259
Travel
    tourism, 3–4, 15, 18–20, 110,
        168, 248
    walking tours, 66
Umwelten, 20–23, 224
Wayfinding. *See also* Cognitive
    mapping, neurophysiological

Wayfinding (*cont.*)
  basis of; Orientation
  being lost, 5, 130, 131–132,
    164–165, 182, 237–238
  in children, 12
  the choice of a route, 130–133,
    149–151
  and dead reckoning, 152–153
  the discovery of the objective, 135,
    153–155
  keeping on the right track,
    133–136, 151–152, 253–254
  mystery tour, 3
  role of cognitive mapping in,
    40–41, 58–59, 124, 146–149,

155, 186–187
  signs for. *See* Design, of
    wayfinding systems
  use of cartographic maps in,
    14–15, 231–235, 241
Whatness, 107–119. *See also*
    Representations
  attributes of, 39, 54
  as description and evaluation,
    54–55
Whenness, 39, 41, 54, 119–123
Whereness, 39, 123–144. *See also*
    Frames of reference; Orientation;
    Wayfinding

77   78   79   80   9   8   7   6   5   4   3   2